Asatru:
A Native European Spirituality

Stephen A. McNallen

⦗R⦘UNESTONE PRESS

Cover Design by Kevin I. Slaughter.
Cover Image by Brad Taylor-Hicks.

ISBN: 9798389786264

The author wishes to extend a special thanks to the people who devoted
many hundreds of hours to putting this book in your hands: in more less
chronological order—Gili, who slogged through the original manuscript and
held me to task; Christina, who put pen to paper with great effect; Brad, for
pulling a thousand threads together. I am grateful to Edred Thorsson and
Richard Rudgely and Nigel Pennick for finding good things to say about me.
Michael Moynihan came to my rescue with Old Norse and much more; he
and Josh Buckley and Kevin Slaughter made the book a thing of beauty. And
throughout, to my wife Sheila for her unfailing support and dedication.

For additional information concerning the
Asatru Folk Assembly, contact: www.runestone.org

Author's Note Concerning Orthography and Pronunciation

In writing this book, I have been forced to use many words from Old Norse. This presents unique challenges, because the Norse alphabet contains a number of letters that are very different in shape and pronunciation from their common English equivalents.

I have decided to use Americanized spelling for the non-English words in this book, especially those in common use among practitioners of Asatru. This is not a volume for scholars and antiquarians. My goal is to bring revived Germanic religion to ordinary men and women in the English-speaking world, and that means making this book as accessible to the average person as possible. Even intelligent and interested readers can be discouraged by words in a foreign language containing letters they never knew existed!

Accessible is one thing; "dumbed down" is another. As a way of encouraging those who want to deepen their understanding, I have given the Old Norse spelling for the majority of these words in the Glossary.

Contents

PART ONE: A NEW-OLD RELIGION

PART TWO: PRACTICING ASATRU

APPENDICES

Part One:
A New Old Religion

Chapter 1

Asatru—A Native European Religion

Asatru is a native, pre-Christian religion of Europe. It is the way by which the Germanic peoples have traditionally related to the Divine, to each other, and to the world around them.

If your ancestors were German, Danish, Norwegian, Swedish, Icelandic, or Dutch, Asatru was their spiritual path before they became Christians. Many people from what is now France, Russia, Spain, and northern Italy—indeed, from all across Europe—also have ancestors who practiced Asatru.

The Germanic tribes wandered all over the map of Europe. From Iceland to Russia, from the frozen north of Scandinavia to the Mediterranean, the Germanic peoples conquered and settled over a span of thousands of years. Today, their descendants are spread around the world. We may refer to ourselves as Americans or English, Germans or Canadians, but behind these labels lurks an older, more essential identity. Our forefathers were Angles and Saxons, Lombards and Heruli, Goths and Vikings—and, as sons and daughters of these peoples, we are united by ties of blood and culture undimmed by the centuries.

Asatru is our native Way. Just as there is a Native American religion and a native African religion, so there is a native European religion—and Asatru is one of its expressions. In the 1960s and 1970s, many Native Americans regained an interest in their traditional religion and made it an integral part of a renewed pride and assertiveness. The American Indian Movement was largely inspired by their traditional religion and their religious beliefs remain an important component of their political, social, and religious identity.[1] During the same period, many African-Americans turned to the religions of their ancestors for strength and connection. At least one intentional community— Oyotunji, in South Carolina—was established where people of African descent could practice the Yoruba tribal lifestyle, including making offerings to their Gods. Today, it is the turn of European Americans to remember that they, too, are a distinct people with a tribal, pre-Christian past. It is only natural that native European religions, including Asatru, will be a part of this social phenomenon. When ancient Gods stir, their people wake and arise.

The word "Asatru" is Icelandic, and it means something like "true to the Gods."[2] Since the Scandinavian version of our ancestral beliefs is the best documented, we take much of Asatru's modern terminology and imagery from the Norse world. The soul of Asatru, however, is not confined to the Scandinavian model, but includes the beliefs of all the Germanic peoples. Indeed, the closer we look the more it becomes apparent that the peoples of Europe all share a strong heritage. Asatru reflects the deeper religiosity common to the nations of Europe as a whole.

About Terms

Before getting into the bulk of this book, we need to explain some terms.

Asatru is sometimes called a "pagan" religion. I seldom use that term, because to the average person it conjures up images of primitives hiding from the lightning and tossing maidens into volcanoes. At best, it suggests people who have no religious or moral system. To

1. For evidence, one has only to look at the *Declaration of War Against Exploiters of Lakota Spirituality* passed unanimously by Lakota Summit V, in 1993. It can easily be found on the Internet. Their concerns are valid and worthy of support by all of us, regardless of our ancestry or religion.

2. See the discussion by Edred Thorsson on p. 2 of *A Book of Troth* (St. Paul, Minn.: Llewellyn, 1989). The word itself was not used in ancient times, but dates from the nineteenth century. I first encountered the word "Asatru" on p. 55 of *Viking: Hammer of the North* by Magnus Magnusson (New York: Galahad, 1976). Until then, I had called my religious belief "Norse paganism" or, occasionally, "Odinism."

the relatively small fraction of the public familiar with the modern pagan or neopagan movement, "pagan" may mean other things, some of them not very complimentary. If we wish to avoid either association, we must not, in general, describe ourselves as pagans. We have enough to do without changing people's negative definitions of words. When I have used the word "pagan" in this book, it is in a historical sense.

More often, the word "heathen" is used when referring to Asatru. I seldom use that term, either, for the same reason—it inhibits communication. While the dictionary definition of "heathen" certainly includes "people following a religion other than Christianity, Islam, and Judaism," the picture in the public's mind is still that of an ignorant, superstitious, or uncouth person.

In practice, I use whatever word will describe us most effectively to the audience to which I am speaking. When talking to people in the New Age movement, I may indeed call us pagans, because that is a term they will know. But to most audiences I refer to Asatru as "an indigenous European religion" or "a native European religion."

Asatru has much more in common with traditional American Indian religion, indigenous African religion, or similar ethnic beliefs than with what passes for paganism in the modern industrialized West. It is the "way of a people"—in our case, the people of Northern Europe. It is a part of our deeper identification, our way of relating to the Holy, an expression of our soul.

Terminology aside, what is Asatru *like*? What is the *feel* of this religion? How, in a few simple statements, might we describe our faith? The sentences that follow are my attempt to convey the attitude, the essence, of our beliefs:

The world is good. Prosperity is good. Life is good, and we should live it with joy and enthusiasm.

We are free to shape our lives to the extent allowed by our skill, courage, and might. There is no predestination, no fate, no limitations imposed by the will of any external deity.

We do not need salvation. All we need is the freedom to face our lives with courage and honor.

We are connected to all our ancestors. They are a part of us. We in turn will be a part of our descendants.

We are also linked to all our living kin—to our families and to every man and woman rooted in the tribes of Europe. These latter are our "greater family."

We are connected to Nature and subject to its laws. The Holy Powers often express themselves in Nature's beauty and might.

We believe that morality does not depend on commandments, but arises from the dignity and honor of the noble-minded man and woman.

We do not fear the Holy Powers, or consider ourselves their slaves. On the contrary, we share community and fellowship with the Divine. The Holy Powers encourage us to grow and advance to higher levels.

We honor the Holy Powers under the names given them by our northern Germanic ancestors.

We practice Asatru by honoring the turning of the seasons . . . the ancestors . . . the Divine . . . and ourselves—in everyday life.

Asatru is about roots . . . about connection . . . about coming home!

Chapter 2

The Blessings of Our Ancestral Faith

Why should anyone care about an ancient religion called Asatru? It sounds archaic, musty, like something out of a museum—something suited for the Viking Age, but not the modern world. What does Asatru offer real people? More bluntly, what's in it for you?

In a society as self-centered as ours, that's the only place to start. Our lives are driven by profit and pleasure, not by idealism or any values beyond our own needs. Don't get me wrong; there's nothing bad about profit and pleasure—but there are bigger things to consider.

Forgetting those grander ideals (duty, honor, right living) for a moment, let's look at what Asatru can do for the individual. I'll use myself as an example.

For me, the benefits of Asatru have been many:

- **An awareness of my connection to my ancestors, and the ability to draw strength from them.** It gives me an immeasurable sense of well-being to know that I am part of a line of ancestors transcending time, space, and mortality. Once I made that spiritual and emotional link, I have never been lonely. But more than that: Through rites such as sumbel (about which more later), we can draw upon the traits of our forebears—their courage, endurance, and strength—and use them to empower us, today.

- **Belonging and fellowship.** Although you can follow Asatru without belonging to any local or national group, much of the richness of our faith lies in the connections it builds to others. It is good to share ideas with like-minded men and women, to sit at a meal alongside them, to call them friend. Humans are hard-wired for family, clan, and tribe—and while it's healthy to enjoy your solitude, even the most independent of us longs for the understanding of a fellow soul.

- **Greater self-esteem and a sense of vast personal potential.** We are kin to the Gods and Goddesses! Their divine spark lives inside us, and our challenge, should we choose to accept it, is to actualize this God-nature and evolve into more than we are now. The holy scriptures of some religions may tell you that you are insignificant, or that you are born to do God's will, not your own . . . but these ideas are the exact opposite of the message of Asatru.

- **Techniques for spiritual growth.** The idea that we have the divine nature within us, and that we can develop that nature so that we become more like the Holy Powers, suggests some work on our part. It doesn't happen on its own. Discipline, will, focus, practice—and of course the difficulties that life throws our way—all contribute to our personal evolution. Spiritual might can be accumulated in many ways. Some of the more apparent ones are performance of the rites of our faith, the successful accomplishment of difficult tasks, and immersion in the esoteric wisdom of our religion.

- **Heightened appreciation for the gift of life.** Asatru is a world-accepting religion. We believe life in this world is a good thing, not something to be scorned as "unspiritual" or something we just suffer through so that, someday, we can go to our reward in the hereafter and get on with the "real deal." *Life is good—better than we can know!* It's noble to want to be worthy of a hero's paradise in Valhalla . . . but first, we need to be worthy of this life in this world.

- **A clear set of standards by which to live.** No, we don't have anything like the Ten Commandments. There are other ways to express a code of behavior, as you'll see in Chapter 13. People want to know what the rules are—but they want rules that make sense, rules that reinforce their highest instincts, rules that trust them to use their wits as human beings (and as kin to the Gods) to make decisions.

- **Answers to the "big questions" of human existence.** As inquiring beings, we want to know the grander scheme of things. We want to understand the larger questions that lie beyond our concerns with food, shelter, and sex—things like our purpose and destiny, where the universe came from, our relationship with the Divine, and what happens after we die. Asatru offers answers.

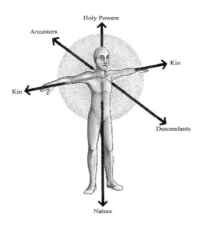

Asatru as Connections

Let me summarize some of the blessings of Asatru in visual form.

I like to describe Asatru in terms of connections: with the ancestors who gave us life . . . with our descendants yet to come . . . with our living kin . . . with the divine powers, or Gods . . . and with the natural world around us. Each of these connections implies certain gifts and corresponding duties.

Think of yourself as suspended in space. Behind you is the past. In front of you is the future. Below you is the earth, the world of nature. Above you is the Divine. Arrows or lines extend from you in these different directions, leaving you at the center of these axes: a vertical axis, a rear-to-front axis, and a left-to-right axis.

Behind you are your ancestors—all those men and women, known and unknown, who passed the torch of life to you. Without them, you would have never been.

In front of you are your descendants, to whom you will give the gift of life. If you had never been, they would never be.

Stretching out to your left and right are your living kin, men and women of your family, and extensions of that family—all who bear your heritage. They are journeying through life with you.

Above you are the Holy Powers—the Gods and Goddesses

Below you lies the Earth, the natural world that sustains us and blesses us with beauty.

Benefits and Responsibilities

What do we get from these connections? And what do we give in return, to uphold our end of the bargain?

First, consider the ancestors. In the traditional view, the ancestors were still a part of the community, although unseen. The family or clan was not limited by space, time, or death.

Today, we think of death as a wall—a solid and impenetrable barrier, though which nothing can pass. Our ancestors viewed it differently. To them, death was more like a thin curtain. Through that veil, the ancestors send us love, inspiration, spiritual guidance. They give us the unexpected bit of luck when it matters the most, that hunch that comes out of nowhere. And of course, they gave us life. We respond to these gifts by remembering and honoring them. We tell their stories to our children, and keep their photographs on the mantel. Perhaps we recall them on their birthdays, or put flowers on their graves.

Looking to the future, we have our descendants. From them, we get love. There are few things sweeter than the love of sons and daughters, and the delights of grandchildren are famous. By their very existence they give us hope for the future. On a more practical side, they can help us and, if need be, take care of us in our old age. Our descendants will remember us when we are gone, sending us love through the veil between the worlds after we are in the grave. Remember, we are all "ancestors in training."

Ideally, our kin should be our ultimate support group. In our drawing, they stand shoulder-to-shoulder with us as we go through our lives together. They give us love, encouragement, and advice. Sometimes their help is as down-to-earth as a loan for a car—or it can be as intangible as the quiet joy that binds us together across the miles and through the years. Modern life has made a hash of our families and forced us to accept substitutes, but nothing beats the organic connection of true kinship. Of course, it is our duty to be open-handed and open-hearted, responding in kind.

Looking above us, we have the Holy Powers. They are our Elder Kin, not our masters. Their connection to us is similar to the one we have with our flesh-and-blood family; they will help us—especially if we bother to build a relationship with them—but often their love is of the "tough" kind. They won't coddle us. We are supposed to imitate their best features and become more like them: wiser like Odin, stronger like Thor, more joy-filled like Freya, more potent like Frey, and so forth. They are our templates for higher evolution. And what do we give them? In the words of one ritual, we give them "our might, our main, our troth"—meaning our personal striving in furtherance of our highest ideals, the gift of our spiritual power, and, finally, our loyalty. We remember them, honor them, and try to become more like them.

Below our feet lies our beautiful Earth, and around us all of nature from the ladybugs in our garden to the stars over our heads. People talk a lot about "connection with nature" these days, but like so many good phrases it has become a mindless mantra that no longer conveys compelling imagery. We need to bring back the immediacy of nature. It is the source of our sustenance, and if we abuse nature or think we can violate its laws at a whim, we will be corrected for our mistake. Earth is the giver of life and of plenty. Nature feeds not only our bodies, but our souls—in the rising and setting of the sun, the magnificence of a field of wildflowers, the smell of rain, the sound of the wind in the mountain pines. All we need do to access this beauty is to notice the world around us. Nature gives us awe, a feeling of connecting with something larger than ourselves. And, of course, it is nature, manifesting as the material universe around us, which provides us with experiences leading to our growth.

Losing—and Regaining—Connection

When we were forced to abandon our natural spirituality, our lines of connection were mangled, twisted, and almost severed. Some bits and pieces remained, but the old wholeness was gone.

Luckily, that which was lost has now been rediscovered. We can experience the love, the fellowship, and the opportunities for growth offered by our ancestral wisdom. All we have to do is come home—to the heart and soul of our heritage. And the next step is to examine the nature of the divine essence in the world, and in ourselves.

Chapter 3

One God is Not Enough

Perhaps the greatest stumbling block for those who would return to the way of our ancestors is the question of polytheism. Most of us were trained from childhood to believe in only one God, so we find it hard to consider that there might in fact be many Gods—and Goddesses, too.

Much of the rest of the world, however, thinks it perfectly natural that there should be many Gods and Goddesses. Hindus everywhere, as well as tribal peoples scattered around Asia, Africa, and the Americas, take polytheism for granted.

Modern science opened the door to the idea of polytheism in the twentieth century, though no one noticed. For decades, physicists have been trying to tell us that the rock-solid world of the materialist has disappeared. In its place, there is a sea of uncertainty. The world is not the sterile interplay of matter and energy described by Isaac Newton or Karl Marx—it is, as Sir James Jeans said, "more like a great thought than a great machine."

Einstein, too, failed to grasp the nature of things. When confronted with the revolutionary world of quantum physics, he declared that "God does not play dice with the universe." We now understand that God not only plays dice with the universe, he is only one of many players!

We rightfully disdain New Age gurus who talk blithely of "quantum" this or "tachyon" that. We'll always have hucksters with us. Nevertheless, the world revealed by twenty-first-century science has changed the way we look at the interplay of consciousness and matter, possibilities of parallel universes, and other topics impinging on philosophy and religion.

A sense of mystery pervades the new physics. For many of us, the peculiarities emerging from relativity, quantum mechanics, and string theory amount to a reawakening of religious awe in a world which had become jaded and pointless. We are now free to seek the hidden truths that underlie existence. The sense of a profound and wondrous enigma surrounds us as we plumb the deepest secrets of the cosmos.

The Improbability of Monotheism

Monotheists need to ask themselves four questions:

1. *Does our observation of nature support monotheism?* Consider nature: storm and calm, ice and fire, plants and animals, life and death, sky and earth, all in endless combinations and complexities. The world around us is packed with forms and phenomena of very different kinds. It seems more believable to ascribe this wide range of forces, things, and events not to one cause but to many. The natural world does not encourage us to believe in a single deity, but in numerous ones. As Vine Deloria, an American Indian activist with a degree in theology once wrote:

> We cannot be absolutely certain that we are dealing with only one god. The fact that monotheism is logically pleasing does not mean that it is an accurate description of reality. The universe, being somewhat discontinuous in other respects, may also conceivably be discontinuous with respect to divinity. Wotan appears to have amazing resiliency; Yahweh's rainbow still shines in the sky; ghosts prowl the British isles; the picture of Jesus is appearing more frequently in unexpected places—and the Hopi have rain.[1]

---

1. Vine Deloria, Jr., *God is Red* (New York: Grosset and Dunlap, 1973), p. 292.

2. *Is human variety consistent with monotheism?* Just as natural phenomena are varied, so is the array of nations and tribes that make up the human race. The way of Asia is not the way of Africa, which is not the way of Europe. Is it logical that one supernatural Power can be the only true God for all of mankind? Is it not more reasonable to assume (as, in fact, each tribe and nation believed until convinced otherwise by missionaries and colonial armies) that each group has its own Gods and its own interpretation of the Divine?

3. *Does the spiritual experience of mankind, as witnessed directly by shamans, mystics, and holy men, support monotheism?* On the contrary, countless cultures assert that the universe is teeming with non-human entities, many of which can be categorized as Gods and Goddesses both major and minor. Deloria notes that religions based on the experience and observation of shamans—wise men and wise women by whatever name— are always polytheist.[2] Monotheism is proclaimed only by religions evolved from philosophical speculation, not from actual contact with the supernatural world.

4. Did the early Christian chroniclers deny the reality of our Gods? The existence of Thor, Odin, and the other Germanic Gods was acknowledged by Christian missionaries and, later, by the Christians who wrote down the Norse sagas. The idea that they are fictional came later. Of course, the position of the Church was that the old Gods and Goddesses were demons— but they never denied their existence outright.

---

2. As Vine Deloria remarks (*God Is Red*, p. 292):"Religious experiences are not nearly as important to Western man as his creeds, theologies, and speculations—all products of the intellect and not necessarily based on experience. Regardless of the experience of a multitude of gods, monotheism has come to be regarded as the highest form of religious knowledge. Yet religions that have achieved a monotheistic doctrine are often rapidly intruded upon by a development of lesser spiritual beings forming a pantheon. When a religion is based in experience whether it be theological or popular, it seems to be of a polytheistic or pantheon-oriented nature."

In summary, monotheism is contradicted by (1) the great range of natural phenomena, (2) the widely diverse peoples that make up humanity, (3) the direct experience of spiritual specialists in every culture who deal with the Otherworld, and even by (4) the testimony of Christians!

Hard and Soft Polytheism

There are two ways of looking at religious systems based on a pantheon of Gods and Goddesses. "Hard polytheism" takes the existence of multiple deities at face value. The Gods are assumed to be real, distinct, and separate. However, hard polytheism does not preclude the idea of some sort of underlying unity or power. Numerous tribal and ethnic religions fall into this category.

"Soft polytheism" teaches that the Gods and Goddesses, though real, are manifestations of some greater and ultimately unknowable source. One of the best examples is Hinduism, which makes room for an unlimited number of deities but believes that all are expressions of an ultimate spiritual source called Brahman or Atman. This impersonal power has no definable form or characteristics and is beyond human comprehension.

Asatru has no set doctrine on hard versus soft polytheism—one is free to believe as he or she wishes.

The Effects of Monotheism

Around the world, the rise of monotheism was accompanied by intolerance and persecution. In the days when people knew there were many Gods and Goddesses, religious wars must have been relatively rare. Each tribe, race, or nation had a relationship with its own pantheon. No single deity or collection of deities demanded the right to rule all mankind. Gods and Goddesses were not typically transferred from one group to another.

Monotheism changed all that. If there was only one God, then the Gods of the unbelievers must be demons, usurping the devotion that rightfully belonged to the One True God. The followers of those Gods/demons were now devil worshipers, and should be killed. Conquest, previously justified by greed, was now motivated by righteousness. It was the beginning of a bloody phase of human history that continues down to the present day.

Anywhere monotheism met polytheism, the followers of the One True God went on the offensive. Monotheism was rarely accepted peacefully. Usually, the war of beliefs lasted for years or generations. It took a thousand years of conflict for the tribes of Europe to give up their old Gods, from the adoption of Christianity by Constantine in the fourth century until the official destruction of Northern European paganism in the thirteenth. Even then, remnants of the native faiths survived in the remote regions, beyond the reach of "law and order."

Consider Islam: the first Muslim invasion of Europe was halted on October 10, 732 CE by Charles Martel at the battle of Tours. The second wave of Islamic aggression was broken at the battle of Vienna in 1683, when an alliance under King Jan Sobieski defeated the Ottoman Empire. The third invasion, in the guise of Muslim immigration supplemented by terrorism, is underway today. Islam fully expects that it will seize the world for Allah, converting, dominating, or killing the rest of us in the process.

Consider Judaism: the Jews in the Old Testament invaded nation after nation and put men, women, and children to the sword—at the command of their God. This habit continues in the modern era, with the mass expulsion of Arabs from their lands during the establishment of Israel. Millions of Christians in the United States believe that God will judge America by its policy toward Israel. Many think nuclear war in the Middle East would be a good thing, because it would bring about the Second Coming of Christ.

And Christianity? We discussed one small part of Christianity's record when we detailed the thousand-year war against the indigenous religions of Europe. Is this a thing of the past? Conservative columnist Ann Coulter writes, referring to Muslim nations, that the United States "should invade their countries, kill their leaders, and convert them to Christianity."[3]

3. Anne Coulter, "This Is War," syndicated column of Sept. 12, 2001. Admittedly, this was written immediately after the attack on the World Trade Center but it does

Looking at this record of intolerance and genocide, it is hard to see any blessings bestowed on mankind by monotheism. We cannot help but contrast this with societies where many Gods and Goddesses are known. Although polytheistic cultures fought wars, they seldom if ever tried to convert their neighbors. When is the last time you heard of an Amazonian Indian sending missionaries to Chicago or Los Angeles to convert the Christians? Religious wars were apparently unknown in Europe until the coming of Christianity, but since that time, it has seldom ceased—as my own Irish relatives can testify.

Polytheism and Freedom

We owe our tradition of freedom to the polytheistic tribes of Europe. Centuries before the founding of the British Parliament, Iceland was governed by a nationwide body called the Althing, which voted on the laws and appointed judges to decide legal cases.[4] Tribal leaders, contrary to modern misconceptions, were not generally born into their jobs; they were chosen by the leading families or by the entire body of freemen. Some tribes did not even have a real leader, except in times of war.

Our ideas of law derive principally from the Germanic world, through the Norse and the Anglo-Saxons (hence "Anglo-Saxon common law").[5] This law applied to all freemen, and to the king or chief as well. Defiance of rulers who thought they were above the law is a common thread running through the old Scandinavian sagas. In fact, Iceland was colonized in the ninth century by Vikings fleeing

indicate an attitude of religious imperialism.

4. Similar assemblies, or things, functioned throughout the Germanic world from the local to the tribal and national levels. The Icelandic Althing maintained a continuous role in government until 1799. On the Isle of Man, the corresponding Tynwald has existed from 979 CE to the present. The Logting in the Faroe Islands was founded in the ninth century and has met annually since the tenth century. All three are Norse creations.

5. Thomas Jefferson, in a letter to Major John Cartwright titled "Saxons, Constitutions, and a Case for Pious Fraud" and dated July 5, 1824, wrote: "the common law existed while the Anglo-Saxons were yet Pagans, at a time when they had never yet heard the name of Christ pronounced, or knew that such a character had ever existed."

the tyranny of Olaf Tryggvason, the Norwegian king who forced his countrymen to accept Christianity or die.

The list can go on and on, but the bottom line is this: when our ancestral religion held sway across Europe, fledgling republics protected the rights of their citizens. After the Church destroyed the people's religion and dismantled the ancient system of checks and balances, royal power grew and human freedom receded. Medieval Christian Europe was a locked-down totalitarian system as absolute as the Soviet Union. The rights we now associate with Western democracies were painfully regained through the centuries, first with the Magna Carta, then with the American Declaration of Independence and its sister document, the United States Constitution.

In a sentence, freedom is a birthright from our polytheistic ancestors in Europe, not something we imported from monotheists in the Middle East.

Monotheism and Polytheism in the Balance

The variety of forces in nature, as well different peoples and cultures, all argue for polytheism and against monotheism. The truth of polytheism is attested by thousands of years of observations by holy men and wise women, mystics, and shamans.

Monotheism has been the main cause of religious warfare, which began in ancient times and continues in today's news from the Middle East (Muslims and Jews), India (Muslims and Hindus), and Northern Ireland (Catholics and Protestants). Our political freedoms are rooted in native, polytheistic belief—and those freedoms diminished when monotheism came to power.

Luckily for us, the way of our ancestors, represented by Asatru, stands before us like an open door! To attain our destiny, to become all that we truly are, we must stride boldly through that portal. It is, after all, the front door to our own home—the spiritual home that served us well for thousands of years and still offers us comfort, dignity, and freedom today.

Chapter 4

Who, or What, Are the Gods?

I s there a God or Gods, or are we alone in the universe? All other issues of destiny, purpose, and immortality hinge on the answer to that single question.

The ancient wisdom of Europe clearly states that there are beings which are far beyond us in abilities, yet nevertheless intimately involved in our origins and destiny. These are the Gods and Goddesses of our faith. Often, I simply call them the "Holy Powers" to highlight two essential truths about them. First, they are holy—special, set aside from the ordinary, awe-inspiring. They exist on the very margins of our comprehension . . . yet, as we shall see, they are intimately involved in all that we are. Secondly, they are powers. They are potent, energy-filled, with capacity for action on a scale we can hardly imagine.

Beyond these two basic facts, there is only so much we can say about them. We can read the stories that have come down through the centuries. We can describe some of their attributes and their associations; for example, we can say that Odin relentlessly pursues wisdom, or that Thor is famed for his strength. We can describe our own relationship to these entities, emphasizing our kinship with them. The true essence of the Holy Powers, however, must be experienced by cultivating a relationship with them and by paying attention as they continually unfold their truths before us.

Stumbling Over a Word

The average person is not emotionally limber enough to consider non-Christian, non-Jewish, non-Islamic Gods to be real. So forget about "Gods" for a moment and consider: if I said there were supernatural beings called *devas*,[1] or *bodhisattvas*,[2] or Ascended Masters,[3] millions of people from India to Indianapolis would agree with me. All these words denote immortal beings of great spiritual power and superhuman abilities. But calling them Gods or even demigods is just too difficult for most of us because we identify the "G word" only with the deity of the Bible.

This is ironic. The word "God" does not come from ancient Hebrew, Latin or Greek. Neither Moses, nor Jesus, nor Mohammed ever uttered this syllable. "God" is a pre-Christian Germanic word originally referring to our deities, not something out of the Middle East. Our modern use of the term comes from the Old English *god*. This word derived in turn from an earlier Germanic term *guþ*, which was originally of neuter gender and could refer to divine beings in general. In Ulfilas's Gothic translation of the Bible, he used it to translate the Greek word *theos* and assigned *guþ* a masculine gender in order to specifically represent the single Christian deity.

You'll notice that throughout this book I have capitalized "God" not only when it refers to the Christian deity but also when it describes our native Gods. This is against all convention, but I am not inclined to favor the God of the Bible over the Gods of the Northlands.

Are the Gods Absurd?

If we do not use the "G word," the Holy Powers suddenly seem much more understandable to the modern mind. After all, millions of people believe the Dalai Lama is a being who has transcended mortality to become a God—and many of those believers are college-educated men and women living in the Western world.

Our cultural conditioning limits our perceptions. Christians believe that a child born to a Jewish girl was fathered by a ghost and was literally God made flesh. The Old Testament says that Moses

---

1. *Deva*—from the Sanskrit, a divine being, "intelligent agent," or a God.

2. *Bodhisattva*—in Buddhism, a powerful "enlightened being" who remains embodied to help mankind rather than attaining Nirvana.

3. Ascended Master—spiritually powerful beings, formerly human, who have risen to a superhuman status.

waved a staff over the Red Sea and parted it so the Hebrews could escape from the Egyptians. Satan, a fallen angel, tries to trap men and women into an eternity of torment. People can go to Hell—forever!— for masturbating, or for breaking dietary rules.

I am not ridiculing Christians and Jews by making these statements. My point is that these beliefs seem bizarre to anyone outside the Biblical religions. If we can rise above our preconceived notions, it is obvious that the beliefs of the Germanic peoples are no more improbable than the Biblical accounts. Yet intelligent, educated men and women will accept the Bible without question, while scorning similar tales from any other source. But why? Why should a beautiful Goddess of love be less believable than the Virgin Birth? Why should Odin or Thor be more unlikely than the vengeful deity of the Old Testament? Why are the miracles of Jesus taken as truth, but those performed by the saints and shamans of a hundred other religions are illusion, lies, or the work of the Devil?

Clearly, all supernatural claims are either equally probable or equally improbable. But unless we are materialists, we have to consider the possibility that all religions—even the ones we call pagan or heathen—might be valid. Conversely, atheists would take the opposite stance and say that all religions are equally wrong: that all Gods, whether Judeo-Christian or pagan, are only illusions and self-deceptions.

Fair enough. We'll leave it to others to explain why they believe in atheism. It is our task to say why we believe in the Holy Powers venerated by our ancestors in Europe—and we shall do so below.

The Reality of the Holy Powers

What makes us think that the Gods of Asatru actually exist?

For hundreds of generations, our ancestors believed the Gods and Goddesses to be as real as their own family, as real as the mountains hovering on the horizon, or the clouds blowing through the sky. It's easy today for us to say that they were ignorant and superstitious, but is that really true? Their brains were not significantly different from ours. In terms of sheer intelligence, our forefathers could have invented the theory of relativity or quantum mechanics a thousand years ago. This didn't happen, of course, because centuries of conceptual foundations had not yet been laid. Discovering quantum mechanics is one thing, but inventing higher mathematics and all of classical physics at the same time, while planning raids and planting crops, is a little much to expect! Lack of brainpower, as such, was not the problem.

Tribal Europeans lived in an environment that selected intensely for intelligence and hard-headed practicality. Stupid people made mistakes that got them killed. Impractical dreamers likewise met tragic ends. Fools, self-deceivers, and the gullible did things that got them eliminated from the gene pool, and thus we can assume that the ancient Europeans would not have believed in the Gods and Goddesses unless they had some reason to do so. We, by comparison, live much more protected lives, sheltered from the natural environment and from our own ignorance. As a result, we are much more likely than our so-called primitive ancestors to believe in superstitions—such as the truth of the evening news or the honesty of politicians, for example.

As I mentioned some pages back, even the enemies of the Gods—the Christian missionaries and later chroniclers—believed they were real. The Christian kings of Norway are said to have met Thor and Odin in mysterious encounters recorded in the sagas. One can argue that these stories are fiction, but the very fact that they were written down reflects a belief that the Gods were not imaginary. Nowhere in the surviving sagas do the Christian writers suggest Odin, Thor, Frey, or any of the other Holy Powers were delusions.

Related to this is the oath the Saxons were forced to swear upon converting to Christianity. In it, the old Gods, "Wôden, Thunær and Saxnôt" were specifically named, thus implicitly recognizing their existence.

The Gods and Goddesses are not confined to the ancient lore, however. They continue to manifest to men and women who call on them today. When we make requests of the Holy Powers, we often get dramatic results. In Christian terms, our prayers are answered: people get healed, children are born, broken lives are fixed, or the future is foretold. In short, belief in the Gods . . . works!

Real, But Different

To say that the Gods and Goddesses are real does not tell us much. The next question, logically, is . . . what are they like?

Aside from rare representations as statues or figures on old tapestries, the only descriptions we have of the Holy Powers are in the myths. Reading the stories, we find Thor pictured as a muscular man with a red beard and flashing blue eyes. Odin is a tall, older figure with a gray beard and one eye, and he sometimes travels in the company of his two wolves and ravens. Frey, on the other hand, is a fertility God, with the appropriate masculine anatomy.

Are we to take these vivid images literally? Modern Asatru leaves this up to the individual. Asatruar are certainly free to accept these descriptions as real, and some choose to do so. Others take them symbolically, as a way of comprehending that which seems incomprehensible. No doubt it was the same in ancient times, with views both simple and sophisticated having their adherents.

Although there are no polls on the subject, I suspect that most Asatruar today think of myth as metaphor. The ancient stories then become symbolic ways of voicing spiritual truths. This is done on a number of levels, like the layers of an onion.

On the surface, myths are entertaining tales that make a moral point or illustrate virtues like wisdom, sacrifice, bravery, or generosity. They tell us something about the nature of the Gods, and they give us guidance for living our lives.

But there is a deeper level. The myths are true in the sense of "those things which never happened, but always *are*."[4] The stories of the Gods become allegories and archetypes rather than history. Their meanings can be dissected through intuition and by comparison with related mythologies.

The next level contains information understandable only to those ready to receive it. Specific techniques of spiritual evolution are encoded in some of the material. For example, the poem called the

---

4. This quote is attributed to Sallustius, a collaborator of Emperor Julian who wrote a text titled *De diis et mundo*. Julian vigorously defended Roman paganism against the attacks of Christianity.

Havamal can be read as pragmatic advice for living a successful life—or as a handbook of initiation. There are many instances of this kind of encoding in the Northern lore.

Finally, the archetypal aspects of the myths constitute a sort of nonlogical "metalanguage," the secret code of the unconscious. In this case the myths communicate with us subtly, without words, influencing our minds and spirits.

Even if the myths are metaphor, the Gods and Goddesses are still very real. But this doesn't mean that Thor is actually a muscular, man-like figure with a red beard, any more than Jehovah is a fatherly figure in a white gown sitting on a golden throne, surrounded by clouds. The description of Thor in the myths gives us a way to relate to the being we call Thor, but it is not him.

The Gods and Goddesses are not limited by the constraints of flesh and blood. So, while it is convenient for us to picture Freya as a beautiful woman wearing a shining necklace, or Odin as having one eye, these are only representations. The Gods and Goddesses themselves are mighty beings, capable of manifesting to humans in any form they wish.

The Gods and Goddesses as Mysteries

I spent many years pondering the nature of the Gods. Inhabitants of a parallel universe or another dimension? Our future selves, cast backward in time? Three-dimensional, sentient projections from the collective unconscious? I have no answers. All I know is that they sometimes manifest in the most remarkable ways.

At this point in my life, I am comfortable with the idea of the Gods as Mysteries. Oh, we can recite their myths and compare them to other deities in the Indo-European pantheons. We can make conclusions from cultic place-names across Northern Europe. In short, we can describe the Gods, but we can never define them.

This is not to say we should not try, for like Odin we are seekers of knowledge, wisdom, and power. In our own individual quests we shall grow closer to the Mystery—but never quite get there. Always it will remain just a little beyond our grasp. I have come to love the

Mystery, for with it comes a sense of awe, of wonder, of a sweetness that permeates the fabric of all-that-is.

The Lore

Throughout the ages, there have been men and women with the power to peer into other worlds. Shamans, mystics, or seers, they have seen wider realities than the one evident to our senses. These gifted individuals have traditionally come together in brotherhoods or sisterhoods dedicated to sharing and expanding their knowledge. Their explorations are the raw material of which religious truth is fashioned; all the rest of religious philosophy is commentary and custom, erected upon this bedrock of experiential knowledge.

Today's seers and clairvoyants are poor imitations of these native psychonauts. Stripped from ancient traditions, filled with the discordant images and thoughts of modern culture, lacking the support of the age-old fraternities of wise men and wise women for support, how could most modern psychics have more than mediocre success? The men and women who gave us the recorded lore of the Germanic peoples benefited from a hundred generations of accumulated experience. Today's seers do not have that deep context. They receive a degraded inheritance that is part wisdom, but also part quackery and self-delusion.

The secrets of our indigenous Northern European mystics are encoded in the myths. The two most important collections of these meta-linguistic masterpieces are the *Prose Edda* and the *Poetic Edda*. Along with the literature of the sagas, the epic poems such as *Beowulf*, and the traditional tales of the folk, the Eddas constitute our lore.

Our lore covers the big questions—the birth of the universe, the existence of the Gods and the origin of humankind, the structure of the invisible worlds surrounding us, our fate after death, the right way to live, human purpose and destiny. But much of this wisdom is open to interpretation, and all of it must be applied with common sense. This is good, because it makes us think for ourselves.

The lore is the accumulated treasure of our wisest men and women over a very long period of time. This is not to say that it is a static thing;

indeed, it is our duty to explore and extend it. The Holy Powers are forever revealing their truths to us, bringing us always closer to them, and with care and prudence we can continually add to this store of wisdom.

The Meaning of the Gods and Goddesses

We opened this chapter with the question of whether or not we are alone in the universe. We answered with a discussion of the Holy Powers. But the answer, as all good answers should do, begs still more questions. What do the Gods and Goddesses mean to us? Should we rejoice at their presence, or cower in fear? What is our relationship to them, and what is the role of humans in the cosmos? We'll turn to these questions in the next chapter.

Chapter 5

The Gods as Kin and Friends

If the Holy Powers exist, what is their relationship to us? Are they friends or foes, masters or guides? What do they expect of us . . . and what should we expect from them?

The precedent from the monotheistic religions is not encouraging. The Old Testament Jehovah is many things—a Middle Eastern potentate, military general, creator, and ruler of the universe. We're told he is also "God the Father," but if so, he's not like the kind of father most of us know. Parents generally do not drown their children in a flood and then, when a few are allowed to survive, promise to burn them all next time!

Things get better in the New Testament. Jesus has a very different personality from Jehovah, but the most persistent image of him is not that of a brother or a father, but of a shepherd who looks after a flock of sheep. This may be comforting, but it is hardly flattering to humans. Sheep may be cute and cuddly, but they're not family. They also get shorn.

Allah is much more like the Jehovah we know from the Old Testament. He demands obedience and worship; indeed, the word "Islam" literally means "submission." No term could better describe the marginal existence of non-Muslims in a Muslim-dominated country.

The great monotheistic faiths view humans as slaves or as property. Native European religion views humans as kin and as friends.

Blood Kin to the Gods

There is a story from our lore that tells how we came to be kin to the

Gods and Goddesses.[1]

Heimdall, one of the Gods, wanted to visit the world of humans. He put on a disguise and changed his name to Rig, then set forth from the home of the Gods.

As he walked along the sea shore, Rig came to a humble cottage. Approaching closer, he could see that it was a rough dwelling lacking decoration and of the simplest craftsmanship. He was not surprised to enter and see a poor and not very attractive couple sitting around a crude fire built on the floor. Ai and Edda were their names, and Rig accepted their hospitality. Dinner was simple, and soon all three of them retired to bed. The traveler took his place between the husband and wife, and so it went for three nights.

Nine months later, Edda bore a son whom she named Thrall. He was as rough as she, and when Thrall grew up he married a girl of his own station and they bred a large family. Their children were no more elegant than their parents. Coarse and ill-shapen, they are the progenitors of the class of slaves and servants.

Again Rig went walking, and in time he came to another house. It was simple, but well built and maintained with care. Upon going inside, he saw a neatly dressed man and woman sitting at the fireplace. Afi and Amma were their names. The two worked industriously, braiding wool and carving tools from wood. Dinner was boiled meat with bread, hardy fare and the best they had. Soon the evening ran late and it was time for bed.

Rig slept between the two of them, and he stayed with Afi and Amma for three nights.

After nine months, Amma presented Afi with a child whom they called Karl. Ruddy and strong, Karl proved capable of all the crafts and skills of the farmer. In time he took a wife, and their many children were also hard workers and practical. From them comes the line of prosperous yeomen.

Rig, continuing his course, found himself before a third house. Its well-built door was open, showing the hospitality of the owner, and it was finely decorated. Walking inside, Rig saw a floor covered with

1. *Rigsthula*, a poem found in the *Poetic Edda*.

clean straw, and sitting by the fire were Father and Mother. They were well dressed, Mother in her fine bleached linen and a bonnet, with a brooch upon her breast, and Father sat leisurely plaiting bowstrings and shaping arrows. When Mother served food it was on fine silver-inlaid trenchers, and their wine was poured into golden cups. The food was plentiful and tasty and they all made pleasant conversation over the meal.

Rig slept between them in their ornately carved bed, and nine months later Mother gave birth to a boy. He was flaxen of hair and fair of cheek, and his eyes were sharp and intense. Mother and Father swathed him in silk and named him Earl. From him come all the ranks of rulers and conquering warriors.

There is more to tell of Earl and of Earl's sons, but their adventures are beyond the scope of our tale. This story makes the point that, regardless of our class or social position, we are descended from divine stock. Heimdall, in the guise of Rig, fathered the three classes from which all Northern folk are descended. The essence of the Holy Powers lives in us. We differ from them not in kind, but in magnitude. We have Godly potential within us.

We are part of the family of the Gods. But, as significant as that fact is, it is only half the story.

Friends of the Holy Powers

We are not only kin to the Gods, we are also their friends.

Looking through the old Germanic literature, we see that this idea of friendship between the Holy Powers and human beings is a popular one. Thor, for example, was given the title "Friend of Men" because he was so approachable by ordinary people. Another man is described as a "friend of Frey." Friendship with the Holy Powers is a lot like friendship between humans, and the same rules apply in both cases.

In the Germanic lands, the most important rule of friendship was to give each other gifts. These verses from the Eddic poem *Havamal* show us how essential this idea was:

Friends should share joy in weapons
and clothes that are evident to one another.
Those who share gifts stay the fastest friends
when things go well . . .

A man shall ever be a friend to his friends,
And give gift for gift . . .

If you know that you have a friend and that he is true,
and that you will get good from him,
share your mind with him, exchange gifts,
and visit him often.[2]

The same custom of exchanging gifts applies to our relationship with the Divine. Befriending the Gods is no different from striking up a comradeship in ancient Norway, or for that matter in America today.

Trading gifts with the Gods was central to Germanic religion. The main ceremony was a blot,[3] meaning a blessing or honoring; it is an exchange of gifts between the Holy Powers and their human followers. The fact that the gifts of humans are intangibles—our loyalty, our strength, our devotion—does not change the equation; we give to the Gods and they in turn give things to us.

The dual nature of our relationship with the Holy Powers—kinship and friendship—carries a number of implications. Kinship implies bonds of duty. Ideally, it supplements these with ties of love and affection, but this does not always work out in everyday life. All of us have family members with whom we can't get along; uncles or cousins or even parents for whom we cannot honestly feel any affection. It is best when we are able to love kin, but even when we can't, we are bound to fulfill our duty to them, regardless of our feelings. Our personal needs and desires are not, frankly, as important as the responsibilities which bind together our families, clans, and tribes.

2. *Havamal*, strophes 41, 42, and 44, translated by James Chisholm in *The Eddas: The Keys to the Mysteries of the North* (n.p.: Illuminati Books, 2005).

3. Pronounced "bloat."

We also have duties to our friends, but except in very special situations (such as the ancient war band) these are not as holy as the obligations we have to kin. What we do have with friends, however, is the choice of giving our affection as we see fit.

The two aspects of our relationship with the Gods, then, complement and reinforce each other. Together, they give us the greatest possible connection with the Holy Powers. As kin, we honor our obligations to them. But since we are also their friends, our good feelings for them help us stay closely bound in ways that ensure the strength of the relationship. It is much like being married. A man and a woman can scrape along with a minimum of passion and love by lowering their expectations and keeping their contract with each other . . . but if they are truly friends and lovers in addition to being two people tied to each other by law and custom, their marriage blossoms to its fullest potential.

Getting Reacquainted

If we are kin to the Holy Powers, why doesn't life go more smoothly? Why do we have so many difficulties? Why are we sometimes defeated by the circumstances around us? Surely this can't happen if we have the super-human might of the Gods on our side—can it?

We have to recall the many centuries which have led us to this point. Yes, we are kin to the Mighty Ones—but we have been estranged from them, individually and as a people, for a thousand years or more. Most readers of this book were not born into Asatru and had at best a hazy idea of the Gods and Goddesses until quite recently. Perhaps some of us knew that our forebears once had a religion of their own, but few of us have had much more than a very rough idea about that faith until relatively recently. Our relationship with our ancestral heritage has been damaged for a long, long time and we are only beginning to repair it.

Moreover, it was not the Holy Powers who turned their back on us, but we as a people who abandoned them. It took about a thousand years to tear the Germanic people from their religious roots, but eventually torture and greed triumphed. The old ways faded from the awareness of all but a very few men and women who secretly kept the spark alive. The Gods and Goddesses never went away, though. They are still here, waiting for us to return to the wise ways of the past. We must renew our relationship with them before we can reap the benefits of our mutual kinship and friendship.

Because we are the ones who opted out of our relationship a thousand years ago, we have to prove ourselves to the Gods. Like a straying husband who wants to come back to his wife, it's up to us to demonstrate our sincerity. We must make the effort to rejoin the family. Even in ancient times, blood relationship was not always enough to qualify an individual for acceptance into the clan. Newborn babies were not officially taken into the family until nine days after birth, by which time they had shown their worthiness by surviving. At that point, the father of the family would give the child a name and recognize it as a member of the group.

We are in much the same situation. We've been separated for a very long time and we must rebuild a relationship that has suffered from severe neglect.

If it is necessary for us to renew our bonds of kinship with the Holy Powers, it is even more important to reestablish our ties of friendship. The Lore makes it clear that friendship requires maintenance. Gifts need to be given, visits need to be made, time needs to be spent in each other's company. Most of us have not even known that the Gods existed, much less that we needed to refresh a friendship long gone dormant!

Fixing our connections with the Gods will not suddenly solve all our problems, but it is a first step on the road back to wholeness. It will bring us benefits in the form of greater connection, increased creativity, and other gifts of the spirit. This does not mean, however, that life suddenly becomes easy!

One key part of the Asatru worldview is evolution. Although we share all the potential of our Gods, we can grow to be more like them only by struggle. In some religions it is enough to believe, accept, and submit, but Asatruar know that this is not enough, that we must prove ourselves by worthy deeds. The Gods give no free rides.

What We Are Not

One does not enslave one's family. It follows, then, that we who are kin to the Gods are not their slaves. Furthermore, since we share in the nature of divinity, it is not right for us to be the slaves of anyone else, either—as that would bring disgrace onto the divine family of which we are a part.

Any religious philosophy which claims that humans are slaves to the divine runs counter to the spirit and practice of Asatru. When we speak to the Gods, we never use postures or gestures symbolizing inferiority or submission. The clasped hands of Christianity,[4] in which the wrists are presented to be bound by the slave-knot, is alien to us. Similarly, the bowing of the Muslim and the prostrations of the Buddhists are not our way. We do not kneel, or bow our heads, or cast our eyes to the ground. Rather, we stand erect and tall, eyes looking straight ahead or skyward, with our arms raised to our sides at a high angle.

Our approach to the Holy Powers is at the same time reverent and familiar. Jean Haudry calls this a "duality of religious attitude." He goes on to describe this as the "fear of offending a god, even involuntarily, but at the same time confidence in and even familiarity with the gods, especially in the case of some of them."[5]

On the one hand they are our kin, and why should anyone be anything other than familiar with our relatives? Nevertheless, we are aware that their power is inconceivably greater than ours. We may be like the Gods in essence, but not in degree. Their holiness, their majesty, gives them an aura that we would be foolish not to respect. To mock them or to put ourselves on their level would be grievous error, and to speak lightly of them betokens ignorance or immaturity. Often we will paraphrase a deity's name rather than speak it outright, out of

---

4. "Paul, a slave of Jesus Christ" . . . "Paul and Timothy, slaves of Jesus Christ" . . . "James, a slave of God and of the Lord Jesus Christ" . . . "Simon Peter, a slave of Jesus Christ." These are the phrases the apostles used to describe themselves in their letters to the early churches.

5. Jean Haudry, *The Indo-Europeans* (Washington, D.C.: Scott-Townsend Publishers, 1998), p. 64.

reverence. We are not yet demigods ourselves, and until we transcend our current level of evolution we would be wise to show them honor.

While we are obviously not equal to the Gods in wisdom or power, we share their blood and we have the capability of becoming more like them. For this reason the imagery of the sheep and shepherd, used throughout the Bible, is offensive to us. The sheep and their keepers are two different species, unrelated and forever separate. We, on the other hand, share an essential similarity to the Holy Powers and we are destined to grow in time to be more like them!

The Elder Kin do not want our abject obedience or our adoration. Our role is to become more like them. They are our models, our inspiration, even our goals. We who are pledged in troth to the Holy Powers are supposed to become stronger, wiser, more willful, more capable of thought and imagination and pleasure. The Holy Powers are not standing in front of us, demanding that we kneel and worship them; they are walking ahead of us, beckoning to us, urging us to follow in their footsteps. If we are children of the Gods, we are children who are expected to grow up and take our part as mature adults.

The idea that we are of the same blood as the Gods opens new vistas. In other cultures, it is the differences between humans and the divine that are stressed, not the similarities. If humans are wholly different from, and inferior to, the powers that govern the universe then we cannot be anything other than subordinates, servants, or slaves. When we learn that we are members of the same family, different in magnitude but not in essence, the relationship changes dramatically. For the first time, the universe becomes open-ended. We are born free, and we are responsible for that freedom! Who can ask for more?

Chapter 6

Ancient Gods in the Twenty-First Century, Part I

We've spent the last three chapters writing about the Gods and Goddesses in general—what they are, how they relate to us, and so forth—but we haven't paid much attention to them as individuals. In this chapter and the next one, we'll take a quick tour through the Northern pantheon and introduce you to some of the main characters. This includes a description of the Holy Powers taken from the myths, a look at the role they play in the bigger picture, and some thoughts on what they have to do with our lives today.

This list is by no means all-inclusive. It's easy to pick out the main players, of course. For example, lots of people have heard of Odin and Thor. But other Gods and Goddesses are less recognizable. Their names may occur only in a line of Viking Age poetry, or in an inscription on a stone in Germany. We know next to nothing about them, despite the best efforts of the scholars.

To make things even harder, many deities were known under several names. Is Skirnir really Frey? Is Hermod actually Odin? Are the dozen or so minor Goddesses that appear to be Frigga's handmaidens only the Goddess herself, in disguise? And can we ever know?

All Gods and Goddesses were not worshipped equally in all times and places. Ullr was fading from memory by the time the old lore was recorded. Odin, on the other hand, seems to have absorbed some of the functions of other deities, including his fellow sky-God Tyr. Many of the Gods Snorri Sturluson describes in his marvelous compilation are known only from the Viking Age; others were worshipped centuries earlier. Odin was more popular in Norway and Denmark, Frey was the chief God honored in Sweden; Thor had his heyday in Iceland.

Keeping in mind all these variables, it is still possible to pull together a coherent and useful list of Asatru's essential deities. That is what I have tried to do here. But before jumping headlong into a recitation of the Holy Powers and their traits, I need to explain about the two main families or clans of Gods, and their distinctive roles.

Aesir and Vanir

The Gods and Goddesses of the Northern world break down into two tribes or families. The Aesir include the major deities Odin, Frigga, Thor, Balder and Tyr, as well as their offspring. In general, the Aesir are more involved with force and rulership. They tend to be associated with the sky—Tyr reflects the ancient Indo-European sky God, and Odin later took his place to some extent. Thor's sky connection is apparent from the nature of his hammer, which is the lightning, as well as his role in fertilizing the fields with rain.

The main Vanir deities are Njord and his two children, Frey and Freya. These three live with the Aesir, so they are described in many of the myths. Other of the Vanir live in Vanaheim, though we know nothing about them. The alfar or elves also seem to be related to the Vanir.

The main focus of the Vanir is fertility—of humans, animals, crops, and even the seas. But they do other things as well; Frey and Freya are both involved in warfare . . . Freya is the mistress of her own special magic called seidr . . . Frey was the divine ancestor of the old Swedish kings. But despite these additional assignments, the Vanir are mainly deities of fertility, prosperity, and pleasure.

Despite this seemingly tidy categorization, many of the Germanic Gods and Goddesses are not clearly Aesir or Vanir; we just do not know enough about them to place them in one group or the other.

Dumézil and his Trifunctional Hypothesis

One of the most important tools for thinking about the Northern deities—as well as the societies that worshipped them—is the "trifunctional hypothesis" of the French philologist Georges Dumézil. He compared social systems and myths across many Indo-European cultures—Rome, the Germanic lands, Vedic India, old Ireland, and others—and found consistent patterns.[1]

In each culture, there was an upper tier—which Dumézil called the "first function"—composed of Gods dealing with sovereignty, law, and priesthood. This function is shared by two deities. One maintains the law, preserves cosmic order, and seeks stability and continuity. In the Germanic pantheon, this is the role of Tyr. The other God of the first function is ecstatic, ever-changing, and mysterious; these words match Odin precisely.

The "second function" is defense, or the warrior function. Thor, swinging his giant hammer like a lightning bolt, is the perfect example of such a God.

Dumézil's "third function" is home to deities of productivity, fertility, and abundance. Frey and Freya, and the Vanir generally, maintain the third function among the Germanic Gods and Goddesses.

Again, this is not to say that the deities identified with the three functions act only in those roles. The boundaries are not absolute: Thor, a God of defense (second function), has a fertility aspect (third function). Frey and Freya, (third function), both operate in a military manner (second function). Tyr, a first function God, is called upon for victory in battle. First function Odin slices through all these categorical boundaries in every direction.

Dumézil noticed that Indo-European societies organized themselves in a manner parallel to their mythological structure. Lawgivers and priests were in the uppermost class; warriors were in the second tier; and farmers, huntsmen, and artisans were in a class analogous to the third function. But since this book is about religion rather than social structure, we will note this in passing and continue our survey of the Northern mythology.

Why should we care about Dumézil's analysis? Often, our knowledge of a Germanic deity is limited by contradictory information

---

1. The best exposition of Dumézil's work as it specifically concerns Asatru is *The Gods of the Ancient Northmen* (Berkeley: University of California Press, 1977).

or poor sources. By studying a God or Goddess in another Indo-European pantheon, we may gain insight into the nature of our own Germanic deities. Verses in the *Rig Veda*, written for Indra, work fine in rituals dedicated to Thor. Celtic and Germanic religions are such good mirrors of each other that, as Hilda Ellis Davidson says in *Myths and Symbols in Pagan Europe*, they are essentially two branches of a common European religion.[2]

For many years, the standard explanation for the mythological war between the Aesir and the Vanir was that the Vanir-faith was the religion of the first Europeans, and that the Aesir were the Gods of invading Indo-Europeans from the steppes of Asia. When the Aesir-worshippers moved into Old Europe, the two parties supposedly fought a war that was described symbolically in the myths. This theory is now out of date, because an examination of other Indo-European mythologies outside of Europe—based on Dumézil's work—shows similar themes. The conclusion: the Aesir and Vanir have always been an integral part of Germanic religion.

Dumézil's trifunctional hypothesis also reminds us of the strong links that unite Indo-Europeans. From Benares to Reykjavik, certain distinct cultural traits underlay the apparent variety of Indo-European regional societies. Looking at these constants, we cannot help but be impressed by the depth and breadth of the pan-Indo-European vision.

With these theoretical considerations out of the way, we are ready to move on to the Gods and Goddesses themselves. In the remainder of this chapter, I will describe some of the Gods and Goddesses that vividly illustrate Dumézil's three categories.

The First Function—Sovereignty, Law, and Magic

Odin

Odin is the preeminent figure in the Norse mythic tales. He is called "Father of the Gods" and "Allfather" in recognition of this supremacy, and he is clearly the God who directs the action of all the other deities

2. H. R. Ellis Davidson, *Myths and Symbols in Pagan Europe* (New York: Syracuse University Press, 1988).

in the Teutonic pantheon. Odin is a mirror of the powerful Germanic chieftain of the Migration Age, an aristocrat among warriors and a master of mysterious magical forces. Odin's wide-ranging expertise—war-maker, magician, poet, seducer, winner of wealth—has won him a reputation of being the "God of everything," as opposed to other Gods and Goddesses of more limited scope.

Odin is a character depicted in bold strokes. His wide-brimmed hat hides the empty socket of an eye plucked out in the winning of wisdom. Two wolves sit by his side, and a pair of ominous ravens circle over his head. Odin's steed is no ordinary horse, but an eight-legged marvel who rides between worlds. Often, the God travels in disguise while accomplishing his mysterious missions; in battle, he may appear as a tall bearded man throwing a magical spear over the ranks of his enemy—thus claiming them for sacrifice. Odin talks with the dead, understands the language of the birds, and fosters heroes only to seemingly betray them at their moment of greatest glory. Odin is power and paradox.

"Odin" is actually a title, meaning "master of the divine ecstasy," and it indicates his skill as a worker of magic. In Germany he was called Wotan, and the Anglo-Saxons knew him as Woden. Additionally, Odin has a multitude of nicknames he uses when working his spells or when traveling throughout the Nine Worlds known to Nordic mystical cosmology.

Let us look beyond the dramatic trappings, and consider the Stirrer of Strife in his larger role as a sort of Germanic *bodhisattva*, a guardian of the cosmic evolutionary process.

In the myths, Odin directs his efforts to preparing for Ragnarok. Translated as the "final destiny of the Gods" or the "reckoning of the Gods," Ragnarok is the great battle at the end of this cycle of time, when the Gods and their human allies will stand against the forces who would destroy not only all the known Worlds, but the all-encompassing World Tree that serves as the very matrix of the cosmos. The prophecies say the Gods will be defeated and the universe will be destroyed, but by the might of their resistance, a new world will emerge. The Gods will be reborn, and the evolutionary drama of existence, action and reaction, cause and effect will continue. It is Odin's mission to prepare for the battle in such a way as to ensure that this rebirth occurs.

Odin's actions in the myths center on quests—for wisdom, for hidden knowledge, and for magical power. He hangs on the World Tree to grasp the might of the runes. He lies three nights with Gunnlod to drink the mead of magic inspiration. He plucks out an eye for the knowledge concealed in Mimir's Well. Odin interrogates long-dead seeresses and queries dead men on the gallows to learn the things he must know to increase his magical prowess, and thus to better counteract the giants.

Paradoxically, although Odin fights to protect the cosmic order, many of his means are disruptive and disorderly—indeed, one of his nicknames (which are called *heiti* in Old Norse) is "Stirrer of Strife." His motivation is not petty mischief; Odin stirs warfare to defeat his foes and to raise up heroes—deliberately furthering the evolutionary process through the highly selective stress of combat. His heroes thrive under his fostering, only to fall at the height of their glory. Superficially, Odin betrays them in battle. But seen from a deeper perspective, he brings them in triumph to Valhalla, where they will feast with him and prepare to fight alongside him at Ragnarok. Those he cultivates, he harvests . . . and in the harvesting, he transforms them into demigods, into the evolved human being.

This brings us to Odin's other great role. While promoting evolution on the cosmic scale, Odin is at the same time the model for the evolution of individual humans. Odin transformed himself in the course of his mythic quests. By seizing the runes and drinking the Mead of Inspiration, as well as in his other attainments, Odin changes himself. He not only knows more and does more, he becomes more. This transformation through magic and by great deeds shows the way for his human sons and daughters who wish to follow in his footsteps. His chosen heroes, plucked off the battlefield and carried to Valhalla, have overcome through will and sacrifice. The magician accomplishes the same thing, but in a different manner. Both become higher beings, realizing their inborn potential as blood-kin to the mighty Gods and to Odin himself.

Odin is not a God for everyone. All revere him, but few will choose to walk the path he treads. For the spiritual aristocrats and the Faustian heroes,[3] however, no lesser patron will suffice.

How about the rest of us? If we're not warriors or mystics, how can Odin be relevant to us? The answer, of course, is that we all need wisdom. All of us have made bad choices at one time or another—choices that have cost us a job, or a chance for love, or which have left us damaged in some other way. Wisdom—the distillation of our experiences, mixed with thought and insight—can minimize these bad decisions and even help us repair the harm we've done to ourselves and others. Odin reminds us that our potential is unlimited . . . if only we are willing to pay the price for what we want. Far from being an anachronism left over from the Dark Ages, Odin is the key to a life of attainment and victory.

Tyr

Tyr, like several of our Gods and Goddesses, is a God of war. Odin stirs strife, and uses war for his long-range goals of preparing for Ragnarok. Freya gets half the battle-slain, and Thor is a fine deity for fighting men because of his strength—but Tyr comes closest to the essence of what it means to call oneself a warrior.

The meaning of warriorhood is perfectly expressed in Tyr's major myth. Fenris, a fantastic giant wolf, threatened the safety of the Gods. Meeting in council, they came up with a plan to put chains on Fenris, but the big problem was how to convince the wolf to allow them to put the fetters on his legs. The Gods promised the wolf that they were just playing a game, and that they would remove them as soon as they could see whether or not he could break the bonds. Fenris, quite reasonably, wanted a guarantee. One of the Gods would have to place his hand in Fenris's mouth. If the chains were removed, fine—and if not, the hand would be bitten off. Tyr unhesitatingly stepped forward and put his hand in the wolf's mouth, knowing full well what would

---

3.Faustian—insatiably striving for knowledge and power.

happen. The wolf was bound, and Tyr lost his hand.

The warrior's lot is to sacrifice for his community. He or she goes in harm's way, knowing that death may be the result, or if not death, perhaps horrible mutilation. The warrior calling can be summed up in a few closely related words: sacrifice . . . courage . . . duty . . . loyalty . . . steadfastness.

Tyr's rune was carved on swords and spears in early Germanic history; it is the original "victory rune."

The One-Handed God is also invoked to guard the Germanic assembly, or thing. He protects human society from the "wolf" of discord, chaos, and law-breakers just as he guarded the society of the Gods by binding Fenris. In the bigger picture, Tyr is a God of "law and order," constancy, and stability. As such, he is associated with the Pole Star, which figuratively sits atop the World Column and remains stationary while all the others revolve around it.

Tyr's connection with law also springs from another source. War, to the Germanic mind, is a sort of trial at which a judgment will be rendered. Victory or defeat hangs in the balance, with success going to the one who has the greatest might. Now, "might" includes not only obvious things like the party with the most fighters, the best strategy, and so forth, but also spiritual or religious factors—the greatest hamingja, or spiritual power, the one who has "right action" on its side. Just as Tyr presides over the thing, so he ensures that the side with the greatest overall might carries the day. Tyr is not just a God of victory, he is the God of a thoroughly deserved victory.

Tyr is obviously relevant to warriors—not just combat soldiers, but also police, firefighters, and every man or woman who goes into dangerous situations in service and sacrifice for others. People who put their lives on the line every day make up a sizeable percentage of any society. But each and every one of us, no matter how humdrum our lives or how safe we think we are, need to cultivate the warrior virtues. One never knows when the wolf will break free of his chains, and people who have never considered themselves heroes will have to place a hand in his mouth.

The Second Function—Defense

Thor, son of Odin and the giantess Jord, is in many ways the opposite of his fearsome father. Where Odin is aloof and foreboding, Thor is known in the Norse poetry as the "friend of man." While Odin is the God of aristocrats and heroes, Thor is the patron of the common man and woman. Odin is known for being subtle and clever, but Thor is famous for his direct approach and his short temper. Just as Odin's key trait is wisdom, so Thor's main feature is his immense strength, and an eagerness to use it.

Thor, as pictured in the myths, is massively muscled. His beard is fiery red. Sparks flash from his ice-blue eyes when he is angry...which is often. In his hands he wields a gigantic hammer named Mjolnir, or "crusher." It never misses when he throws it at his enemy, and it returns to his hand by magic. Mjolnir's impact is the stunning blast of the lightning, and in this respect Thor is brother to Jove and Indra, who toss lightning bolts in their respective pantheons. To handle such a fearsome weapon, Thor wears iron gloves and a belt that doubles his strength.

The tribes of Germany knew Thor as Donar, and to the Angles and Saxons he was Thunor.

Thor is the archetypal warrior, tasked with defending those entrusted to his care. Odin's strongest son protects the worlds of the Gods, and that of humans, from all threats. These include numerous giants—Thor is often "journeying in the east" seeking his prey—but his arch-enemy is the World Serpent, Jormungandr. This sea snake is so long that it stretches all the way around the world on the ocean floor. When Ragnarok comes, Thor will battle this monster, and each will kill the other.

Thor's hammer came to symbolize protection and holiness. This power extended to actual ritual hammers, to hammers carved into stone monuments, and even to hammer-like gestures made with the fist. Its might was called upon at life's transitions. At birth, it blessed the new baby. During weddings, it was placed in the bride's lap to ensure her fertility. At the end of life, the hammer hallowed the funeral pyre. Finally, carved into stone, it guarded the graves of the dead.[4] Miniature amulets in the general shape of Mjolnir—some stylized, others realistic—were worn as necklaces for protection, or to give the wearer Thor's strength and boldness. While hammer-shaped amulets go back far into antiquity, they also seem to have become a specifically pagan answer to the cross of Christianity. Indeed, Thor was thought of as the protector of our religion, and it was Thor, not Odin or the other Gods, who was spoken of as doing single combat against Christ. Today, a thousand years later, the hammer amulet is still the most recognizable symbol worn by those who follow Asatru.[5]

Thor, and his hammer, have an important secondary significance—the fertility of humans, the fields, and livestock. It remains a powerful phallic symbol. To this day, "hammer" is a crude slang term for the penis. We've already mentioned the use of Thor's hammer in the wedding ceremony. When the lightning flashes over the fields, it brings the life-giving rains that make the crops grow. The rain becomes, mythically, the lovemaking of the sky and the earth, or Thor and his wife Sif. The power of the hammer manifests in many ways, from war to sex, from the strength to wield a weapon to the mysterious might of the male member.

In our pampered modern world we sometimes belittle physical force. We lull ourselves into believing that we are beyond all that, that reason and persuasion has made the display of "brute strength" unnecessary and stupid. However, only the fool does not respect the strong. We live in an intricate web of laws and customs designed to prevent the use of violence, but not everyone gets the word. As long as there are humans there will be violence, and often that violence will be the elementary force of fist, foot, and elbow. We still need strength and the will to use it in our defense, and in defense of those we love. Thor can be our guide to lives of strength, and the boldness to use it.

---

4. Following a successful campaign by the Asatru Folk Assembly and other heathen organizations, the Hammer of Thor was added to the list of symbols approved for engraving on Veteran's Administration headstones in 2013.

5. In 1970, I had my first hammer cast by a local jeweler, as I knew of nowhere they could be purchased. Today, there are dozens of sources listed on the Internet.

This is not to say that all strength comes from muscle. Strength to endure, perseverance, and will power are all characteristics exhibited by Thor, and as we seek to build these into our lives we can call upon Thor for inspiration.

Fertility will always be a concern of humans. Without fields that bear crops and animals that give birth to young, we will die, despite our modern toys and affectations. Without children, our family lines will dry up and there will be no descendants to remember us, to tell our stories, to pour libations on our graves. The names of our ancestors will be forgotten, and we as a folk will fail. If Thor's lust (and that of some other deities) abandons us, our lives will be sterile in every sense of the word. The blessings of Thor are as relevant in the twenty-first century as they were in the tenth.

The Third Function—Fertility, Pleasure, Wealth

Freya

Freya is the best-known Goddess of the Germanic folk. This is understandable; beauty and love demand our attention across the centuries. These are Freya's best-known domains, but they are only part of the complex nature of this Goddess.

Freya's beauty is enhanced by her marvelous necklace, Brisingamen. The myths tell us that she made love with four dwarves in exchange for this piece of jewelry. We should not, however, be hasty to dismiss the Goddess as a whore. The most famous dwarves in the Norse mythic lore are the four that hold up the sky—Nordri, Austri, Sudri, and Vestri, or North, East, South, and West, respectively. The symbolism is significant: they are the four main directions personified, and they represent great esoteric wisdom and power. In winning Brisingamen, Freya gained these gifts, and we should no more condemn her than we condemn Odin for sleeping with Gunnlod three nights to win Odroerir, the Mead of Inspiration. Like Odin, Freya was engaging in an act of erotic magic for a specific purpose.

Just as Odin is lord of rune magic, Freya has an occult art all her own. It is called seidr, and involves trance work, spells, and foretelling the future. Seidr differs from rune magic in several important points, not the least of which is that it involves a loss of control, a suspension of the will, in a way that rune work does not. Despite these differences, Odin craves the knowledge of seidr, and it is Freya who teaches it to him. The two styles are very complementary, and modern would-be Germanic magicians often pursue a working knowledge of both in order to be well rounded.

In still another parallel to Odin, Freya is active in the warrior realm. She does not fight on the battlefield, but she gets first choice of the slain warriors, whom she brings back to her hall much as Odin claims his own heroes. Also, according to some traditions, Freya is the leader of the valkyries, the magical women who carry Odin's heroes to Valhalla. Freya and Odin cooperate when it comes to harvesting the souls of the dead.

Comparing Freya and Odin, we see that both of them operate in many areas. Both are workers of magic, both have to do with war, and to a lesser extent both are involved in the winning of wealth and sexual pleasure. Of all the Gods and Goddesses, Freya is the only one who has taken to herself as many functions as Odin.

Freya's relevance to modern men and women is obvious. Love, lust, pleasure and wealth are still as much on our minds as they were in the Viking Age and before. Why not incorporate them into a legitimate religious context so they can be expressed in ways that are helpful, rather than harmful to the individual and to society? Why not get rid of the hypocrisy and guilt and deal with them in a positive and life-affirming manner? The gifts of Freya are an integral part of our ancestral religion—and they fill important human needs that transcend the centuries.

Frey

Frey is Freya's brother. Together, they are the most important representatives of the family of Gods and Goddesses called the Vanir.

Frey personifies fertility, prosperity, peace, and pleasure— especially pleasure of the sexual variety. Snorri Sturluson, in his *Prose Edda*, says it well: "Frey . . . rules over the rain and the shining of the sun, and there-withal the fruit of the earth; and it is good to call on him for fruitful seasons and peace. He governs also the prosperity of men."

Statues of Frey—both the large wooden ones in temples and small ones designed to be worn as amulets—featured an erect penis. His animals are the stallion and the boar, both famous for their strength and virility. The best-known story about Frey tells of his wooing the giantess, Gerd. While sitting on Odin's seat which looks over all things, Frey sees Gerd and is instantly smitten. He persuades Skirnir to ride to the land of the giants and plead Frey's case for marriage. Skirnir offers Gerd one gift after another, but the maiden is not interested in his proposal. Finally, Skirnir chants a terrible curse against her and, at last, Gerd agrees to wed Frey. For his success in convincing Gerd, Frey gives Skirnir his magic sword.

Frey's principle powers lie in the realms of fertility, wealth and pleasure, but he can be a fighter as well as a lover. There was a story about him, now lost, in which he battles a giant named Beli with an antler and kills him. Frey had no sword for the duel because he had given it to Skirnir, as recounted above. It is said that Frey will greatly miss his sword at Ragnarok, when he will fight and kill the fire giant Surt.

In addition, Frey has connections to kingship and sovereignty. Under the name Yngvi-Freyr, he is known as the divine ancestor of the Yngling dynasty of ancient Sweden. The combination of fertility, warrior might, and rulership make Frey the most well rounded of the Gods, next to Odin.

Farmers, gardeners, herdsmen, and all who make their livelihood from the land, can call upon Frey's help. All who want prosperity—and who does not?—should seek the blessings of Frey. Men who want to be more virile can seek his intercession . . . and women, as well, who want more fulfilling relationships. Billions of spam email ads for Viagra and penis enlargers testify to an enduring need for Frey's gifts.

Beyond the Three Functions

Odin and Tyr as Gods of magic, law and sovereignty, Thor as defender,

Frey and Freya as deities of wealth, reproduction and joy—these categorizations work very well. The Gods and Goddesses covered in this chapter are also among the best-known and most important among the Holy Powers recognized by our ancestors. But there are many other deities, some of them very significant indeed, who do not so easily fall into Dumézil's classification. In the next chapter we will take a closer look at them.

Chapter 7

Ancient Gods in the Twenty-First Century, Part II

In the previous chapter we took a tour of some of the most vivid images in the Germanic lore. Who could not be impressed by figures such as the wise Odin, boisterous Thor, life-giving Frey and Freya? But there are many other powerful Gods and Goddesses, and no study of our ancestral faith is complete without considering them.

Frigga

Odin's wife, Frigga, plays her part in the myths much more quietly than her questing husband. In the stories that have come down to us, she remains in the background. When she does assert herself, however, she is not afraid to contradict Odin. In the Eddic poem *Grimnismal*, she takes the side of Agnarr over his brother, Geirrod, who is Odin's favorite. Frigga uses trickery to thwart Geirrod and ensure Agnarr's kingship. She uses her wiles against Odin in another story, where she tricks him into naming the tribe of Langobards and thus obliges him to give them victory in battle.

But above all, Frigga is the Goddess of childbirth, motherhood, marriage, and domestic life. Along with Freya, she is listed in the sagas as one to call upon when a woman is in labor.

The lack of material on Frigga in the literature does not mean that her role was in any way undervalued. Our ancestors, or any tribal people for that matter, would consider childbirth and motherhood to be crucial. We know, too, from the surviving tales that Frigga is wise and that she had great powers. Like Freya, she possesses a cloak of feathers with which she can go on magical journeys. If Frigga seems neglected in the lore, it is partly because, as a female, she would have been singled out for special attacks by the triumphant Christian religion. Additionally, Freya's dramatic character overshadows her in Snorri's accounts.

There is also the possibility that, like many deities, Frigga may have been known by other names. For example, there are the little-known Goddesses often considered her handmaidens, who might actually be Frigga functioning in particular roles. They are: Saga, renowned for her wisdom; Eir, a healer; Gefjon, a virgin (virgins who die are said to be with her); Fulla, also a virgin, who looks after Frigga's personal belongings and keeps her secrets; Sjofn, who turns the minds of men and women to love; Lofn, who brings together those for whom marriage is forbidden or banned; Var, who hears oaths and takes vengeance on those who break their vows; Vor, who is so wise that nothing can be concealed from her; Syn, who guards the home against intruders and who defends people in court; Hlin, who protects those in need; Snotra, who is also wise, self-controlled, and of gentle manners; and Gna, who runs errands for Frigga on a horse that flies through the air and over the sea.

Our society needs Frigga's blessings today, when families are torn by lack of commitment, infidelity, financial stresses, drug and alcohol abuse, and hedonism. Frigga is the one who can help us create a calm and loving atmosphere in our homes, and who reminds us to be the best parents we can be. Ultimately, everything depends on the home and hearth: without the family, the tribe and nation die.

There is another reason we need the good graces of Frigga in the twenty-first century—much more than our ancestors did in the tenth century, for that matter. Frigga is our mother Earth. During the Migration Age or the Viking Age our ability to disrupt her processes was nil. We could (and did) chop down forests and exterminate wild animals, but the Earth was able to renew itself. Today, our destructiveness is incalculably greater. We need Frigga's blessings, but we have responsibilities toward her, in turn. Unless we repair our relationship with our holy Mother, nothing much else matters.

Idun

Idun, wife of Bragi, is the keeper of the golden apples that bestow youth on the Gods and Goddesses. In the only significant myth concerning her, Loki is coerced by a giant into allowing Idun, along with her marvelous apples, to be stolen. Loki is then forced by the Gods to make things right by retrieving her, which he does by turning himself into a bird and flying away with Idun and her apples.

Apples are symbols of eternal youth and fertility in a number of ancient cultures, including the Germanic and the Celtic. Magic apples and nuts from the Otherworld are found in the Irish tales, where they grant youth, vigor, and immortality to those who eat them. Germanic graves sometimes contain apples with an apparently symbolic function (the famous Gokstad Viking ship burial is one such case). In *The Saga of the Volsungs*, Frigga sends an apple to King Rerir, who desperately wants a son. Rerir shares the apple with his wife, and the result is the famous line from which the hero Sigurd would be born.

What does all this have to say to moderns? We don't have the apples of eternal youth, but we can hope for health, and for the ability to resist the decay of the aging process for at least a while. It's important to realize that "old age" is only partly determined by the calendar. There are plenty of people sixty years old who can literally run rings around youngsters a third their age. Suppose the calendar says I am "sixty years old," but I can run three miles and do sixty push-ups. The man next door, however, can't walk up the stairs without exhausting himself— but the calendar says he's "forty years old." Who is really older?

A lot of this is purely physical, but it all starts with attitude. Men and women today can call on Idun for a youthful outlook on life, and on the health to enjoy the wonderful world in which we live. Maybe we can't live forever, but we can *live* until we die!

Actually, there are scientists who say that anyone who can live another fifty years, and have an income that allows them to afford new technology, can live for the next few centuries. We are on the edge of incredible breakthroughs, if we don't blow up the planet or pollute ourselves to death first. Idun is the ideal patroness for research in human longevity, as well as for those of us who seek to make use of these new scientific developments.

But there's more. Idun's apples, Odin's mead quest, and certain spiritual techniques from elsewhere in the Indo-European world have something in common. All three suggest a system for expanded consciousness, vastly enhanced powers of the mind and spirit, and transformation of the physical body so that the aging process is stopped. Is this possible? It sounds fantastic, but at the very least there is an unexplored branch of the Germanic lore that may make our lives richer, more powerful, and longer. Idun and her apples—along with Odin's mead—are symbols of this formerly hidden part of our ancestral spiritual tradition.

Balder

Balder, son of Odin and Frigga, plays a part in the central theme in Northern lore. It is his death that ushers in the battle at the end of this cycle of time, Ragnarok.

Balder is described in glowing terms—Balder the beautiful, the one with the white brow, the mild God who is loved by all. It was startling, then, that he should have dreadful dreams. Frigga sought to protect her son, and took oaths from all things in the world to not harm him. This of course makes him invulnerable, and the rest of the Gods took sport in standing in a circle around Balder and pelting him with stones, axes, spears, and any other harmful things that came to hand. Each missile bounced harmlessly off Balder, leaving him intact and smiling.

It turns out that Frigga had obtained promises from all things . . . with the exception of the mistletoe, which she thought too young to make an oath. Loki learned of this, and, shaping a dart of mistletoe, contrived to have Hod, the blind God, join in the mirth by throwing it at Balder. Balder dropped dead when it struck him. He was given a magnificent funeral, and efforts to get him out of Hel began at once. These efforts ultimately failed, and Balder remains there until after Ragnarok.

Victorian-era writers made Balder something of a "pretty boy" among the Gods, painting him as somehow different from the rest of the rough-and-tumble Germanic deities. Others have even made him into a sort of Nordic Christ. These interpretations fail. For one thing, the name "Balder" means "warrior." This is substantiated by a version of the myth in the writings of Saxo Grammaticus that portrays Balder as a mortal warrior who fights great battles to win the hand of a beautiful woman. Finally, the picture of the Gods standing around Balder and throwing weapons at him has been identified as a warrior initiation by some scholars.

Could it be that Balder is not a soft-spoken bringer of peace at all, but just another Germanic God associated with war? Tyr is the archetypal warrior, and Odin uses war as an evolutionary strategy for producing heroes. Where does Balder fit into the scene?

Balder teaches us (and warriors everywhere) the lesson of luck. He is of noble lineage and possesses many traits that make him beloved by everyone. His mother, queen of the Goddesses, tried to protect him as soon as she discovered a threat to his life. All these things come together to give Balder a high degree of luck, of hamingja—yet there is a fatal flaw in the protection woven around him, in the form of Frigga's failure to get an oath from the mistletoe. Balder is good, and his luck is good, but they're not good enough to thwart the threat against him.

The outcome is tragedy. Balder, the young warrior, is struck down by blind chance in the form of a sightless God named Hod.

Soldiers today have a saying: "It doesn't matter how good you are, if you're not lucky."

The story of Balder is most obviously relevant to soldiers, law enforcement officers, firefighters and others who risk death for the sake of others. But the general principle of luck as a tangible quality, as something dependent on your hamingja or overall spiritual might and therefore something you can shape, is true for all men and women.

Ullr

Thousands of skiers and other winter sports enthusiasts know the name of Ullr, one of the most ancient Nordic deities. These folks are hardly devotees in any serious sense, but nevertheless they flock to Ullr-related festivals around the country and many will have raised a glass or two to this God of winter, of skis and bows, of hunting, and of shields.

Skiing in the United States was largely founded by immigrants from Germany and Scandinavia. Along with their knowledge of winter sports, they brought traditions from the old country—including the lore of Ullr. The fact that they were good Catholics from Bavaria and Protestants from Norway made no difference at all; they saw no harm in sharing a bit of their heathen heritage.

Today, a whole new generation of men and women true to the Gods of their ancestors are taking up winter sports. When they call on Ullr, they're not just having a good time, they're connecting with a deity who is entirely real.

For some modern followers of Ullr, skiing through the powder-covered trees, or snowshoeing, or tracking game in the snow becomes a religious experience. The silence, the immediacy of nature, the stunning beauty all immerses them in the Holy.

Ullr is usually described as wearing skis and carrying a bow. It appears that he is an archaic deity of hunting and of winter. It's all very well to lie in wait for game in gentle weather, but winter hunting has a special mood to it. When temperatures fall below zero and the ground is deep with snow, the tribe's existence depends on whatever it has set aside, plus meat from the hunt. Life and death become two sides of the same coin—death for the game means life for the people. Killing is done with reverence. Prey and predator are joined in a holy dance.

Ullr was an ancient God by the time the Viking Age began. He is mentioned in some of the oldest poems in the *Poetic Edda*, and is absent in the younger ones. Snorri, author of the *Prose Edda*, tells no stories about him, presumably because they had faded into the forgotten past by the time Snorri wrote. But the archaic God of winter, of death, and of the bow speaks to us with the persistence of the hunter, making his tracks on our souls, drawing us to the dark woods and the snow.

The shield is another item associated with Ullr. We read in the lore that it is good to call on him in single combat, so martial artists will also find him to be relevant to their lives and passions.

Certainly, skiers and hunters and all who love the outdoors in winter, plus martial artists and archers, can relate to Ullr. But we don't have to think so literally. Maybe you're just a person who needs to persevere, or maybe you need to obtain victory over a foe, and perhaps you took inspiration from the winter wilderness on a trip twenty years ago. You, too, may want to call on Ullr. We all have a winter place inside us, where we stalk some need or another with the bow of our instincts and the arrow of our will.

Heimdall

Asgard, the world of the Gods, contains Odin's well-known dwelling, Valhalla. It also holds the halls of many of the other Gods and Goddesses. The world in which we humans live is called Midgard, literally "the world in the middle." Access between Midgard and Asgard (and presumably between Asgard and the other worlds, too) is by way of the wondrous bridge, Bifrost, which we mortals perceive as the rainbow.

Naturally, such a strategic point cannot be left unguarded, and that is where Heimdall enters the picture.

Heimdall is the sentry of the Gods. He stands watch at Bifrost Bridge, ready to blow on his horn when the giants and their allies march against the Gods at Ragnarok.

According to the Eddas, Heimdall is the perfect guard: he never sleeps, his ears are so sensitive that he can hear grass grow, and he can see to the end of the earth.

Obviously, Heimdall plays an important role at Ragnarok. Other than that myth, there are two stories that give us a bigger perspective on this enigmatic God. In one, he battles Loki to recover Freya's necklace, Brisingamen, which Loki has stolen. This is no ordinary struggle; in it, both characters shift into animal forms and fight on rugged rocks surrounded by the ocean's waves. Heimdall is victorious, and Freya gets Brisingamen back. This story, recorded in the Norse poem *Haustlong* and copied in the *Poetic Edda*, is one of several clues that link Heimdall to the Goddess of Love.

It is the other tale, however, that is most important to us. In the Eddic poem titled "The Lay of Rig," Rig—Heimdall in disguise

—wanders through Midgard and stays as a guest in three homes in which live three married couples. In the first, he fathers the class of thralls, or slaves. In the second, he engenders the free yeomen, or karls. The class of leaders, or jarls, results from his stay in the third household. I've told this story in greater detail elsewhere in this book.

As Edred Thorsson points out in *Futhark* while discussing the rune *mannaz*, there are two things we may conclude from this account.[1] From the standpoint of the Germanic peoples as a whole, Heimdall established the organic social order of our traditional society. Note that all three classes are worthy in their own right and have their part to play in making the society function. All three share the divine spark as descendants of Heimdall. From the perspective of the individual, all Northfolk share the essential nature of our Gods (having the same "soul structure" or soul components). The implication of this kinship is that our destiny is to grow ever more like the Gods themselves.

Heimdall, then, is the personification of the *mannaz* rune. This rune name means "man" (meaning not necessarily a male, but merely, "a person"), but the inner meaning is the illuminated man, the initiate into the Mysteries, the "perfected man"—perfected not in the sense of being a finished and unchanging product, but in the sense of possessing the same inner structure as the Gods themselves. We have the same nature as the Gods, but on a much (much!) smaller magnitude.

There are two ways in which Heimdall is of concern to us today. In a more limited sense, he is the natural God of anyone who works in the security field—from the ordinary guard patrolling factory areas at midnight or controlling entry into a public building, to Border Patrol agents and the thousands of employees of the Department of Homeland Security.

But don't we all need vigilance? We all watch over our homes, and over our children. Each of us looks out for our interests and guards against threats to our livelihood, our status, and our reputation. With our senses sharp, we sweep our surroundings for anything or anyone that might harm us. The Eddic poem *Havamal* is full of advice about

1. Edred Thorsson, *Futhark* (York Beach, Maine: Weiser, 1984), p. 60.

wariness and prudent self-protection. To that extent, Heimdall is a God for every man and every woman.

When we consider the esoteric aspects of Heimdall revealed in the "Lay of Rig," we see that the White God is our ancestral link with the Divine. As such, he reminds us of our Godly potential. Any one of us who aspires to self-transformation, to the realization of our holy heritage, can look to Heimdall for inspiration. Such a spiritual aim transcends the centuries and makes Heimdall our God today just as he was our ancestors' God a millennium ago.

Sif

Sif, wife of Thor, is overshadowed by her blustery husband. It's hard to compete with the God of Thunder when it comes to getting attention! We know little about her. Sif plays a role in a tale where Loki, mischievous as ever, cut off her beautiful blond hair while she slept. Thor, furious, threatened to smash Loki with his hammer, but Loki promised to set things right. And indeed, he does. Journeying to the realm of the dwarves, Loki convinced two of them to make a replacement for Sif's glorious mane out of real gold. Unlike ordinary gold, however, when placed on her head it grew just like natural hair. The dwarves also made two other treasures of the Gods: Frey's magic ship, Skidbladnir, and Gungnir, Odin's spear.

It has been speculated that Sif's locks represent the crops growing in the fields, and that cutting them stands for the harvest. Some scholars find problems with that explanation, but it would be logical for Sif, wife of Thor, to be a Goddess of the growing fields, considering Thor's connection with fertility. The rain-yielding thunderstorm could have been seen by our ancestors as the lovemaking of Thor and his beautiful wife.

Every woman who has been married to a man resembling Thor— and that would be many women indeed—can identify with Sif. Their relationship, such as we can see of it, may be more like that of the average couple than the bond between Odin and Frigga. Sif holds her own as a model and patron for many wives.

In her role as Goddess of the fertile field, Sif reminds us where food comes from. We're used to finding our fruits and vegetables in neat piles in the produce section of the grocery store, and our wheat all made up into loaves of bread on shelves in aisle 7B. The Goddess with the golden hair whispers in our ears that life is more fragile than we know, and that hunger has been a scourge for humans for most of our existence. The earth must be treated with respect and care if she is to yield her bounty for the consumption of man.

Aegir, Ran, and Njord

Take a look at any map of Northern Europe and you will see that the Germanic peoples were surrounded by the sea. Our earliest origins were along the base of Jutland and the adjoining Baltic and North Sea coasts. The Danish peninsula, and for that matter all of Scandinavia and northern Germany, were profoundly influenced by the oceans, from which they drew much of their food and which were essential to long-range commerce. To understand what the sea means to people who live by its shores, one has only to look at Ireland. Irish coastal villages, especially those bordering the wild Atlantic, developed a lifestyle, economy, and traditions centered on the waves and the depths beneath them.

Three Nordic deities are associated with the sea. Their functions are similar, but there are significant differences between them.

Aegir and Ran are husband and wife. They dwell beneath the sea, where they entertain the other Gods and Goddesses at feasts. Aegir is renowned as a brewer—an association that apparently has to do with the sea foam's resemblance to the froth atop beer or other fermented beverages. On one occasion, Thor goes on a quest to obtain a huge kettle from one of the giants and deliver it to Aegir, who could use it for brewing.

Aegir's wife, Ran, uses a net to trap drowned sailors and bring them to the hall, where she and her husband entertain them. They presumably share feasting and laughter much as Odin's champions in Valhalla. A popular belief in Iceland was that a drowned person had been especially well received in Aegir's hall if he was seen at his own funeral feast.

Njord is also a God of the sea, but in a different sense than Aegir. Aegir, the brewer and hall-master on the ocean bottom, receives the drowned voyagers who are gathered in Ran's net. Njord's position is somewhat different. He is the father of Frey and Freya, the Lord and Lady of the Vanir. We might reasonably expect him to be, like them, involved with prosperity and the accumulation of wealth and this is indeed the case. Njord is the God of ships and shipping. His hall is named Noatun, meaning "the place of ships." He presides over the sea as a place that provides a double harvest—in the form of fish to keep men from starving, and as a road for trade to bring goods that make life easier, richer, and more interesting.

As we have seen throughout this chapter, some things do not change much from century to century, or even from millennium to millennium. Men and women still cross the sea, and ships still sink. Ran still collects the drowned in her net, and those who would have a good welcome there may, like the saga hero Frithjof, carry a bit of gold to pay one's way into the hall. Saxon ship-masters were rumored to sacrifice captives to placate the forces of nature—a practice, by the way, that modern Asatruar have not adopted!—and even as you are reading these words, a sailor on some storm-tossed sea, perhaps rounding the Cape of Good Hope or crossing the Skaggerak, is praying to the God he knows for a safe landing. If you're in the navy or a hand on a merchant vessel, an oil platform worker, or just a passenger on a ship, pour a horn of mead or beer to Aegir and his wife.

Many people travel by sea, and so Aegir and Ran will get their share of devotees. Professional fishermen, those workers who harvest the fish just as surely as farmers gather crops from their fields, might well be followers of Njord. Likewise, men and women who run shipping companies, or who work for such companies, or who manage import-export businesses, might understandably have an interest in the Lord of the Enclosure of Ships.

In a broader sense, all of us owe Aegir, Ran, and Njord a debt of gratitude. Our welfare depends on commerce, of course, and just about everyone eats fish. But there's more. All higher forms of life on Earth depend on the sea. The oceans absorbs carbon from the atmosphere, release oxygen, and determine our climate by circulating water from one place to another on a planetary scale. Life arose in the sea. The blood in our veins and the amniotic fluid that surrounds us before birth are tokens of this watery nativity. The deities of the sea give life, and if their realm falters, death will follow for us and for all our works. The oceans, and the numinous beings they represent, deserve our love and our deepest reverence.

Easter (Ostara)

Easter or Ostara was a Goddess of the Angles and Saxons. We know of her only from the writing of a Benedictine monk named Bede, who described her in his *De temporum ratione* (On the Reckoning of Time).

According to Bede, Easter (*Ēostre*) was a Goddess honored at the Spring equinox. Her name derives from the Saxon word for "east," and from a Proto-Germanic term meaning "illuminate" and "daybreak." We can conclude that Easter was a Goddess of the dawn and of the onset of springtime. Most Asatruar in the twenty-first century call her "Ostara," from the Old High German. I have given more prominence to the Saxon pronunciation because it is identical to the name of the Christian festival and thus is more familiar to people outside our faith.

Easter is not known in Scandinavia, and she derives much of her modern popularity from the fact that Christianity borrowed her festival (and her name!) for their celebration of the resurrection of Jesus. Most of the symbols and customs we associate with the Christian holy day—eggs, bunnies, chicks, and sunrise services—make much more sense in the context of a life-bringing Goddess of the Spring.

Anyone who has endured a harsh and gloomy winter will understand the joy that comes with springtime. The dawn of the first day of the season, when at last the day defeats the night, must have been a time of rejoicing. The resurgence of life was proof that the community had, after all, survived the rigors of winter without starving or freezing. Even today, when our lives are much more secure than those of our ancient ancestors, we feel this instinctive response to the birth of light and warmth. Easter isn't just for the ancient Saxons now, but for all who follow the ways of our people in the present age.

Nerthus

Nerthus is a Germanic Goddess of the earth. She is mentioned in Tacitus's *Germania*, written in the first century CE. Her worship may have centered on the island of Zealand, in Denmark.

Tacitus writes that Germans drove a wagon bearing Nerthus, concealed in a draped sanctuary, through the community. Wherever she went, there was peace and festivities. Weapons were put away. Eventually, the wagon was driven to Nerthus's sanctuary, where the wagon and its contents were washed in a holy lake and the servants who had attended it were—according to Tacitus—drowned.

Many scholars believe the name "Nerthus" is linguistically related to "Njord"—the name of a male deity we know from the Viking Age. One possibility is that Njord was once a hermaphroditic deity. A more popular theory is that Njord and Nerthus were originally brother and sister, much like Frey and Freya. This suggests that Nerthus was one of the Vanir—which makes sense, given her role as Earth Mother and life-giver.

Nerthus is not the only Germanic deity to be drawn around the community in a wagon. Many centuries after Tacitus, the image in the wagon was not Nerthus, but Frey—again making a connection between Nerthus and the Vanir.

Now, two thousand years after Nerthus gave her gifts to our ancestors, life on Earth teeters on the edge of disaster. Extinction is stalking countless thousands of species in one of the greatest die-offs our planet has ever experienced. Our seas are polluted and fish populations are plummeting. The climate is changing at a rate never before known. More than ever, we as a society need to reconsider our relationship with Nerthus, the giver of life.

Loki

Loki may be the most controversial character in the Norse myths. At one extreme, there is the temptation to treat him as a mirror of the Biblical Satan, but the comparison is faulty. While Loki is certainly exasperating, irritating, and mischievous, he is not the arch-fiend, the Prince of Darkness, that haunts Christianity . . . at least, not in the beginning.

If "Loki as Devil" is one extreme, the other is "Loki the Trickster." Tricksters are found in many cultures, where they break the rules of normal behavior. Often, the things they do end up having positive results even if their intention was malicious. Tricksters are frequently able to change their gender. They can be foolish and clever at the same time. All these statements apply to Loki. Eventually, however, Loki commits crimes so horrendous that he ends up in a category all his own: the murder of Balder and the onset of Ragnarok make his deeds of mere mischief seem utterly insignificant.

When Loki enters the myths, he is usually found stirring trouble. He steals Thor's hammer, or robs Freya of her necklace, or arranges the theft of Idun's apples. Sometimes he behaves stupidly, as in *The Saga of the Volsungs* when he wantonly killed an otter lounging by the river. He finds out, too late, that the otter was really Hreidmar's son in animal form—thus initiating the dread cycle of events surrounding the cursed treasure of the Nibelungs. Loki usually fixes the problem he has created, though the other Gods usually force him to do so. Sometimes the Gods come out ahead, as when Loki, after cutting off Sif's hair, returns from the home of the dwarves with her new hair of gold, a magic ship for Frey, and Odin's spear.

Loki is not so much evil as he is greedy and weak, at least in most of the myths. In defending Loki's role, one can point out that he keeps the action going. When things get stale and static, Loki can be depended upon to cause a crisis that will precipitate a whole new sequence of events, for better or worse.

There is a qualitative change in this pattern when he instigates the death of Balder. Loki fashions a dart from the one thing in the world that could harm Balder—the humble mistletoe. Placing the missile in the hand of blind Hod, he guides the throw that strikes Odin's most-beloved son dead. This is a cosmic catastrophe, and brings on Ragnarok.

Loki flees the angry Gods, but is eventually captured and chained to a rock where a serpent continually drips burning venom on him. His wife Sigyn holds a cup to catch the poison, but when she goes to empty it the drops fall on Loki, and his writhing is the cause of earthquakes.

At Ragnarok, Loki will be free—as will the Fenris wolf and all the other monsters that hate the Gods. Loki will steer the dread ship Naglfar, made of the fingernails and toenails of the dead. He and Heimdall will fight against each other for the last time, and both will die. The end will come—so that there may be a new beginning.

To the very end, Loki's role remains an ambiguous one. Though Balder's murder is a heinous crime, bringing sorrow to all beings except Loki, one could argue that it had to happen for the cosmos to move on. Even Ragnarok has its purpose, just as we have our purpose in delaying it and, when it comes, to fight on the side of the Gods—and against Loki.

There was no devotion given to Loki in ancient times. No place-names marked ritual sites for him, no human bore names related to him, there were no priests or priestesses of Loki. Some modern practitioners of Asatru have apparently considered this an oversight, and one occasionally hears toasts to Loki at Asatru gatherings today. However, I strongly discourage this in the Asatru Folk Assembly, and I do not permit horns to be raised to him in my presence. My experience is that Loki-toasts are followed by discord and all-around bad luck.

Throughout this chapter, we have taken many Gods and Goddesses and shown how they are just as relevant today as they were long ago. Loki, too, is relevant; not as a model, or as a patron, or as a friend—but as a warning.

A Few Other Gods and Goddesses

In this survey, I have focused on the Gods and Goddesses who play a substantial role in the myths. They are well-developed characters with functional specialties—fertility, wealth, battle, magic—and we can relate them to the priorities governing our own lives. Other deities are more enigmatic. Some are little more than names, and have no surviving tales to tell us about their character, and why we might want to approach them.

Because my purpose is to demonstrate the modern relevance of the Gods and Goddesses, I will not devote much time to these more obscure deities. However, a quick listing of some of them will give you an idea of the richness of our ancestral lore, and indicate how much has been lost through the ages:

- Nanna is the wife of Balder, son of Odin.
- Forseti is a son of Balder and Nanna, and a reconciler of disputes.
- Vidar is a son of Odin, very strong, who will slay the wolf Fenris at Ragnarok.
- Bragi is famous for his eloquence and poetry.
- Skadi skis through the winter landscape while hunting with her bow.
- Vali, son of Odin and Rind, is a good fighter and a sharpshooter.
- Hod is a blind God who throws the dart that kills Balder.
- Saxnot is one of the divine ancestors of the Saxons.
- Friagabis, "Giver of Freedom," was the Goddess of the Frisians.
- Mani, while perhaps not exactly a God, is the personification of the moon.
- Sol, likewise, is the personification of the sun.

The Holy Powers and Us

Our ancestors called on the Gods and Goddesses for every conceivable reason, most of them immediate and tangible: for good crops, victory in battle, easy childbirth, cure from sickness, success in love, good weather, and a hundred other things. Our situation has changed a lot in the last thousand years or so. We are more protected from snow and ice, our children are usually born in hospitals surrounded by medical professionals, and most of us rarely face life-threatening violence. Despite these differences, most things have remained the same—we need food, shelter, love, and lives that are fulfilling. And though we seldom think about it, catastrophe and death strike people all around us, every day. The fundamental realities are much as they have always been, our needs and wants are remarkably constant, and the Gods and Goddesses whom our ancestors revered are still as pertinent today as ever.

Are our native Gods, the ones that speak to us from old manuscripts and rock carvings, still relevant? Absolutely.

Chapter 8

Che Chousano-Year War

The struggle to convert the Germanic peoples began in the fourth century with Ulfilas preaching to the Goths, and ended seven hundred years later with the burning of the temple at Uppsala in 1087.[1] The process was seldom peaceful. When persuasion failed, or when local chieftains could not be bribed, no method was too extreme. Followers of Asatru were murdered, maimed, exiled or fined. Temples were destroyed and pagan priests slain. Hostages were taken. Far-flung settlements were threatened with economic isolation and starvation.

Some tribes accepted Christianity with comparative ease. The Goths and Lombards, for example, converted even before they were integrated into the Roman Empire during the Migration Age. Unfortunately for the Church, several Germanic tribes adopted a version of Christian belief that became known as the "Arian heresy," so named because it was formulated by the theologian Arius. The Goths in particular were attracted to this sect because it reinforced their identity as a people, rather than detracting from it.

In Scandinavia, the Church wasted many years preaching to the common people. Despite the easygoing tolerance of local Germanic kings, who generally allowed missionaries to carry on their work unmolested, the Church achieved little. Christianity was simply too alien to take hold in Germanic culture. The Germans believed in

---

1. The war between Asatru and Christianity was part of a more comprehensive war against European paganism spanning about a thousand years—from the Christian persecutions of pagans in Rome to the nominal victory over the Baltic religion of Romuva in the 1300s. This thousand-year war has gone largely unnoticed, not to mention unappreciated, by the world.

heroic self-assertion, relentless courage, and stoic toughness. They had no need to be "saved" from anything. Such an aristocratic mindset had little interest in a doctrine from a foreign land, which arose among people who were neither kin nor ancestors to the Northmen, and which preached submission! Clearly, pitching the Christian message to ordinary men and women of Germania was not going to work. Another strategy was needed.

The new approach was twofold. First, Christianity was superficially "Germanicized" to make it more palatable to the Northern taste. Second, this new version of Christian belief was then sold to the chieftains rather than to the common folk. Jesus now became a warrior prince and his apostles were transformed into his loyal war band. Heroism became a part of the new doctrine, and the newly-recast Christ became the greatest hero.[2]

Often, the scheme succeeded. Ambitious kings and up-and-coming chieftains allowed themselves to be baptized, and their folk—loyal to their leaders and trusting their wisdom—followed their example. Of course, these leaders often had plans of their own. Becoming a Christian was like joining the Masons or the country club, only better. It allowed the kingdom and its ruler admission to the medieval equivalent of the European Union, opening doors to trade and political alliances that otherwise would have remained closed.

The most convincing reason for kings to be baptized, however, was the Christian outlook on royalty itself. Kings ruled by the grace of the Almighty, and to disobey them was to defy God Himself. This "divine right of kings" had no counterpart in German experience. The pre-Christian tribes had kings typically chosen by the elders. Their nomination was ratified by the freemen. Some tribes had no king until war threatened, at which time they elected one. Once chosen, the king was still subject to the law, and his power was hedged in by the freemen on the one hand and the council of elders on the other. This system of checks and balances came to an end with the coming of Christianity, which centralized royal power at the cost of everyone else. In almost

---

2. The best account of this entire process is found in James C. Russell, *The Germanization of Early Medieval Christianity* (New York: Oxford University Press, 1994).

every respect, the rights of ordinary men and women shriveled when our native paganism was replaced by the alien creed.

The conversion of self-serving leaders often brought about the baptism of their followers. But not always—an unwilling people might choose war and death rather than conversion. One of the best examples is the war of resistance against Charlemagne, king of the Franks.[3]

Charlemagne launched a war against the pagan Saxons in the year 772 and fought a total of eighteen battles in northwest Germany. He began by attacking a holy site, probably the ritual site known as the Externsteine, near what is now Paderborn. There, Charlemagne destroyed the Irminsul, a large, wooden treelike structure representing the all-encompassing World Tree of Northern lore. By thus defiling a religious shrine, Charlemagne made it clear that his war was not merely political, but religious. He fought to the river Weser and destroyed a number of Saxon settlements on the way. Having temporarily achieved his aims, he took hostages and turned his fury on the Lombards of northern Italy.

Although defeated on the field of battle, the pagan Saxons dispersed and fought on as guerrillas under their king, Widukind. In 775, Charlemagne tried again to pacify them. He swept through the offending villages, overwhelming all that stood against him and destroying Saxon strongholds. Thinking his job done, he forgot about the Saxons and resumed his war against the Lombards.

But Widukind's pagans proved resilient. As soon as Charlemagne turned his attention to the Lombards, they regrouped and took the Frankish garrison at Eresburg. Once again Charlemagne fought them, and this time he drove Widukind into exile. Consolidating his victory, the king reorganized Saxon society by replacing the traditional tribal leaders with royalty of his own choosing.

In 782, Charlemagne established a uniform code of laws over both the Franks and the Saxons. Because it harshly punished pagans,

3. The war against the Saxons is described with passion in a little-known volume titled *The Franks: A Critical Study in Christianisation and Imperialism* by F. J. Los (n.d.; my copy was given to me by the Odinist Movement of Miami in the early 1980s). Los (1898–1974) was a professor of history and geography in the Netherlands.

the people again rose up in revolt. Widukind returned from exile and defeated a Frankish army at Suntelgebirge. In retaliation, Charlemagne brought 4,500 pagan Saxon leaders to Verden, on the Aller River, and had them murdered. This massacre sparked two more years of relentless war. Finally, in 785, Widukind surrendered. Sporadic revolts against Charlemagne and Christianity continued for nine more years, however.

Two hundred years later, the Christianization of Norway provided another case study of the religious repression. Olaf Tryggvason became king of Norway in 995, and immediately began tightening his grip on the various regional rulers. Olaf also insisted that the entire country worship Christ, and he enforced his will by the sword. Snorri Sturluson's epic *Heimskringla* describes the conversion in great detail. The saga tells how Olaf went from district to district baptizing the Norwegians, burning temples, and killing or exiling all who stood firm in their ancestral faith.

Snorri's account highlights many of the martyrs who died under torture rather than become Christian. Eyvind Kinnrifi had his internal organs cooked when Tryggvason ordered a bowl of red-hot embers placed on his stomach. The king forced Raud the Strong to swallow a poisonous snake—after which the king confiscated all Raud's wealth. Olvir organized religious rites observing the coming of springtime; Olaf had Olvir killed and all his co-conspirators murdered, mutilated, exiled, or fined depending on their degree of complicity.

On one occasion, a man named Iron Beard was hosting ceremonies in honor of the Gods, and as a gesture of good faith he invited Olaf to attend. Olaf deceitfully agreed to come. When all had arrived and the door was bolted, the king produced his axe and demolished the statue of Thor, then killed Iron Beard. The rest of the people were given the choice of baptism or death.

But like their Saxon cousins, the Norwegians were stubborn. Tryggvason's efforts did not succeed in wiping out all resistance. Years later, another King Olaf—this one known as Olaf the Stout—employed these same methods of converting the heathen. Like his namesake, Olaf the Stout made many martyrs for Asatru. One of these was an outspoken man named Guthroth, who spoke against Olaf's trampling the traditional liberties of the folk and his constant violations of the law. For this offense against the king, his tongue was cut out.

Threats, tempered with bribery, were enough to sway the decision in other lands. According to tradition, Iceland adopted Christianity in the year 1000. Missionaries had splintered Icelandic society into two factions, one Christian and one Asatru. Law and order were breaking down; several killings had already occurred and more seemed to be on the way. A resolution was needed if the country was not to dissolve into chaos. When the Icelandic assembly met in that fateful year, the question was put to Thorgeir, the Lawspeaker. After deliberating for a day and a night, he announced that there was to be one law in Iceland, and one religion: Christianity. Those true to the old Gods and Goddesses were allowed to practice in private, but if witnesses proved they had done so, they would be banished from the country for three years.

Dag Strömbäck, in *The Conversion of Iceland*, tells us what was happening behind the scenes.[4] Olaf Tryggvason had taken all the Icelanders in Norway hostage and had threatened to kill them. His hand was temporarily stayed when he was convinced that persuasion could be used to bring Iceland to Christ. An unfavorable decision at the Althing, of course, might change Olaf's mind and cost the hostages their lives. Strömbäck believes that Tryggvason might even have mounted an all-out invasion of Iceland if the Christians had not won the decision.

But there's more. Ari Thorgilsson writes in *The Book of the Icelanders* that money changed hands between the Christian chieftains and the Lawspeaker. While Ari does not specifically accuse the Christians of bribery, the context of his remarks makes it unlikely that this payment was a fee for other, legitimate services. Sadly, Thorgeir the Lawspeaker may have been the Judas of Asatru.

Whether Christianity displaced Asatru peacefully, by force, or by

---

4. See pp. 30–31 in Dag Strömbäck, *The Conversion of Iceland: A Survey* (London: Viking Society for Northern Research, 1975) for details on the likely bribing of Thorgeir the Lawspeaker.

threat and bribery, two things were constant: (1) the practice of our ancestral religion was banned and those who disobeyed were put to death, and (2) political freedom was diminished in the face of royal power and the dictates of a tyrannical church.

An impartial look at history shows that Christianity won because of greed, force, and a well-organized army of missionaries supported by Vatican gold. The new creed had the power that comes with clear, dogmatic doctrine and a ruthless desire to persuade others of its truth—or to kill them if they could not be persuaded.

Surprisingly, some good things came from the Christianization of Europe. The evangelizers brought a form of writing that helped preserve our sacred lore. The Germans could write with runes, but runes were designed for working magic, not for ordinary communication.[5] Further, the technology of parchment and papyrus was a huge advance over writing on wood, stone, and bone.

Two hundred years after Asatru had officially disappeared, Snorri Sturluson penned his essential collections of myths. It may be that Snorri was simply a Christian of his era who had an abiding love of his national culture—but I often wonder if he was not one of the last surviving members of an indigenous religion that had gone underground in response to Christian persecution. In either case, today's modern revival of Asatru would have been much more difficult, and much poorer, had Snorri not preserved the lore while (supposedly) writing a manuscript on the art of poetry!

Perhaps there is a larger plan at work here. It would be typical of Odin, wise and powerfully paradoxical, to allow the doctrine of the Christ to overrun Germania—for a while. Thanks to this temporary "conquest" we acquired skills that our ancestors lacked. With these tools we can forge the sword needed to shatter the chains that bind us, and go onward to our destiny among the stars.

---

5. This is not to say that runes were never used for sending messages in daily life. Archaeologists have found graffiti and short notes scratched on wooden staves from the Viking Age, and later, a lengthy manuscript detailing the laws of Scania (the *Codex Runicus*) was written in runes. Such mundane usage, however, indicates that the old magical-religious system was in decline.

Those who would think the old ways gone forever, those who believe that Christianity has permanently consumed the Gods of the North, need to put things into the perspective of time. We have been Europeans for thirty or forty thousand years. For about ninety-seven percent of that time, we followed a religion other than Christianity. There is no proof that Christianity was anything more than a passing phase.

Odin, on his seat high in Valhalla, is laughing.

Chapter 9

How the Gods Came to North America

About forty years ago, I pledged my loyalty to Odin and the other deities of the Northlands. What followed in the ensuing decades was a persistent and ever-evolving attempt to revive our ancestral European religion. That struggle continues to this day.

If it is true that we learn more from our mistakes than from our successes, then the reawakening of Germanic religion in America has much to teach us. My private devotion became a movement—at first narrow, then broader and better informed—with implications for all who care about the direction of our culture and the fate of the European peoples in general.

This narrative is a personal one, based on my experiences as the founder of three successive organizations devoted to the practice and promotion of Asatru. It is a report of my own history and of lessons learned, and makes no claim of being an encyclopedic account.

The Viking Brotherhood—The Beginning

I decided to follow the Gods of the Vikings in either 1968 or 1969, during my college years. This decision arose from two things: my perception that the God of the Bible was a tyrant, and an admiration for the heroism and vitality of the Norsemen as depicted in popular literature.

This pagan epiphany did not spring from the leftist/hippy/Age-of-Aquarius counterculture of the 1960s. Quite the opposite. I was attracted to the Vikings by their warlike nature, their will to power, and their assertion of self. My own views bore no resemblance to "peace, love, and good vibes." I was a cadet in the Reserve Officer Training Corps and aspired to a career in the U.S. Army's Special Forces.

Neither did my allegiance to the old Gods come from the racially tinged writings of the Australian, Alexander Rudd Mills, or from Canadian Else Christensen, or from the early twentieth-century German rune mystic Guido von List (as at least one critic has alleged). In those early days, my interest was driven by my idealism, and by my youthful desire to do brave deeds.

My devotion to Odin and the other Gods and Goddesses remained a private and lonely faith for about two years. As far as I knew, I was literally the only person on Earth who stood alongside the Elder Gods.

Soon, however, I felt the need to find others like myself. I took out advertisements in *Fate* magazine and other "pagan-friendly" publications under the (rather embarrassingly dramatic) name of the "Viking Brotherhood." In the winter of 1971–72, the first issue of *The Runestone* saw print. I produced it with a rickety typewriter and a mimeograph machine, and the first run was of eleven copies.

So far as I have been able to ascertain, the Viking Brotherhood was the first organization in the United States devoted to the elder faith of the Germanic peoples. It was recognized as a tax-exempt religious organization by the Internal Revenue Service in the summer of 1972.

Two or three months after this publishing debut, I reported for active duty as an army officer. I attended the infantry officer course, then earned my parachutist wings and the black-and-gold Ranger tab. *The Runestone* limped along, gradually improving in quality and reaching between one and two hundred subscribers. I was astounded at its success! Who could have imagined there were so many other people out there who loved the old Gods? The consuming obligations of army life occupied me for the next four years, and the Viking Brotherhood remained a minuscule organization, devoid of grander ambitions, until its transformation in 1976.

The Viking Brotherhood in Retrospect

The Viking Brotherhood was focused on the image of the warrior, and on the assertion of individual will and freedom that the warrior epitomizes. In many ways it was a reflection of where I was at that point in my life.

A photograph of me taken in that era shows a serious young man. His eyeglasses betray the scholar within the infantryman's uniform. No doubts fog his face; the self-exploration and introspection of the Sixties did not sway him from his chosen course. He is a romantic and a warrior, sincere and well-meaning but largely ignorant of his own depths. He has a capacity for intellectual and spiritual breadth, but it is by no means fully tapped. In a way, that photograph was not only Steve McNallen; it was the Viking Brotherhood itself.

I would evolve, and so would Asatru, in the years to come.

Many aspects of the complex and rich Nordic belief system—the feminine, the magical, the agricultural, the broader Indo-European context—were largely ignored during those early days. I was just beginning to shift out of this narrow vision during the period between 1972 and 1976.

It was in about 1974 that I began to realize that there was an innate connection between Germanic paganism and the Germanic people. I had resisted the idea as being somehow racist, but I could not ignore the evidence. Within a year or two I had shifted from a "universalist" to a "folkish" position—even though neither of those terms would enter our vocabulary for many years.

The Asatru Free Assembly

After my release from the army in 1976, I moved to Berkeley, California. I had learned the term "Asatru" from *Hammer of the North*, a book by Icelandic scholar Magnus Magnusson. At last I had a name for my beliefs! The Viking Brotherhood soon became the Asatru Free Assembly, or AFA.

In Berkeley, a group of us met in the back of Dick Johnson's insurance agency at 1000 University Avenue—the office is now a store selling Indian saris, in itself a statement on the dispossession

of European-descended people in North America. Dick took the
religious name of Aluric.

Twenty years later, in the New Jersey Pine Barrens, I befriended
another man who had taken the name Aluric (and for the same
reasons as Dick). By coincidence, this "new" Aluric had worked at a
pizza parlor a few blocks from Dick's office during the years we were
meeting there—but never knew of us. This was neither the first nor the
last peculiar coincidence I was to encounter while carrying the banner
of the Holy Powers.

During the ten years of the Asatru Free Assembly's existence we
devised a religious calendar, composed and performed a multitude of
rituals, and published booklets and audiotapes. Beginning in 1980, the
AFA hosted an annual event called the Althing (a tradition which
Valgard Murray of the Asatru Alliance has continued down to the
present day). Local congregations, or "kindreds," were formed around
the country.

We established several special-interest groups or "guilds" to meet
the needs of warriors, women, and brewers. Each of these guilds had
its own newsletter, and a richly varied Asatru literature soon began to
proliferate. The existence of a guild dealing with rocketry and space
travel testified to the fact that we were not locked into the distant
past. (For a few years we had the custom of opening each Althing
with a rocket launch, just to remind ourselves that the Faustian reach
expresses itself differently in each age.)

The Asatru Free Assembly held to a middle ground on the
controversial role of ancestry in Asatru. On the one hand we were
proud of our European heritage, actively espoused the interests of
European-descended people, and felt that Asatru was a uniquely
Northern European way of perceiving the Holy. On the other hand
we opposed totalitarianism and racial hatred, convinced that decency
and honor required us to treat individuals of all racial groups with
respect. Forces from either extreme periodically tried to budge us off
this position, but we successfully held our ground.

When the Asatru Free Assembly crumpled in 1986, I was working
as a peace officer in the county jail, and my wife kept books for an oil

company. She and I were logging around sixty hours and forty hours per week, respectively, on Asatru-related matters. We knew we could not continue putting out this effort without financial compensation, which would allow us to cut back on these mundane jobs. When we approached the membership, the general reaction was negative. Some accused us of trying to "establish a priesthood" or of being "money-hungry." Surprised and bruised by this rejection, we tried cutting back on membership services to make the job more manageable. This in turn caused more complaints among some AFA members.

We soon realized this was a losing battle. We were at the end of our financial and emotional resources. The AFA was disbanded, with the ashes turned over to Valgard Murray, leader of the Arizona Kindred, who used them as the foundation for the Asatru Alliance.

Looking Back on the Asatru Free Assembly

The Asatru Free Assembly had evolved far beyond the old male-dominated, warrior-oriented Viking Brotherhood: we honored the Goddesses along with the Gods. Women, originally rare in our ranks, played an important part in our activities. The AFA understood that warriors have a role, but that they are only part of a healthy community. The continuity between Germanic religion and the broader Indo-European family was acknowledged. I coined the term "metagenetics" to refer to the link between spirituality and heredity, and we produced a body of literature that served as a valuable foundation for the future.

It is important to realize that everything we did was new. There was no model for our actions. Revisionists with their own agendas have attempted to minimize the role of the AFA, claiming that we were only one of many groups extant at that time, but this is not true. For all practical purposes, the AFA was Asatru in America until the mid-1980s.

The Wandering Years

Disappointed by our experience with the Asatru Free Assembly, my wife and I eventually moved to a semi-deserted mining town in the mountains of California, earned teaching credentials, and tried to find meaning in our lives without the AFA. I taught science and mathematics to junior high school students, visited exotic countries during the summer, and tried to forget about organized Asatru.

I interviewed Tibetan resistance fighters in northern India, gave blot to Thor in a high Himalayan pass, and spent time in the jungles of Burma with freedom fighters of the Karen people. Some of the articles I wrote during this period were published in *Soldier of Fortune* magazine. These experiences helped me to develop sympathies not just for my own people, but for others around the world. To this day I am active in the Tibetan freedom struggle, and AFA publications have given me a chance to voice support for Burmese, Nigerians, and southern Sudanese—all working for the independence and freedom of their respective tribes, nations, or ethnic groups.

Even in my travels I could not escape the Gods. I was sitting in a guerrilla camp in Burma, talking with a young German who worked as a physical therapist most of the year, but spent his summers teaching Karen soldiers how to be snipers. The German saw my Thor's hammer necklace and asked me about it. I explained its religious significance— at which point he produced a similar one from under his shirt. Years later, in Bosnia, I was to see hammers worn by some of the young men in the international section of the Tomislav Brigade.

I also joined the Army National Guard during this period. My unit was called up during the Rodney King riots in Los Angeles. I am undoubtedly one of the few men in America to have stood on the famous corner of Hollywood and Vine with a loaded M-16 rifle. One of the best things about these years—indeed, about my life—was the chance to work with soldiers, doing a job I loved.

I never lost my love for the Gods, either, but it was very difficult to do any religious work in my wandering years. Even a simple prayer before meals was painful, too much a reminder of the past. I was scarred, and angry, and bitter.

But I got over it. Healing always comes—and sometimes circumstances force our hands.

The Asatru Folk Assembly

In 1994, I saw signs that a corrupt faction was making inroads into the Germanic religious movement in the United States. Individuals and groups had emerged which denied the innate connection of Germanic religion and Germanic people, saying in effect that ancestral heritage did not matter.

This error could not be allowed to become dominant. I decided to re-enter the fray and throw my influence behind Asatru as it had been practiced in America since the founding of the Viking Brotherhood back in the 1970s. I formed the Asatru Folk Assembly—which became known as the "new AFA," as distinct from the Asatru Free Assembly, or "old AFA."

My re-emergence had been brewing for some time. Already, my scars healing, I had begun writing about the Gods again, putting out a small, digest-size version of *The Runestone* for interested readers. I suppose, looking back, that my eventual return was inevitable in any case.

Our new organization soon made original contributions to the Asatru scene. *The Runestone* and the guild newsletters became thicker and more professional than ever before, and for a while we arranged for a distributor to stock them on newsstands.

One of our more daring experiments was the "Asatru Community Church," which offered public services every other Sunday in Nevada City, California. In our own way we were trying to carry out Edred Thorsson's dream, expressed in the pages of *A Book of Troth*, of having a hof (or building for worship) in every major city in the country. The Community Room of the Nevada County Library was a far cry from a building of our own, but it was a start!

We designed the format of the service to be comfortable for people with Christian backgrounds, but at the end of a year we had little to show for our efforts. The most important thing about the Asatru Community Church was that it tried to reach beyond our usual target audience, to the public at large. I am convinced that Asatru must do this if it is ever to be more than a tiny cult on the fringe of American life.

Kennewick Man

The AFA's greatest fame, or notoriety, came with the Kennewick Man case.

When a set of Caucasian-looking bones was found in the shallows of the Columbia River, the anthropologist who examined them thought they must be the remains of a white settler. When radiocarbon dating showed them to be about 9,300 years old, it was time to take a second look at American prehistory.

Because the skeleton was found in the city of Kennewick, Washington, the media quickly dubbed their original owner "Kennewick Man." The name stuck.

The US Army Corps of Engineers (on whose property Kennewick Man had been found) decided to turn the bones over to local Indian tribes under a law called NAGPRA—the Native American Graves Protection and Repatriation Act. Since the skeleton did not seem to be Indian, and since it was far too old to have been the ancestor of the recent and historically mobile tribes in the area, this was simply politically motivated pandering on the part of the Corps of Engineers.

The AFA filed suit to stop the handover. Since there was a very considerable chance that these were the remains of an ancient European, it was only right that a native European religious organization should have a say in what happened to them.

We were, of course, outgunned from the beginning. Our lawyer, working pro bono, was up against the massed legal might of the Federal government. They had millions of dollars to spend; we had at most a few thousand. They had white guilt and political correctness on their side; we were identifiably members of that nasty, genocidal, oppressive European race.

The AFA didn't have a chance, but we scored a few points. We were the first to contest the government's definition of "Native American" as anyone whose remains were here before 1492 CE. We noted that any Viking burial—such as those of Leif Erikson's colony, for example—would be turned over to the nearest Indian tribe under those guidelines. Much later, Judge Jelderks used precisely our argument to demolish the government's faulty definition.

This controversial case earned the AFA a huge amount of publicity. Hundreds of newspapers over the next few years carried articles about us, and several books mentioned our role. Some of the reporters and authors attacked us with lies, but some were balanced and objective.

One commonly heard statement was that the AFA claimed Kennewick Man was a Viking, or that he was Nordic. This was completely false. Another writer stated that a prominent Christian Identity figure was an AFA spokesman, which is ludicrous to anyone familiar with the American right wing. Perhaps the strangest article accused us of being a racist cult based on a belief in the lost continent of Atlantis!

The fact is, if the American media wants to tell lies about you, they will simply do so and there is not a lot to be done about it. People who urged us to sue the perpetrators did not stop to ask themselves where we would get the hundreds of thousands of dollars needed to take such a case through the courts.

One result of the Kennewick Man case is that scientists are finally taking a serious look at the possibility that ancient Americans migrated to this continent via the "Atlantic Crescent," an equivalent to the Bering land bridge over which Mongoloid peoples crossed.[1] Even more significant, in some ways, is the Discovery Channel program (and ensuing DVD) stating without reservation that Europeans were in North America 6,000 years before Asians came over the Bering Strait. A spear point found in 1996 at Cactus Hill, in Virginia, bridges the gap between the Clovis style of projectile point common in America and the artifacts produced by the Solutrean culture of Spain and France—some 17,000 years ago. This and other evidence ranging from identical caches of spear points dusted with ochre on both continents, plus DNA evidence, cinches the case for a very early European presence in North America.

Soon after the discovery of the Kennewick Man skeleton, a group of leading scientists sued for the right to study Kennewick Man. Judge Jelderks eventually ruled in their favor, and the remains were not given

1. This theory is outlined in Dennis Stanford, *Across Atlantic Ice: The Origin of America's Clovis Culture* (Berkeley: University of California Press, 2012).

to the Indians.

Where Do We Go from Here?

"Destiny" is a strong word, but nothing less can describe what I see for the future of the AFA.

The AFA's mission statement is a bold one: "to promote, practice, and further evolve the religion of Asatru, thus forging it into a powerful and effective tool for building a better world."

Note the activity implied in that sentence. We are not content to quietly follow the Way of our Gods and our ancestors; we intend to actively reach out to others who are ready to "come home." Nor are we trapped in the past. While we are true to the ancient spirit and the essence of our faith, we are also ready to bring Asatru into the twenty-first century.

Over the last five years the AFA has carefully built an infrastructure that will help it become the large, mainstream religious organization implied by its mission statement.

One essential component is our clergy program. For several years now, our clergy course has turned out men and women qualified not only to lead religious ceremonies, but also to offer spiritual guidance and comfort. Clergy members conduct naming rites for newborns, join couples in marriage, and bless homes. They visit the sick, bury the dead, and inspire the living to live better lives.

Parallel to the clergy is a network of AFA representatives we call "Folkbuilders." Their task is to connect with our members and promote the AFA in their assigned areas, coast-to-coast and around the world. Folkbuilders organize events, answer questions, and build the evolving Asatru community.

Together, these two institutions are bringing Asatru to the mainstream in America and elsewhere.

Other AFA projects serve the same end. For example, we compiled a compact Asatru handbook for military personnel. Service members of other faiths have their sacred texts, and it only seemed right that Asatruar have this same degree of spiritual support. We included portions of the Eddas, a selection of prayers, the poems associated with the runes, and much more—all crammed into sixty-some pages designed to fit in the pocket of a combat uniform. A secondary purpose of this manual is to show unit commanders and chaplains that Asatru virtues are compatible with military service and that, in fact, the values of Asatru make us useful additions to any military unit.

But how about our veterans, or Asaturar who fall in battle? The Department of Veterans' Affairs has historically provided headstones for those who have served the nation, at no cost. These tombstones come engraved with the cross, the star of David, and a number of other religious symbols. The AFA has now arranged to have the hammer of Thor—recognized everywhere as a prominent Asatru icon—approved for our own military personnel. If Asatruar are willing to fight and die for their country, shouldn't they be allowed to have the symbol of their faith over their final resting places?

Projects like these are gradually bringing Asatru to the attention of Middle America—and its equivalent in other countries. The increasing quality of our membership reflects this transition.

Aside from attracting the mainstream, the most encouraging sign in the AFA is the growing sense of community. Initially, much of this was "cyber-community," which many of us understandably consider an oxymoron. This feeling of being part of a group has matured over the years, however. More and more of us have met in person. Even our online relationships have grown deeper and broader. We console each other in times of death, and celebrate the birth of new children. We share favorite books, career tips, and recipes. We make plans to meet down at a local pub, or to attend an event the next state over. Locally, we gather for rituals and for birthday parties, or to load a truck for someone moving to a new home. Community? We're getting there.

Asatru has come a long way since I dedicated myself to the service of Odin, some forty years ago. We've grown up. Now we're ready to grow in numbers, and in influence.

Chapter 10

The Universe:
Its Origin and Evolution

The creation myth of any people reflects their attitudes toward the Divine, themselves, their place in the universe, and their values. This is as true of the Germanic people as any other.

When we examine the Nordic tales about the origin of the universe and of humans, we immediately notice several things. They support the idea of human worth. They establish the equal value of men and women. And—remembering, of course, that they are metaphors— we find them more consistent with the spirit of modern science than perhaps any other ancient cosmology.

First, let's examine the account as described in the Eddas.[1]

In the beginning, there was nothing but a yawning void called Ginnungagap. From the northern part of this vastness, waters flowed toward the middle, and as they flowed they turned to ice. Buried within the ice was a yeasty essence, the very substance of potential life. A drizzling rain continually fell upon it, so that it formed layer after layer of hardened rime.

From the southern part of the expanse came fire and sparks, stretching toward the middle of Ginnungagap. The heat fell upon the ice and, where it melted, the yeasty fluid began to stir with life and this life took on the shape of a manlike being. He was called Ymir. A man

1. Every tribe and nation has its own story of the beginning of things. The one told here does not purport to speak for all humanity, but only for the Northern Europeans. Odin, Vili, and Ve did not give life to humans in general, but only to Northfolk; to claim otherwise would be to say that our lore is the "one, true creation story" and that the creation mythologies of other nations are false. We leave such claims of the one true way to the monotheists.

and a woman were born from the sweat under his left arm, and one leg begot a son on the other. From Ymir and his offspring come the race of frost giants.

A giant cow also emerged from the melting ice. She is called Audhumla, and four rivers of milk flow from her teats. This milk fed Ymir. As for the cow, she lived by licking the blocks of salty ice. She licked for three days, and from the ice she shaped a man with her tongue. The man's name was Buri, and he was handsome and strong. His son was named Borr, who married Bestla, a giant's daughter. Borr and Bestla had three sons: Odin, Vili, and Ve. They slew Ymir and from the parts of his body they constructed the world. His blood became the sea, and his flesh the earth. Mountains are made from his bones, and the dome of the sky is the inside of his skull.

Later, Odin and his two brothers were walking along the seashore when they come across two trees, an ash and an elm. Odin gave them the breath of life, Vili granted them wit and the ability to move about, and Ve bestowed upon them senses. The ash became a man called Ask, and the elm became a woman who bore the name Embla.

Taken at face value, the story is peculiar, even absurd. Giants made of ice, cosmic cows, and a world made from the body of a frost giant—it's easy to dismiss this as the childish fantasies of a primitive race.

When we look at it in terms of symbols, patterns, and processes, though, we see something much more sophisticated.

One of the first things we notice is that the universe is not created ex nihilo, that is to say, out of nothing. It is not the creation of a God. Rather, the cosmos arises through a series of natural processes involving primordial fire and ice. This contrasts sharply with the Biblical account, where God creates the world over a period of seven days simply by willing everything into existence. Since God created everything from nothing, it all belongs to him—the Earth, all the stars in the far-flung galaxies, every lonely atom of hydrogen drifting in the interstellar emptiness. Humans, too, are a part of this creation and thus we all belong to God. We are his property and he can do with us whatever he wants. We are supposedly given free will, but if we exercise it we are punished. Free will is a cruel joke when bestowed on a slave who can only peer through the bars of his cage.

The Germanic creation myth has an entirely different premise. The worlds arise from the laws of nature, without divine intervention. Indeed, we can hardly call the Eddic account a "creation myth," since there is no creator involved! (Odin, Vili, and Ve, who constructed the world from the corpse of Ymir, are at most "rearrangers," not "creators.") Likewise, humans are not brought into being from nothingness, nor from an inert substance like clay or dirt; they are fashioned from something already alive—the two trees found on the beach by the Gods.

In the worldview of our ancestors, then, neither the universe nor the humans inhabiting it are property of the Gods. We belong to ourselves. Free will is not given to us; it is a natural result of our being. We are kin and co-workers with the Gods, not their property.

Another thing we notice is the scientific tone of the Eddic story. Consider the beginning of all things: first, there is great yawning abyss, Ginnungagap, which translates as the "magically charged void." Only in recent times have scientists discovered that what we think of as a vacuum is actually a seething cauldron of forces. Subatomic particles are continually popping into existence, then disappearing back into the invisible fabric of the universe, many times every second. "Empty space" is not empty; it is the energized "quantum foam" underlying all existence. Calling it a "magically charged void" sounds like a poetic description of subatomic reality.

Note, too, the timespan involved in the Germanic version. In Genesis, God supposedly created everything in six days—which, if taken literally, is ludicrous given the scientific evidence. The Eddas, on the other hand, speak of vast periods of time. In the *Prose Edda*, Snorri records that Nifelheim, the World of Mist, existed for "many ages" before the formation of the Earth.[2] This scenario is much more

---

2. "It was many ages before the earth was shaped that the Mist-World was made," according to *Gylfaginning* (The Deluding of Gylfi), Chapter 4. See *The Prose Edda of Snorri Sturluson*, translated by Arthur Brodeur (New York: American-Scandinavian Foundation, 1967), p. 16.

in line with the facts than creating the cosmos in just over an average work week.

Switching from quantum mechanics to biology, we find that the Germanic description of the beginning of life is startlingly modern. It begins when the "yeast" contained in Niflheim's primordial waters is activated by light and heat from Muspelheim. This sounds much like the "primordial soup of organic matter in water" stimulated by sunlight, from which life on Earth is generally thought to have come.

Once formed, life develops in a progressive way. At first it is androgynous—Ymir and Buri each begets his descendants upon himself. Later, distinct male and female sexes appear, symbolized by Buri's son Borr, and the generation of frost giants. Finally, an advanced form of consciousness manifests in Odin, Vili, and Ve (whose names stand for Inspiration, Will, and Holiness, respectively). This sequence from inanimate matter, to asexual reproduction, to sexual production and to higher forms of awareness follows the pattern of evolution revealed by the biological sciences.

I am not suggesting that ancient texts be used as a key to scientific knowledge. In fact, I believe the opposite, namely, that we should depend on scientists for the ultimate truth about how the universe, as well as life on Earth, came to be. However, it is uncanny that the Eddic accounts are precise metaphors for modern theories concerning the formation of the cosmos and the evolution of life. This is something that could not have been known until modern times, and it testifies to the wisdom of our ancestral lore.

Taken at face value, the Norse creation myth is naïve and absurd. When seen as metaphor, however, we see layer after layer of profound truth. The essential message is that the People of the North are not the property of the Gods. Instead, we are beings with free will and with a link to the Divine—the product of a long line of evolution that began when energy quickened life from matter in the void.

The Nine Worlds

After fire and ice have done their work, and after Ymir has been dismembered to form the Earth and sky, what remains are the nine worlds. These are nestled in the branches and the trunk of the immense World Tree, known as Yggdrasil. The worlds may be thought of as states of being, or like the worlds visited by shamans on their journeying. In a more rationalized mode, we might identify them with the "parallel universes" hypothesized by physicists.[3]

The descriptions of the nine worlds, just like the myths themselves, are metaphors. Edred Thorsson considers them as states of consciousness or levels of being.[4] What you or I would actually find there may not much resemble the accounts in the Eddas. Like the Gods themselves, they are mysteries that can be plumbed only by the daring few.

What follows is a quick survey of the worlds as found in the mythology. In this survey, I will focus on their exoteric rather than the esoteric significance. Whatever the true nature of these realms, we need to have a basic understanding of them to make the traditional tales more comprehensible.

Magic horses, like Odin's eight-legged steed or the horses of the valkyries, can carry riders between the worlds. Frigga and Freya, however, own magical cloaks made of feathers that enable them to make these journeys. Bifrost, a luminous rainbow-like bridge, provides a path between Midgard and Asgard.

The world most familiar to us is the one we live in, Midgard—literally, the "middle enclosure." It includes not just the planet Earth, but our entire universe or dimension. A number of religions speak of our world as lowly and unworthy—a place of suffering, from which they seek to escape to Heaven or Paradise. They are wrong. Midgard is a place of beauty and wonder, where everything "comes together," the realm of experience and action. Even the Gods like being in Midgard!

Asgard is where the family of Gods called the Aesir live. Here are the dwellings of the various deities, the best known of which is

3. A good scientific introduction to this concept is *Parallel Worlds: A Journey Through Creation, Higher Dimensions, and the Future of the Cosmos* by Michio Kaku (New York: Doubleday, 2004).

4. Edred Thorsson, *The Nine Doors of Midgard* (Smithville, Texas: Rûna-Raven, 2003), pp. 41–44.

Odin's hall, Valhalla. The Vanic deities Njord, Frey, and Freya also live in Asgard.

The light elves live in Light-Elf Home. Snorri describes them as being more beautiful than the sun. Of course, the very word "elf" will make some readers snicker. The word comes from the Old Norse *álf*, and refers to a much more serious being than the cute and fanciful inhabitants of children's tales. Sometimes the *álfar* are classed with the Vanir, and other times they are considered the male ancestors.

Dark elves live in Dark-Elf Home. They are wise, and are skilled craftsmen. Snorri identifies the dark elves with the dwarves—who, despite our modern ideas, were not originally thought of as being small.

Hel is where the dead—those who do not join their God or Goddess—end up. It is not a place of punishment, but of rest and inactivity, where the dead continue in a vegetative state with very little consciousness or will. Hel is ruled over by a Goddess also named Hel.

Muspelheim is a realm of fiery energy, one of the two primordial worlds that gave birth to the cosmos. It is the abode of the fire giants, the most important of which is Surt, who will destroy the world at Ragnarok.

Nifelheim, the "world of mist," is the other primordial world. It is the origin of the waters which solidified into ice and interacted with Muspelheim's fires at the beginning of things.

Vanaheim is the home of the Gods and Goddesses called the Vanir. Although the best known of the Vanir live in Asgard, there are presumably many others in Vanaheim who play no role in the myths.

Jotunheim is the world of the giants, or etins. Their influence is destructive and oppositional, and in particular they are the antithesis of the evolving life of Midgard and Asgard. Thor, as mentioned in our discussion of the Gods and Goddesses, is our protection against intrusions from Jotunheim.

So what does any of this mean to today's Asatruar?

Most of us don't spend a lot of time worrying about the elf-realms, or about Nifelheim, or Muspelheim. But some of the worlds are very important to us on a personal level. Midgard, of course, is our home—and it doesn't get much more personal or important than that.

We live here, and hopefully learn here, and build lives of achievement and worth. Although it's easy to get wrapped up in our routine and forget the wonder all around us, Midgard is marvelous. We should learn to savor each day and count it as a unique blessing.

Asgard, likewise, gets our attention. This is the realm of the Gods and Goddesses, which we hope to join after death. Some of us aspire to feast at Odin's table. Others look forward to drinking with Thor in his hall. The other deities have their own dwellings, many of which are listed in the Eddic poem *Grimnismal*. All of these are potential afterlife destinations for those loyal to the Aesir and Vanir.

Hel matters to us because it is a place to avoid. We strive for the realms of the Gods after death, but those who lead lives characterized by low levels of consciousness may find that they have lost their chance.

So what about the rest of the worlds in the tree? While they are ignored by most men and women, there are some who take a keen interest in them. Those who seek to imitate Odin—the mystics and magicians who seek after hidden knowledge—explore all these worlds for what they have to teach those who want to transcend the human condition and become demigods in their own right.

In this chapter we have considered the origin of the universe, the progressive development of life, and the multidimensional array of worlds in the cosmic Tree. We are left with an overwhelming sense of freedom, an unfettered view of all-that-is. This wide vista of human potential arises from the fact that we are naturally evolved, un-created beings with free will and with the liberty to explore all worlds in accordance with our desire and our ability. As kin to the Gods, the cosmos is our playground and we will dance among the stars.

Chapter 11

Many Gods, Many Peoples

All native religions arise from the soul of a particular people. They express that people's relationship with the Divine, with each other, and with the world around them. Such religions are an intimate product of the group's total experience as a distinct people, and can only be transferred to other peoples in the most superficial sense.

Some religious systems claim to be the "one true faith" for all mankind. Christianity is one such belief; it combines elements from Judaism, Egyptian religion, Gnosticism and other sources and has the nerve to lay claim to the devotion of all humanity. Islam makes the same error. Judaism, interestingly, claims only to be the Way of the Jewish people—but still considers the Jewish people to be the Chosen people of the "one true God."

We call religions of this sort "universal" because they try to encompass the whole world under one faith.

Adherents of native religions know that this whole approach is wrong. There is no one religion for all the world—nor should there be. The various branches of humanity arose under different conditions, underwent different experiences, and have their own unique way of being in the world. It is only right that we should approach the Divine in the manner native to our own branch of the human family . . . in the way of our own ancestors. To claim that there is, or can be, or even should be a universal religion flies in the face of our genuine diversity.

Obviously, this is not a judgment for or against any particular native religion. All native religions are valid—indeed, they are the very best religions possible—for the peoples from whose essence they spring. My ancestral religion is definitely best . . . for me. The Sioux religion is definitely best . . . for the Sioux.

God is Red?

The idea that there is a built-in connection between specific groups and their religion is a heresy in today's world, but the proposal is not a new one. The various Indian nations have long claimed that their religions are proprietary—that they "belong to" the tribes in question and should not be transferred to outsiders.[1]

This issue revolves around the presence of a new tribe—the "wannabes," who "wanna be" Indians. These are men and women, usually of European descent, who adopt Indian religion and culture. Peace pipes and smudge sticks are sold in New Age book stores. Dreamcatchers are even more ubiquitous; they clutter the checkout counter at the local dollar store and dangle from rearview mirrors on millions of automobiles. Non-Indians make big money sponsoring sweat-lodge experiences, drumming sessions, and vision quests. Perhaps the worst abuses are the sun dances done on Astroturf, and the sex orgies conducted under the guise of Cherokee tribal ritual.

Many Indians are angry about this, stating correctly that this is their religion, the way of their ancestors, and that it is not for outsiders. People of all races and cultures are genuinely welcome at powwows, but participation in tribal ceremonies is something else altogether. There comes a point when whites are politely told to go away, that it's time for private matters at which only Indians are welcome.

Some Indians are more forceful, turning New Agers away from sacred sites, overturning their teepees, and passing out flyers denouncing cultural genocide. At the Lakota Summit V in June of 1993, about five hundred representatives from forty different tribes and bands unanimously passed the "Declaration of War Against

1. There is some dispute over what to call the peoples explorers found when they arrived in America. The politically correct term is "Native American," but many of these people call themselves Indians, or simply describe themselves by the name of their tribe. Some activists, notably Russell Means, specifically reject the label "Native American." I have used "Indians" instead of "Native Americans," not out of any disrespect, but because I don't think politically correct white liberals should get to define other peoples.

Exploiters of Lakota Spirituality."

Mohawk newspaper editor Doug George commented:

> If you look far enough back, you'll find the Celts and the Anglos [sic] and the Saxons and the Jutes all have similar rituals of thanks-giving based on the cycles of the moon and the growing seasons of the Earth. That is what needs to be revived. Maybe we can use this as a kind of spiritual judo. When people come to you with a desperate need to know more, just turn that around and say the solution is within your own self. The solution is in your own community.[2]

Drinking from Our Own Well

Many Asatruar are with us today because an Indian suggested they look at the way of their European ancestors rather than clinging to Native American religion and culture.

My friend Stefn is one such person. Here is his story:

> In 1975, I was at a powwow on the Rosebud Sioux Indian reservation in South Dakota. My girlfriend and I and another couple had been there for a couple of days enjoying the dancing, drumming, and craft-work. I had struck up a conversation earlier with a gentleman who turned out to be one of the Sioux elders who had helped organize the event.
>
> Later on that evening, he came over to me and asked me if I had had a good time. I answered, "Yes, very much so." Then he said, "I'm glad to hear that. But you'll have to leave now." Afraid that I had violated some rule or committed a social faux pas of some kind, I asked why. He replied, "Because we're about to perform a religious ceremony and it's only for Indians." I replied that I understood.
>
> As we were walking away, he walked beside me. At the entrance, he put his hand on my shoulder, smiled, and said

2. "Quoted in "A Theft of Spirit?" by Christopher Shaw, *New Age Journal*, August, 1995, pp. 84–92.

to me, "You're not going to find what you're looking for here. You need to drink from your own well." I shook his hand, and left.

It would be another twenty years before I would understand what he meant by his statement. I had discovered Edred Thorsson's *A Book of Troth* in a bookstore and was reading through it when the Sioux elder's words came back to me and struck me like a thunderbolt. This was it! I was finally drinking from my own well. I had found my way home.

Another friend, Ed, has this story to tell:

I was talking with a family counselor who happened to also be a Hopi medicine woman. In the course of our conversation, I mentioned that I admired Native American culture and wanted to study the wisdom of her spiritual path. Looking at me with a little smile in her eyes, she asked, "Do you have any Indian in you?"

Pausing only a moment, I replied that, no, I was just about a hundred percent German.

Her response was immediate: "Honey, the Indian way is my way, not yours! Here, let me show you some people who can help."

She put me in contact with the Asatru Folk Assembly, and I've been here ever since.

The Wisdom of Vine Deloria

Vine Deloria, of the Standing Rock Sioux nation, was a man of courage, humor and vision. I was privileged to exchange letters with him, but unfortunately I never got to meet him in person.

As a distinguished Indian activist, author, and theologian, Deloria wrote more than twenty books on the history and the plight of his people. One of his most important works was *God is Red*, in which he eloquently suggests that different groups should naturally have different religions.[3] Here are some quotes from that book:

> [T]he idea that religion was conceived as originally designed for a specific people relating to a specific god falls well within the experience of the rest of mankind and may conceivably be considered a basic factor in the existence of religion.

> [Perhaps] a religious universality cannot be successfully maintained across racial and ethnic lines . . . ethnicity will almost always triumph.

> Most tribal religions make no pretense as to their universality.

> The very concept of a Chosen People implies a lost religious ethnicity. Most probably religions do not in fact cross national and ethnic lines without losing their power and identity. It is probably more in the nature of things to have different groups with different religions.

This concept extends far beyond both Asatru and American Indian belief, encompassing all native religions as a general principle.

In 1995, I sent Dr. Deloria some material on Asatru, and he sent this letter in return:

> Dear Stephen:
> Thank you for the letter and the materials on ASATRU.
> I applaud this movement and your organization for taking the initiative in bringing back the traditional European religious beliefs and practices.

> [Referring to "wannabes"] To tell you the truth, these New Agers just look silly even when they try very hard to perform Indian ceremonies. I have always felt sorry for them. It

---

3. Vine Deloria, Jr., *God is Red* (New York: Grosset and Dunlap, 1973). Highly recommended!

would be like me dressing up in Roman Catholic cardinal's costumes and swinging pots of incense in the air. But they are very hard to discourage, particularly when American culture teaches that if you are sincere, you can do anything you want.

I will certainly refer people to your organization.

Good luck with your endeavors. I hope your movement grows so we don't have so many part-Cherokees hanging around our communities.

With best wishes,
Vine Deloria, Jr.

Genetics and Beyond

So what factor is it that links us—any of us, European, Asian, African or whatever—with the ways of our ancestors? It's not just culture. I've seen a Tibetan teen in India wearing a tee shirt emblazoned with the portrait of a rap performer and sporting plastic "bling" around his neck, and Irish-American youth imitating Mexican farm workers. No, there's something deeper than culture, something that is an essential part of who we are, that ties us to those who have gone before us.

Genetics provides part of the answer. Most people know that superficial features like hair and eye color are determined by heredity. What few realize, however, is that less tangible qualities are also passed on genetically. Intelligence, temperament, values, and reactions to basic sensory stimuli are also partly inherited. According to one study, even political party preference is to some extent heritable! (Of course, this doesn't mean that there's a Republican or a Democrat gene, but that certain underlying traits of temperament and worldview can be passed on through heredity.) Our genetics, that very special gift from the ancestors, is a powerful thing.

But there is more to all this than genetics. Past a certain point, DNA is incapable of explaining the strange things we find. Studies of identical twins raised apart yield coincidences that baffle investigators. These twins often both possess the same obscure habits—unusual things, like wearing rubber bands on their wrists and habitually popping them. Sometimes their lives are strangely parallel; they may marry people with the same names or the same birthdays, and own pets with the same names—things that are very unlikely to be influenced by genetics as we know it.

There is an invisible bond that connects people who are genetically similar—a bond of mind and soul that is beyond genetics, that is, *metagenetic*.

I wrote an essay in 1985 with the title "Metagenetics," and made significant additions in a 1999 article called "Genetics and Beyond: The Ultimate Connection." In this latter piece I defined metagenetics as the "hypothesis that there are spiritual or metaphysical implications to physical relatedness among humans which correlate with, but go beyond, the known limits of genetics."

It comes down to this: we are of course connected to all of humanity and indeed to all life, but we are not connected equally. A mysterious law of similarity dictates that we will be most closely linked to people with whom we share a genetic bond. The ties that bind us are not accidental, nor are they dependent on our external environment. Our bonds are genetic, and beyond that, metagenetic.

This truth has profound religious significance. Indigenous religions place emphasis on the ancestors and on the identity of the group. In Asatru, as the story of Rig reminds us, we know that the Gods themselves are among those ancestors. The idea that there should be "different groups with different religions" no longer seems strange. Indeed, it becomes inescapable.

The Folk

The word "folk"—or "Folk"—is vital to understanding the revival of Asatru in the modern age.

In Old Icelandic, *fólk* is variously translated as "people," "people of a household," "kinsfolk," "crowd of people," or "host," that is, an armed group of people.[4] This word is used to denote many different degrees of closeness, from one's immediate family to much larger and more general groups of people.

Modern Asatru uses this term to mean several different things. On the smallest scale, we might use it to refer to the Asatruar at a specific gathering, or attending a particular ritual. We would say, for example, that "The folk passed the horn and toasted the memory of their departed friend." In this case the folk are local people, men and women pledged to the Holy Powers, who know each other personally.

On a larger scale, we speak of the totality of all who follow our ancestral faith as being the folk. This would include Asatruar in Texas, Norway, Rhode Island, or wherever they might be on Earth—or beyond it, since someday there will be Asatruar on other planets. We can also use the term "Asafolk" when we speak of all adherents to native Germanic religion.

All Asatruar of whatever denomination constitute the Folk Within. By this we mean that they are consciously following the native belief of the Germanic peoples and, metaphorically, stand within our ranks. They are aware of their ancestral heritage and are busily practicing it.

But what about all those men and women who share our ancestry but not our faith? What about all the Germans and Scandinavians who are Lutherans? Or the atheists and Buddhists and Scientologists whose blood hearkens back to our native lands, but who do not know or care about their heritage? How do they fit into this, and what do we owe them?

They are the Folk Without . . . those who share our essence and thus are also related to the Gods, but who stand outside our ranks. We are, nevertheless, connected to them and we owe them a high degree of concern and loyalty. One of our obligations is to let them know that our (their!) native belief is alive and well, and that it is an option for them if they are interested.

If this seems ethnocentric—well, so it is. All native religions are

---

4. Geir T. Zoega, *A Concise Dictionary of Old Icelandic* (New York: Dover, 2004), p. 145.

by definition centered on a particular *ethnos*, and to deny this fact or to claim that it should be otherwise is to be politically correct to the point of blindness. There's nothing wrong with ethnocentricity; people with healthy instincts naturally prefer their own family. Ethnocentricity does not imply hostility or negativity to anyone outside the group. It simply means that one gives kin first priority.

Properly understood, the kinship bonds such as those found in Asatru and other native religions should only enhance, not lessen, our respectful attitude towards others. A basic law of life is this: love your own, and respect others unless they demonstrate by their actions that they are not worthy of your respect.

The Gods and their Folk

I think of the Holy Powers and we, their sons and daughters, as being somehow part of the same thing. This hypothesis is intuitive, speculative, and personal. It is also very hard to verbalize. The closest I can come is this: think of some shape—a sphere or a cube, for example—that has more dimensions than the three spatial dimensions of length, width, and height that we can perceive.[5] Let's say that some parts of this sphere or cube are visible in our world, while other parts remain invisible to us because they project into higher dimensions. The Gods and Goddesses are like those higher-dimensional parts of us . . . and we are like the part visible in three-dimensional space. In a sense, the Gods are our representatives in Asgard, and we are their representatives in Midgard. We are connected. We are part of the same thing. They depend on us, and we depend on them.

Most modern people think that religion is just a matter of choice—that, as Vine Deloria said, "if you are sincere, you can do anything you want." They might get up tomorrow morning, look in the

---

5. Mathematics can describe geometrical forms with more dimensions than the three spatial ones we can perceive with our senses or picture in our minds. One of these is a *tesseract*, or a four-dimensional cube. We cannot visualize this, but we can visualize (and even make a model of) a projection of a tesseract into three-dimensional space. (It looks like one cube suspended inside another, with lines connecting the corresponding corners of the two cubes.) If you drew this on a piece of paper you would have a two-dimensional drawing of a three-dimensional model of a four-dimensional cube!

mirror while brushing their teeth, and say to themselves: "You know, I think I'll take up Amazonian shamanism this week."

Can they do that? Of course. This is a free country, at least in these trivial ways, and you and I can adopt any religion that catches our fancy. It's easy: you go on the Internet and read some articles, and then find someone who teaches some classes, and you're in! No one will think less of you for it.

But even if you have the "right," is it really the right thing to do? Most people never stop to think that there might be a way that is best for them, because it reflects what they are—a member of a specific group of people sharing common descent . . . a group connected in powerful ways by culture, heredity, and metagenetics . . . a group bound by blood to a particular set of Gods and Goddesses.

Religion should not be like a hat or a coat that you find in a store, take a liking to, and decide to purchase. Rather, it should be like your arm, or your head—a part of who you are from birth.

The Gods and their people are one.

Chapter 12

Fate or Freedom?

The popular image of our pre-Christian ancestors is that they were unsophisticated fighters and drinkers who never thought about the finer points of philosophy. Historians or scholars who comment on the mental world of the Germanic people may observe that they were "fatalistic," and leave it at that.

This picture is wrong on several counts. In this chapter we'll take a look at the Germanic ideas of time, causality, and free will versus determinism.

Humans have always wondered about these things. Are we free agents, or only actors in a play whose script has been written in advance by the Gods, or perhaps by an impersonal fate?

If we have free will and the power to exercise it, then our deeds make a difference and our lives have meaning. If not, then our personal significance is negligible. The question of "fate or freedom" pours over into other areas such as morality (Can we be held accountable for our actions?) and politics (Why should we care about political freedom if free will is only an illusion?).

To understand how Asatru answers these questions, we must first understand the lore of our ancestors.

All of Germanic cosmology can be summed up in only two features, Urd's Well and the World Tree. The relationship between them expresses the concepts of time, space, causality, fate, and the ethical values of the ancient tribes.[1]

---

1. The best explanation of this cosmology and its philosophical implications is *The Well and the Tree* by Paul C. Bauschatz (Amherst: University of Massachusetts Press, 1982).

The Tree

Our ancestors spoke of the mythic World Tree, Yggdrasil, and envisioned it as a gigantic yew.

Yggdrasil is both the framework and the content of the manifest, multidimensional universe. In its branches nestle all the worlds of Gods, giants, dwarves, and elves. Our own world, Midgard ("the enclosure in the middle") is also in the tree.

The Well

Yggdrasil has three roots. One is found in the home of the Gods. Another looks out onto the land of the Rime-Giants. The third root extends into the misty world of Nifelheim, where the roiling well Hvergelmir gives birth to thundering rivers with names like "Storming," "Loud-boiling," and "Fearsome."

Just as there are three roots, so are there three wells. Other than the aforementioned Hvergelmir there is Mimir's Well, from whose wisdom-giving waters Odin drank after plucking out one of his eyes for the privilege. The third is the Well of Urd, and it figures very largely in the account that follows.

While the lore describes three distinct wells, such repetition is common in myths and we can think of them as three aspects of a single mythic well. In our discussion of fate and freedom, I'll refer to it as Urd's Well.

Time and the Norns

Our myths describe three female beings called the Norns. They are much like the Fates of Classical mythology, and are reminiscent of Shakespeare's three "Wyrd sisters" in the first scene of *Macbeth*. Urd is one of these Norns. She has two companions named Verdandi and Skuld, and together the three encompass the Norse ideas of time. Urd translates literally as "that which has become," or the past. Verdandi is "that which is becoming," or the present. Skuld means "that which should be." While the past and the present can be easily defined, the future is only tentative, or conditional—it is not determined in advance. We'll have more to say about the Norns in a moment.

Causality and Free Will

Urd's Well is the repository of all past actions. Into it go the deeds of Gods, humans, and the other beings in the worlds. These deeds are symbolized in the mythology by dew falling from the branches of the tree into the water of the well, for good or bad. However, they do not simply lie there, static and forgotten. They roil and weave, connecting people and things in inconceivably complex ways. Chaos theory gives some insight into these complicated links, and many of us will have heard, for example, that the flutter of a butterfly's wings on one continent can cause a hurricane thousands of miles away. (This sounds like an exaggeration designed to illustrate a point, but then I am no mathematician!)

So how much control, if any, do we have over what happens to us? Past events continue to affect the present, but the individual's choices must also be figured into the equation. Can a man or woman overcome the momentum of the past by heroic will? Maybe or maybe not, depending on the magnitude of the events in the Well. Our ability to shape the outcome is a function of skill, wisdom, and prowess on many levels, ranging from physical strength to the intangible power one acquires through spiritual growth. Sometimes our overall might is great enough to prevail, but other times the odds are against us, and we are overwhelmed.

In other words, the final outcome depends on cause and effect, both as manifested in Urd's Well (from the past) and in the power of the person or group on whom these influences are acting (in the present). There is no moral judgment or divine fiat involved—just the working of a multitude of interwoven events both great and small.

The Role of the Norns—Active or Passive?

In seeming contrast to the cause-and-effect model I've outlined here, many Asatruar believe that the Norns decide our fates, in a literal and deterministic sense. This seems supported by the literature, where the Norns are said to determine the fates of men. Snorri, in "The Deluding of Gylfi" (*Gylfaginning*), has the High One say of the Norns that

These maidens shape men's lives. We call them the norns.
There are yet more norns, those who come to each person at
birth to decide the length of one's life, and these are related
to the gods. Others are descended from the elves, and a third
group comes from the dwarves.[2]

It seems, then, that there are the three "major Norns" or "cosmological
Norns" we have discussed so far—Urd, Verdandi, and Skuld—but there
are also a host of lesser norns (note the lower case) that interact with
humans from infancy. The latter are of varying quality. The best are
related to the Gods, lesser ones are kin to the elves and the dwarves.

In the *Voluspa*, we read of the Norns that

One is called Urd, the other Verdandi,
the third Skuld. Scores they carved,
laws they laid, lives they chose.
They worked orlog for the sons of men.[3]

A superficial reading of this and similar material suggests that
life's major events are determined in advance. This deterministic view
may have prevailed among the common folk; there was neither Internet
nor an authorized handbook of religious dogma, and opinions would
vary from person to person. To some, it must have seemed convenient
to let the Norns take the blame for events. But what about a deeper
understanding of the concept?

Throughout the sagas and heroic lays, the Norns played roles that
were similar if not identical to those of the fylgja, hamingja, and the
valkyries. Elsewhere in this book we discuss all three of these not as
distinct entities, but as part of the individual soul complex. Might not
the Norns likewise be a hidden part of our own selves, rather than
independent beings dictating our fate?

2. Snorri Sturluson, translated by Jesse L. Byock, *The Prose Edda* (New York: Penguin,
2005).

3. *Voluspa*, strophe 20, translated by James Chisholm in *The Eddas: The Keys to the
Mysteries of the North* (n.p.: Illuminati Books, 2005).

Edred Thorsson seems to think so. He writes: "The Nornir are the medium through which action is received and transmuted into a projectable but essentially unaltered form and returned to the sphere from which that action was received."[4] He restates this elsewhere: "the Norns are not causal agents, but rather the numinous organisms through which the energies of actions are received, transformed, and re-directed back to their source."[5] In short, what we are dealing with here is a metaphysical law much like karma. Insofar as the Norns give us anything at all, they give us what we have earned through our deeds. They need not exist as beings independent from our own psycho-physical complex in order to carry out their task. However, this interpretation of the Norns (or the norns) is not a matter of required belief; Asatruar are free to think of them as external entities if that makes more sense to them. But whether part of our own being or not, their role is ultimately passive.

Germanic "Fatalism"

It is sometimes said that the Germanic peoples, and particularly the Norsemen, were "fatalistic." As we can see from the pages above, this is not true. The idea of events being predetermined, with humans relegated to the role of actors in a script written in advance, is alien to the Germanic mind. No God, no inherent structure of the cosmos, forbids free will or sets limits on human activity. However, as we have seen, that does not mean we can do whatever we want, whenever we want. Although we are free from divine coercion, we are not free from cause and effect. The man whose leg is trapped by a fallen rock is not free to walk away—not because God, or the Gods, or the Norns are forbidding it, but because he does not have the ability to overcome this obstacle.

Philosophically, this means that to an extent limited only by

4. Edred Thorsson, *Futhark: A Handbook of Rune Magic* (York Beach, Maine: Weiser, 1984), p. 47.

5. Edred Thorsson, "'Fate' in Asatru," *Green Rûna*, 2nd ed. (Smithville, Texas: Rûna-Raven, 1996), p. 28.

our power, we are free to "make our own fate."[6] There is a word in Old Norse for this fate we fashion for ourselves; it is called *ørlög*—Americanized in modern Asatru as "orlog." Literally, it means the "primal layers" placed in the Well by the Norns.

Heroism

It is our freedom that makes heroism possible. In any contest we are expected to exert all our strength, skill, and will to gain victory. If we triumph, the experience increases our personal store of spiritual power.

And if we do not win? Defeat, not victory, is the true test of the hero. We may not be able to control circumstances, but we can control the way in which we react to them. An enemy can take away victory and even take away our lives, but the hero does not allow the opponent to take away his or her poise, calm, and dignity. This is why characters in the sagas make casual jokes while dying, and why Viking hero Ragnar Lodbrok concludes his death song with the words "Laughing, I die"—the ability to die with calm and consciousness shows self-possession and, paradoxically, the inability to be truly defeated.[7]

Asatru insists we assume the burdens—and accept the rewards—of free will. We are not puppets or pawns, but free men and women acting in the complex arena of the present under the influence of the past. We fight life's battles, and in the process grow physically, spiritually, and mentally. For those who have mastered themselves and conquered their fear of death, life gives opportunities for shining heroism.

6. While reading through *Taking the Quantum Leap: The New Physics for Nonscientists* by Fred A. Wolf (New York: Harper Perennial, 1989), I found a more "scientific" affirmation of free will. The "Uncertainty Principle" of Werner Heisenberg says that we cannot precisely know the location or motion of any subatomic particle because the very act of observation affects these qualities. Hence, the universe is not deterministic and there is room for free will. The flip side of this, as Wolf points out, is that we cannot predict the outcome of our actions. That's fine with us—the ethic of Asatru is to accept the risk of the unknown and to boldly act to work our will.

7. *The Saga of Ragnar Lodbrok* and the "Lay of Kraka" containing Ragnar's death song are hard to find. The standard print version referenced in other works is *The Saga of the Volsungs, the Saga of Ragnar Lodbrok together with the Lay of Kraka*, translated by Margaret Schlauch (New York: American-Scandinavian Foundation, 1964).

Chapter 13

Values, Virtues, and Ethics

If, as we saw in the last chapter, we have free will and therefore have responsibility for our actions, how shall we choose to live our lives? What guidelines, what set of rules, are we to follow?

Asatru has no equivalent to the Ten Commandments. Unlike Jehovah, Odin didn't appear on a mountaintop with a list of "Thou shalt nots" carved in stone. Does this mean we are not bound by moral laws, free to act on any whim that pleases us?

It's amazing how many people believe that. Almost everyone who thinks of pre-Christian religion at all assumes that its followers were hedonists, libertines, men and women who followed no moral code. The reality, of course, is nothing of the sort.

The difference is one of mindset: Christianity, Judaism, and Islam believe men and women need a precise list of rules, usually framed in a negative sense—"thou shalt not" do certain things. Asatru sees it differently, and teaches adherence to principles originating in the customs of the tribe and nation, where people have evolved effective ways of relating with each other over thousands of years. There are no Ten Commandments in our faith, but the sagas, heroic epics, and Eddic poems offer hundreds of examples of idealized behavior.

Nevertheless, several attempts have been made in modern times to condense Asatru's rules for living into a compact set. In the old days, this wasn't necessary because everyone was immersed in the traditional culture. Tales of the Gods and Goddesses, of heroes and villains, were told around the hearth and the campfire; the old wisdom was everywhere. Today this supporting matrix has been largely demolished, and simple statements of morality can play a useful role. We expect to get our information in a quick and condensed form, and few of us will thumb through the sagas to find just the right episode to use as a reference.

At least three lists of moral or behavioral principles have evolved in modern Asatru.

The Nine Noble Virtues

The Nine Noble Virtues were formulated in the early 1970s by the Committee for the Restoration of the Odinic Rite (later known simply as the Odinic Rite).[1] Two or three versions have appeared over the years, but the original list is given below. The comments after each virtue are my own.

Courage—Without moral and physical courage to defend the right, the other virtues would be overwhelmed.

Truth—Truth is the pole-star, our guiding light, our unwavering recognition of the universe as it is.

Honor—It is good to strive for glory, acclaim, and the reputation that comes from great deeds.

Fidelity—The fulfillment of duties to friends, kin, and the Holy Powers is the very heart of Germanic morality.

Discipline—If we cannot command ourselves, we cannot command our lives, and still less can we command others.

Hospitality—The open-handed and hospitable lead the best lives, while the miserly and mean suffer from their closed hearts.

Industriousness—The happiest people are busily engaged in

---

1. The earliest source I have is the pamphlet *This is Odinism* (London: The Odinist Committee, 1974), p. 13.

constructive work in harmony with their inner needs.

Self-reliance—Each of us should accept the aid of family and friends when needed but, likewise, each must do his or her share and avoid being a burden on others.

Perseverance—Often life's victories are won by stubborn refusal to give up. We are beaten only when we quit trying.

The Noble Values

In the early 1980s, seeking a better balance, I composed the Noble Values.[2] They are meant to be not so much virtues—in the sense of single words designating an abstract moral quality—as values, or statements about choices we believe to be true:

Strength is better than weakness.

Courage is better than cowardice.

Joy is better than guilt.

Honor is better than dishonor.

Freedom is better than slavery.

Kinship is better than loneliness.

Truth is better than dogma.

Vigor is better than lethargy.

Ancestry is better than rootlessness.

---

2. According to my archives, these first appeared in a twenty-page booklet titled *The Values of Asatru*, authored by myself in 1985 and published by the Asatru Free Assembly.

The Noble Values remain an official statement of the Asatru Folk Assembly today.

The Twelve Thews

A more recent attempt to define right behavior in Germanic religion is the list of thews—roughly, tribal customs—presented in 1998 by Eric Wodening in his manuscript *We Are Our Deeds: The Elder Heathenry, Its Ethic and Thew*. I have used modern English terms instead of the Old English of his original, and the explanatory sentences are my own interpretations:

> Industriousness—Be productively engaged in life. Avoid laziness. Strive to accomplish good things.

> Justice—Let fairness be your hallmark. Treat others in accordance with what they deserve, and give each person a chance to show his or her best.

> Courage—Fear is natural, but it can be overcome. Train yourself to do the things you fear, both physically and morally.

> Generosity—An open hand and an open heart bring happiness to you and to others. The miserly are miserable.

> Hospitality—Travelers should be greeted with food, drink, and a warm place by the fire. See that your guests never want.

> Moderation—Enjoy all good things, but do not overindulge. No one admires a glutton, or a person whose appetites are out of control.

> Community—Cooperate with kin and friends, do your fair share, and fulfill your responsibilities. Remember that the community includes not just the living, but all the ancestors and the descendants as well.

Individuality—Although we belong to a community, we are also individuals with distinct personalities and clearly defined rights. Respect the individuality of others, and insist on respect in return.

Truth—Be honest and straightforward in all your dealings. Avoid deceit and deception.

Steadfastness—Learn to persist, to endure in the face of adversity without discouragement. Do not be blown about by every changing wind.

Loyalty—Be firm in your commitment to others. Have a true heart.

Wisdom—Learn from your experiences. Grow in the understanding of the world, and of the human heart. Comprehend as much of the universe as you can in the years available to you.

There is a lot of overlap between the Nine Noble Virtues, the Nine Values, and the Twelve Thews. All express a common spirit distilled from the Eddas, the sagas, and the history of the Germanic people. We are to live lives of nobility and worth—and in doing so, we serve the very purpose of life.

The Asatru Folk Assembly Statement of Ethics

The Statement of Ethics was composed by the Clergy Board of the Asatru Folk Assembly, as a complement to the organization's Declaration of Purpose. In many ways it integrates the spirit, if not the fine print, of the three lists of values and virtues given above.

We believe that members of the Asatru community should be guided by the following principles:

1. The Aesir and Vanir Principle

We believe in and honor the Gods and Goddesses of our Germanic ancestors, the Aesir and Vanir. We believe that they hold special value for us. We seek their good fortune and we work to develop and maintain mutually beneficial relationships with them. We honor the Aesir with our dedication and spirituality; we honor the Vanir with our deep respect and dedication to preserving and protecting Midgard. We believe that through ritual, dedication, generosity, honor, and hard work, our lives and consciousness will be touched by the Holy Powers.

2. The Folk-Community Principle

A community based in ancestry and common culture is a better society in which to live. We in Asatru hold that our ethnic culture is vital and worthy of protection and promotion. We believe that we each have a personal responsibility to consider the Folk good and to assume a personal role in promoting and protecting it. We believe that each of us must work to keep our heritage alive. For the best community, we must:

a. Work to make justice and law rule among our folk.
b. Express good will towards, and cooperation with, members of our community.
c. Work for a better tomorrow. We believe that we have an obligation to create a better future for our Folk and to shape a brighter future for our children.
d. Give back to the community that has given to us.

3. The Ancestry Principle

We are a community united by descent from common

ancestry. We value this unique heritage and seek to maintain a vibrant connection with our ancestors. We each should strive to know about our ancestry and commit to that which defines our common folk community.

4. The Family Principle

Healthy families are the cornerstone of folk society and its strength and prosperity is derived from them. We in Asatru support strong, healthy family relationships. We want our children to grow up to be mothers and fathers. We believe that those activities and behaviors supportive of the family should be encouraged while those activities and behaviors destructive of the family are to be discouraged.

5. The Organization Principle

A disorganized community is a weak community. In the world we live in today, being disorganized is akin to inviting death. Organize or die. We must build our community and its ability to promote and defend its own interests. The community must be able to focus resources and bring benefits to our members. We are committed to building thriving folk communities, growing leaders and encouraging cooperation among our folk. The leadership roles of our community should be respected just as individual rights must be.

6. The Personal Excellence Principle

One should strive to grow in capabilities and wisdom. One should maintain good physical and mental health. One should know right and wrong and how to reason about them. One should be well-read both in the lore and in a wide range of subjects that will help one understand and utilize opportunities in Midgard and beyond. One should know how to apply what one knows. We believe that the pursuit of knowledge, the accumulation of wealth, the practice of skill, the building of family, and the leadership of men and women are worthy endeavors.

7. The Honor-Your-Oaths Principle

Living honorably requires fulfilling one's oaths at all costs. Never enter into oaths lightly; understand the consequences of oaths before making them and live up to your obligations that result from oath making.

8. The Warrior Principle

We believe that our members should strive to be ready for the challenge to defend our Folk, Gods, and Goddesses with both cunning and physical skill when needed. We should be prepared to stand against those forces which would seek to destroy our Gods and Folk.

9. The Life-Is-Good Principle

Living, loving, expanding, thriving, and acquiring wealth and prosperity: we should grasp and experience these things in life. One of the things that is important in life is its mystery. In Asatru we have the ability to, and should strive to, transcend mundane human existence by cultivating our unique connections and relationships with our Gods and Goddesses, our ancestors, and the spirits of the land, and by studying our culture, our Lore, the runes, and the mysteries of the Nine Worlds.

I've shown you a number of options as you strive to put together a set of Asatru values, virtues and ethics for your life. It may seem a little overwhelming; certainly it's a lot more complicated than the simple set of ten commandments supposedly handed to Moses on Mount Sinai. That's the price of freedom—you have to make decisions and exercise your own judgment. The good news is that you have a lot you can choose from while still staying within the general framework of our ancestral religion!

Chapter 14

Our Many Souls: Life and Mind

Christian dogma is that we have only one soul that leaves our bodies at death and goes either to eternal punishment or everlasting reward. Asatru, however, observes that our souls are made up of a number of parts that serve different functions during life, and go to different places after death.[1] Some of these soul-parts apparently cease to exist almost instantly. Others dissolve gradually, and some move on to other dimensions. The question of "What happens when we die?" is one we will examine in another chapter, but first we must familiarize ourselves with the various bits and pieces that make us who we are.

In the following pages, I will begin with some familiar soul components and then move on to those that are less well known. We'll start with the physical body, then move on to the ego, or our sense of self. Next, we will take a look at the conscious mind, followed by the more shadowy world of the personal and collective unconscious

In the next chapter, we embark on more adventurous seas and investigate the enigmatic life energy, the ecstatic condition, personal spiritual and magical power, and finally those soul-parts that seem to be independent of us, but that may actually be part of our totality as human beings.

The Physical Body, or Lik

The first part of the soul we'll discuss is—the body! In Old Norse it is

---

1. Jean Haudry, in his book *The Indo-Europeans* (Washington, D.C.: Scott-Townsend Publishers, 1998), p. 24, describes the notion of a soul consisting of only one part as being "relatively recent" among the Indo-Europeans and "probably of foreign origin."

called the *lík* (pronounced "leek," Anglicized as *lik*).

We habitually think of the body and soul as being two distinct things, or even opposites. We regard our flesh as spiritually insignificant, a mere garment we wear on Earth and then discard when we leave this world. The body is not thought of as being us in any important way.

Nevertheless, many people seem quite interested in the physical body. They sweat on treadmills, lift weights, get facelifts, and swallow handfuls of food supplements. We may call them health-obsessed or narcissistic, but maybe they instinctively realize something the more "spiritual" types don't: denial of the body brings neither happiness nor spirituality. The body matters.

Asatru goes a step farther and says that the physical body is crucial to the development of other, less tangible components that make up the whole human being. It may or may not be, strictly speaking, a "part of the soul" but it most certainly is a part of what Edred Thorsson calls the "psycho-somatic complex"[2]—referring to the body and the soul working together as an integral whole.

Even at the molecular level, the body expresses a spiritual essence. Our DNA is the encoded experience of our lineage in the physical world. Our genetic template transmits information across space and time to literally shape us. Science has shown that heredity influences not only physical traits, like the shape of our ears and the color of our eyes, but also mental traits such as personality and temperament. When we consider that even our personal values are partly hereditary, it becomes apparent that the link between the body and the spirit is a profound one.

All spiritual evolution depends upon the body. We learn our lessons slowly and painfully, one at a time, through a lifetime of challenge, defeat, and triumph. In religious philosophies like Hinduism, this process may take millions of years—even millions of incarnations! And each moment of this growth occurs . . . in a body. From birth to death, we learn how to deal with others; how to master our cravings;

---

2. Edred's writings on the soul in Germanic thought are essential reading for any serious student of our ancestral philosophy. The best source is the entirety of Chapter 12 of his book *Runelore* (York Beach, Maine: Weiser, 1990).

how to live fully; how to die bravely, mindfully, and with dignity. None of this could be done without a body. Without a body, there is no experience of this world. Without experience in this world, there is no evolution. If for no other reason than this, the body deserves to be honored by the spiritual traditions of mankind.

People around the world use many practices to help them evolve to a higher level. Breathing exercises are among the most important. But how can you perform breathing exercises without lungs, or a nose? Most cultures use ritual dances to induce altered states of consciousness. How do you dance, or shake a rattle or beat a drum, without feet and legs and arms? The power centers called chakras in yoga or "wheels" in Asatru are developed by vocalizing certain syllables, and through body postures—but you certainly won't be sounding any syllables without a throat, or assuming any body postures if you don't have a body to begin with!

All this is related to the fact that we who follow the traditional ways of Europe love the world. Earth, this holy home our ancestors called Midgard, is where evolution happens. All the parts that make us who we are come together here. Every day is another opportunity to be, to become, to love, to fight, to laugh, to cry—to grow upward, toward our great destiny. All of this happens . . . in the body!

Using the Lik for Your Advancement

The body is an absolute necessity for accomplishing anything in this world, but beyond that, the condition of the body can either help or hinder your spiritual quest. If your body is strong, flexible, and in all-around good working order, if it is clean on the outside and free of debilitating toxins on the inside, your progress will be faster. Some disciplines carry this to great lengths, but even following the simplest rules will help.

Keep your body strong. Use resistance exercises, such as weights, to develop muscular strength and endurance. Run or swim to build your cardiovascular strength.

Keep your body flexible. Stretching is particularly important for spiritual development, because flexibility and relaxation aid the flow of subtle energies throughout the body.

Keep your body clean, inside and out. Your skin is your largest organ, so wash it daily. A weekly sauna will help eliminate poisons from your system. Eat foods that are nutritious, and when possible choose foods that are natural or organically grown.

Give your body a good environment. Spend at least some time outside daily. Get a little sun (but not too much!), breathe some fresh air, walk in the forest, let your body and soul remember what the natural world feels like!

The Ego, or Ek

The ego is our awareness of individual existence as a self. It is that part of us we identify as "I." During our lifetimes, the ego is usually located in, and identified with, the physical body. The Old Norse term for the ego is the *ek*.

Buddhism says that the ego is a transient illusion. Christianity demands that the ego be subordinated to God, or to Jesus. I recall a religious tract from my youth that urged us to "take ego off the throne of our heart," and put Jesus in its place—complete with drawings of just how this would look, in case we didn't get the idea.

This is the very opposite of Asatru. Unlike Buddhists, we like existence in this world. And unlike the authors of the little Christian tract, we'll stay firmly seated on that throne in our hearts. We want neither to "dissolve the illusion of ego," nor to surrender it to any outside force.

A strong ego demands our personal freedom, our existence as sovereign and distinct personalities. Any philosophy that advocates blending, merging, submitting, or surrendering our sense of self is anathema to the spiritual truths of our European ancestors.

On the contrary, the traditional wisdom of ancient Europe tells us that it is possible to enlarge our sense of self, by realizing that we are actually much more than our everyday "I-ness" would have us think.

This deserves further explanation. To the materialist, we are only a fleeting consciousness that temporarily inhabits a physical body. When the body dies, nothing remains. In contrast with this limited view, Asatru teaches that we are made up of the powers, energies, and various subtle soul-components outlined in this chapter and the next. All these can be cultivated and strengthened by various spiritual practices. Those who are persistent can tap into these unseen parts of our being, realizing that each is a part of who they are, and thus attain an expanded sense of self.

An example of a portion of ourselves that we do not normally experience would be what Carl Jung called the "unconscious." Although we are not usually aware of the unconscious (which is why we call it the unconscious in the first place!), we can learn to explore it, and eventually integrate its contents into our psyche—attaining what Jung called "individuation." Exploring the soul-components of Asatru is much like this. The idea in both cases is not to become something essentially different from what we are, but to realize who we truly are in the first place—and to gain the capabilities that come with allowing all our soul components to inform our awareness.

In the native European view, then, the ego or ek is only "bad" if it is limited by our small, superficial notion of who we are. Even then it is not really evil, only incomplete—for even a restricted sense of self is better than "becoming one with God," "dissolving into the infinite sea," or "merging with the Oversoul."

Using the Ek for Spiritual Growth

Most people have a very poorly developed ego. This may not seem true, since we all know plenty of egotists whose every thought is of themselves. But, strangely enough, being egotistical is not the sign of a strong ego—in fact, it is often quite the opposite. Egotism is born of fear and desperation. What we hope to cultivate, however, is much more meaningful: a definite, constant sense of one's identity as a distinct self. For the average person, "I" changes with every passing emotion and scattered thought—while what is needed is true awareness and permanence.

Few thinkers have understood the difference better than P. D. Ouspensky, who was associated with G. I. Gurdjieff's "Fourth Way." The theory and techniques outlined by Ouspenksy in *The Psychology of Man's Possible Evolution* will be useful to all Asatruar who seek to develop a functioning ego.[3]

Because the ego is, among other things, "the part of us which wills," it is important to develop your will power. There are many misconceptions about will, but the best approach I have seen is in the works of Roberto Assagioli, who formulated a school of thought called "psychosynthesis." Any books by him or by his students (Assagioli died in 1974) are valuable guides for those who would grow stronger wills.[4]

Another way to strengthen the ego is to learn the art and practice of victory—*sigr*, in Old Norse. Winning is a powerful form of self-affirmation. Learn to be victorious in as many ways as you can: intellectual, athletic, and so forth. The true depths of the Norse term *sigr* have, I believe, never been clearly stated and much wisdom awaits those who penetrate its secrets.

A caution: nothing here should be construed as advocating the narrow, deceptive, and self-satisfied glorification of one's self. There is all the difference in the world between egoism and egotism. One is puffery, the other genuine development. Those who have come far are humbled by how far they have yet to go, and they will not belittle those who have accomplished less.

The Logical Mind—the Hugr

In the Northern lore, Odin has two ravens that fly forth every day and report back to him at night. Their names are Huginn (Thought) and Muninn (Memory). They represent two soul components, called the hugr and the minni, respectively. These correspond roughly to what psychologists would call the "left-brain" and "right-brain" functions. First, let's look at the hugr.

The hugr deals with left-brain cognitive skills—reasoning, logical thinking, judgment, counting and measuring. It is linear and analytical, and works sequentially rather than holistically. Think of *Star Trek's* Dr. Spock and you'll have a good idea of what left-brain functioning is like.

3. P. D. Ouspensky, *The Psychology of Man's Possible Evolution* (New York: Vintage Books, 1981).

4. One I like is *What We May Be* by Piero Ferrucci (Los Angeles: Tarcher, 1982).

Many of us are driven by our emotions. We don't use logic to make decisions, but instead use it to rationalize the things our emotions tell us to do. This is not always a big deal in daily life, but it creates a haze of self-deception that surrounds our actions—and ultimately this works against our success or even against our survival. We must see the world as it really is, not as we might like to imagine it. When we are driven by the emotions, we are less likely to be in control, less likely to be working our will in any conscious way. The idea is not to suppress the emotions, however. Passion is good! But when our logical mind is in control, our command of our mental faculties is more definite, more deliberate.

Using the Hugr for Spiritual Growth

As you study our ancestral spirituality, stay anchored in what is objectively known about the ancient ways. Study the scholarly evidence presented by historians, anthropologists, linguists, and archaeologists. Learn to tell the difference between facts and subjective flights of fancy. Teach yourself to see what is, not what you might want to see. Apply these standards not only to the exploration of our Lore, but to other subjects as well.

To learn objectivity, pick an issue on which you have strong feelings. Now study the other side of that issue—not pouring through it with the idea of refuting the arguments, but seriously challenging your preconceived notions. Try arguing on behalf of that other side in an imaginary debate. Take up games of strategy such as chess, the Viking board game of tafl, or historical war gaming. Study mathematics, logic, or one of the "hard sciences" like physics or chemistry.

Memory—the Minni

"Memory," as we mean it here, can be roughly equated with the right brain functions, those mental faculties expressed in images or symbols rather than precise words or numbers.

One part of this memory is individual, based on personal experience and filtered through the emotions and the situational context. This memory is often subjective and difficult to analyze in any useful manner.

Our memory includes another part, as well—the reservoir of images and instincts originating outside of our personal experience. This is comparable to Jung's collective unconscious. The minni, then, encompasses both the personal and the transpersonal.

Much of this storehouse of images and patterns is common to the human race as a whole, while other portions are specific to the Germanic or European peoples. It may also be called ancestral memory, metagenetic memory, or the Folksoul. Sometimes, symbols or symbolically significant events can trigger recall of this material, and much of this can be spiritually useful. For example, working with the runes or performing ritual acts can strike a resonance with this soul component, giving us insights of value.

Content of both the individual and collective memory often expresses itself though feelings, intuition, and images.

Using the Minni for Spiritual Growth

Just as Odin left one of his eyes in Mimir's Well so that he could know the secrets contained in its watery depths we, too, must explore the personal and collective memory. We must come to know those parts of ourselves that are hidden from our sight, including those parts we would prefer not to face! When done in a psychoanalytical context, this work of self-exploration is best accomplished through Jungian analysis. This is a highly specialized process and most of us are not able to undertake this work for ourselves. Nevertheless, any of us can gain by becoming familiar with Jung's writings on archetypes, symbols, and dream analysis. You can take this work farther by keeping a dream journal and working with the unconscious content revealed while you sleep.

However, a way more in keeping with that of our ancestors is to study the magnificent system known as the runes, and actually internalize these mysteries using the "Rune-Thinking" exercises given throughout *The Nine Doors of Midgard* by Edred Thorsson.[5] Some

5. Smithville, Texas: Rûna-Raven, 2003.

parts of rune study are very linear and logical—memorization and contemplation of the basic meanings of the rune staves, for example. However, there comes a point at which the runes speak to the soul of the student in ways that touch upon ancestral or metagenetic memory. This creative and nonlinear opening of the hoard of archetypal images is the very essence of memory in the sense we are using it in this discussion.

Vital Breath—the Ond

The vital breath, or *önd* as it is called in Old Norse, is a subtle energy which seems identical with the Hindu concept of *prana*, as well as the Japanese and Chinese ideas of *ki* and *chi*, respectively. When German occultists in the early twentieth century wrote of the "rune might" that coursed through their bodies, they were apparently sensing the flow of this energy.

This life force obviously plays an essential role in the physical body, but it is also the key to developing advanced levels of consciousness and spiritual power.

From this point onward in our discussion, the ond is crucial. All the exotic soul components covered in the next chapter depend on this subtle energy. It is the key to unleashing the ecstatic state, or wode. It is a factor in the growth of the individual power known as hamingja. Even our relationships with seemingly independent entities like the valkyries or "fetches" is facilitated by this mysterious energy.

Using the Ond for Spiritual Growth

The vast amount of information on manipulating and accumulating *prana*, *ki*, or *chi* is relevant to the quest for the vital breath. Key among these are the breathing exercises used in yoga. Known as *pranayama*, they range from the very simple to the complex. You should start with the basics and only then, preferably with the help of a teacher, begin exploring the more advanced routines.

Probably the simplest exercise of this kind is to observe your breath as it flows in and out of your body. The technique called *hong sau* or *ham sa* is excellent for this purpose. Precise instructions can be found in many books and websites dedicated to yoga.

There are also activities for sensing the flow of energy in different parts of the body, particularly the hands. By briskly rubbing your palms together, separating them, then slowly bringing them near each other again, you can feel what seems to be an energy field between your hands. There are many variations on this experiment, all of which teach you to perceive and control the flow of energy throughout your body.[6]

Practice "breathing" energy into different parts of the body—the stomach, the knee, and so forth. This is done by visualizing energy entering the chosen portion of the anatomy as you inhale. It sounds very strange if you have not tried it, but with a little practice it becomes very easy. Some writers recommend this as a way to speed the healing of injuries.

Some martial arts have much to teach us about the vital breath in the forms of *ki* and *chi*. The emphasis differs from style to style and from teacher to teacher. One place you will definitely find it is in the Japanese art of aikido, which—as the two letters in the middle of the word suggest—is all about using the power of *ki*.

Another tool for using the vital breath is stadagaldr or "posture magic"—the Nordic equivalent to the *asanas* or yoga positions. Stadagaldr involves assuming positions imitating the shapes of the rune staves, sounding the appropriate verbal formulas, and channeling the "rune might" through the body. Persistent practice gives many sorts of physical, mental, and spiritual benefits.[7]

In the next chapter, we will continue our investigation of the soul. So far, we have been on more or less familiar territory—the ego, body, mind, and the energy found in the breath. All of these, except the energy associated with the breath, are things we have known about all our lives. In the coming pages we will build on this foundation as we look at some soul components which are considerably stranger.

6. Years ago, I learned a lot from *The Centering Book* by Gay Hendricks and Russel Wills (New York: Prentice Hall, 1975). No doubt there are many other volumes available today.

7. The two best volumes on this subject are *Rune Might* by Edred Thorsson (Smithville, Texas: Rûna-Raven, 2004) and *Rune-Magic* by S. A. Kummer (Smithville, Texas: Rûna-Raven, 1993).

Chapter 15

Our Many Souls: Power and Potential

I n the last chapter we discussed some parts of the soul, starting with the physical body (lík) and working our way up through the ego (ek), two aspects of the mind (hugr and minni), and the vital breath (önd).

Now things are going to get a little stranger. We have daily experience of most of the soul components covered so far; even the önd is familiar to yoga practitioners and martial artists. But now we are going to consider parts of ourselves we didn't even know we had!

The Ecstatic State—Wode

The next soul-component is actually a state or condition, rather than an identifiable structure. Ecstasy or wode arises, at least in part, from cultivating the önd, or vital breath—and it is the key to activating and strengthening the more extraordinary components in the pages that follow.[1] The ancients seem to have included it as one of the parts of the soul for that reason, and I have followed their lead.

Ecstasy allows us to touch, however briefly, the world of the Gods—and indeed to act as a God. In this supernormal condition we gain insights and have powers that are denied us in normal consciousness. Wode lies at the root of the ancient Germanic mystical tradition.

However, relatively few of us will choose to participate in these high flights of the soul. Mystics, magicians, and shamans have always

1. There are many kinds of ecstasy, and my use of the word in this chapter specifically means the Germanic phenomenon of wode rather than any more general definition.

been a small percentage of the population. Just as we do not expect the average Catholic to have visions of the Virgin Mary, we do not anticipate that many Asatruar will delve into the mysteries of Odin or Freya. Most of us are content to honor our ancestors and the Holy Powers, living our lives as honorably and productively as we can, and leave the deeper mysteries to the few.

Nevertheless, some will explore these forbidding inner landscapes—and all of us should at least know that these things are a part of our Lore.

Wode is the domain of Odin, father of the Gods. His name is actually a title meaning "master of the wode." He continually seeks wisdom and magical power, partly because it is his responsibility to prepare for Ragnarok—the great battle at the end of this cycle of time—but also because he pursues wisdom for its own sake. Odin is the supreme model for personal evolution, our guide on the path to the *Übermensch* or super-human, and our inspiration to be and to do more.

Magical power, superhuman consciousness, wisdom, and even the poetic arts are tightly knotted together with the idea of wode in the Northern mind. In this altered state, our left brain and right brain act as one integrated whole. The enhanced capabilities that come with ecstasy allow us to construct, strengthen, or communicate with the exotic soul components we'll be discussing later in this chapter. With it, we become a transformed being fully capable of utilizing all our soul-selves. It allows us to imitate Odin, and share in the essence of Godhood.

If this sounds like more than you bargained for, remember that this is the path for a very few. No one will compel you to take this route. But supposing you did want to walk the Way of Odin—how would you go about it?

Using Wode for Spiritual Growth

In Asatru, the ecstatic condition is linked with magical incantations, the singing of songs, and poetic verse. All of these have three features in common: (1) alterations in the pattern of breath, (2) a specific rhythm, and (3) some sort of associated imagery. These functions use both the "left-brain" logical mind and the "right-brain" image-creating mind, synchronizing their activity to induce a state of wholeness and lift consciousness to a higher level.

Therefore, to experiment with wode, compose poetry. Seek out the meter and alliterative style of the ancient Norse skalds, or poets. Infuse your verse with the traditional poetic metaphors called kennings, and meditate on the meaning and imagery they convey. Use your poems ritually, and recite them with passion.

The story of Odin's winning of the Mead of Inspiration refers to two other methods for attaining ecstasy. In this tale, Odin persuades the giantess Gunnlod, who guards the mead, to share the holy liquor with him by spending three nights in love-play with her. The sought-after mead is much more mysterious than the mere honey wine drunk by mortals. A powerful concoction, accompanied by sex-magical techniques amounting to a kind of "Teutonic tantra," would be a powerful inducement to ecstasy. Individuals who have a strong background in the safe use of herbal lore and tantric technique may be qualified to experiment along these lines.

Luck, Personal Power, and So Much More!—Hamingja

Hamingja is the Old Norse word often translated as "luck." More precisely, it has three different but related meanings: (1) the total spiritual power of a person, (2) the ability to magically take on an animal shape, and (3) luck in the ordinary meaning of the word.

The first meaning—personal spiritual power—is primary. Hamingja is comparable to the *mana* of Pacific cultures. It can be thought of as a magical "charge" bestowing a sense of presence, wisdom, influence, and success on those who possess it. According to old belief, hamingja even played a role in combat; the individual with the greatest hamingja would be victorious.

We increase our hamingja through "right action"—making wise choices and doing right deeds. Unlike Christian grace, which is bestowed at God's pleasure, hamingja is one hundred percent earned.

We can understand how the uninitiated, with no deeper religious or esoteric knowledge, would connect this personal power with the idea of luck. To the outside observer, it would seem that certain people were lucky. A closer look would reveal that these people had the "luck" that comes from proper preparation—not just in the obvious material world, but in the spiritual realm as well. In Asatru, "You get the luck you make."

The word hamingja originally referred to shapeshifting ability. Turning into an animal—or, more realistically, making someone perceive that you have done so—requires a great deal of magical power, so we can see how the same term came to be used to describe both spiritual/magical might on the one hand, and taking on an animal shape on the other.

Using Hamingja for Spiritual Growth

There are many ways of increasing one's personal spiritual power.

The simplest is to consciously try to live by the virtues and values of Asatru as listed elsewhere in this book—the Nine Noble Virtues, the Noble Values, or the Twelve Thews. Each evening before retiring, go over the list and see how you did during the day. Where were you weak? Where were you strong? What can you do tomorrow to improve on any one of them? Don't get disappointed if you have fallen; just pick yourself up and try again tomorrow. Many small deeds, done with consistency and mindfulness, train the character over the weeks, months, and years. This is a lifelong project!

Beyond a general training of the character, there are specific spiritual or magical acts that help build hamingja. Blessing your food, greeting the rising sun, honoring the full moon, pouring a libation to the ancestors or the Holy Powers—all these are examples, along with more elaborate rituals done either with others or alone. The traditional Asatru rites called blot and sumbel, described elsewhere in this book, are valuable aids in developing spiritual might.

Immerse yourself in the traditional lore by reading the Eddas and great heroic epics like *Beowulf.* Memorize stanzas from the *Havamal* and the *Voluspa.* Lean a Germanic language—modern German, or a present-day Scandinavian tongue, or best of all Old Norse.

You can add to your hamingja by successfully fulfilling

oaths—swearing to accomplish some particular deed, great or small, and carrying it through. This practice builds will, self-discipline, and self-knowledge. The amount of hamingja gained is proportional to the difficulty of the deed undertaken. There is a great danger here, however: breaking an oath takes away the same amount of hamingja as you would have earned by fulfilling it. For this reason, make your oaths with great forethought.

Along with taking many small actions in everyday life, consider something that was greatly valued in our traditional culture—heroism! In ancient times, heroes fought great battles, won kingdoms, or slew monsters. Ragnar Lodbrok and Sigurd the Volsung killed dragons. Thor fought the Midgard Serpent and Tyr placed his hand in the mouth of the Fenris Wolf. Today's monsters are different, but just as dangerous, and there are great deeds to be done that have nothing to do with swords. Save an ecosystem, risk your life to serve your kin, found a multi-million dollar foundation to serve our Folk, overthrow a tyrannical regime, change a paradigm!

The Fetch, or Fylgja

With our discussion of the ecstatic condition (wode) and the personal power (hamingja) we moved beyond the boundaries of most people's experience, transitioning completely from the mundane to the metaphysical.

The fetch, or fylgja, continues this journey and takes us deeply into the shamanic and magical realm.

The fetch is a mysterious entity. From the way it is described in the old sagas, you'd never suppose that it was a part of the soul. On the contrary, it appears to be an independent being, often manifesting as a woman—perhaps gigantic in stature, or fantastic in appearance—or even as one of Odin's battle maidens, a valkyrie. Sometimes the fetch can show itself as an animal that corresponds to the personality of the person with whom it is connected. Bears, wolves, deer, and mice are only some of the forms taken by the fetch in its animal aspect. In many cases the fetch acts in a protective role.

None of this sounds much like a part of the soul, does it? However, despite this apparent degree of autonomy, the fetch may actually be a hidden part of ourselves.

Modern psychology gives us something very similar to the fetch in the archetype Carl Jung called the *anima*. It typically manifests in dreams or in visionary experiences as a powerful female figure. Although it seems to be a separate entity from the person to whom it manifests, it is nevertheless a part of that individual, one unknown to the waking consciousness. The fetch is very much like this; you might think of the fetch as a livelier, three-dimensional, "more real" version of the anima.

The fetch has several important functions. It serves as a channel for spiritual power, numinous knowledge, and love. The Gods and Goddesses communicate to us through the fetch. The fetch sometimes provides "second sight," or information about events yet to come. Along with its gifts, it often places obligations or responsibilities on the person to whom it is attached.

The fetch also provides protection, a fact that becomes significant when we note the popularity of "angels" in modern popular culture. Dozens of books have been published in recent years, recounting cases in which men and women encountered beings they describe as guardian angels. Indeed, Christian doctrine commonly teaches that every human being is assigned a guardian angel at birth.

But what are these angels, anyway? We find a clue in the old Icelandic story called *Njal's Saga*, where, in chapter 100, Sidu-Hallr says that he wants the archangel Michael as his *fylgju engill—fylgja* being the Old Norse word for the fetch. The guardian angel of Christian lore, then, is nothing more than the Germanic fetch in new clothes. As a result, all these modern accounts of angels are evidence for the truth of our traditional belief.

The valkyries of our Lore are pictured as beautiful women, daughters of Odin, who ride through the battlefield and choose fallen warriors. These they carry back with them to Valhalla, there to feast and fight until the great battle of Ragnarok. Other times, the valkyries are described as ferocious, corpse-devouring demons of death and battle who weave magical chants as contending armies prepare to clash. A closer look, however, shows that they are nothing more (or less) than a form of the fetch. Like the fetch, they impart protection, magical knowledge, and foresight. They serve as lovers to their chosen hero. Like the fetch, they are the means of communication between humans and the Holy Powers, the Gods and Goddesses.

There are two kinds of fetches. One is born with the individual and stays with him or her throughout life, departing only at death. In the Old Norse literature, this individual fetch was called the *manns fylgja*. It was the summary of all that the person was or had done—the complete expression of the person's deeds and duties.

Parallel to the individual fetch was the *kynfylgja*, or the fetch of the entire lineage. This was usually attached to the head of the clan, and was transferred to someone else—traditionally, the chief's son— at death. Its function was much like that of the personal fetch; the *kynfylgja* was the storehouse of the might of the clan and was made stronger by great deeds done by clan members.

Using the Fetch for Spiritual Growth

The fetch is the key to the highest known levels of spiritual evolution. It is this entity—in the form of the valkyrie—which enables us to cross the fiery Rainbow Bridge into Valhalla and take our places with the einherjar, Odin's chosen heroes. In actuality, this is a metaphor for our own transformation into demigods—sovereign, powerful, and, for most purposes, immortal.

Becoming aware of the fetch, then learning from it and using these encounters for spiritual progress, is the work of a lifetime. There are parallels in other mystical systems (Aleister Crowley might have called it "attaining the knowledge and conversation of the Holy Guardian Angel"), but fetch-work is firmly a part of the ancestral Way of the Northern peoples.

Everything that promotes all-around spiritual development will facilitate the growth and eventual manifestation of the fylgja. There is little I can add to this except to mention that there are specific rituals that can be used by properly prepared individuals to encounter the fetch. Perhaps the best is given in *The Nine Doors of Midgard* by Edred

Thorsson.[2]

The Soul—A Summary

Some writers describe more soul components than I have dealt with here. My intent has been to make a complex subject as simple as possible, and to explain the use of these soul parts for spiritual evolution. Most people will never consciously experience some of the more esoteric fragments that make up the complete human being, but all of us—even if we do not walk these higher paths of development ourselves—should be aware they exist.

There has been a logical progression in the analysis used in these two chapters. The first parts I covered—the body, the vital breath, mind, and memory—all help one reach a condition of ecstasy or wode. The use of this inspired state in a ritual context helps the individual accumulate more personal spiritual power, or hamingja. This might ultimately develops the fetch and permits full communication with it.

For all this apparent complexity, there is an underlying simplicity. As Stephen Flowers (Edred Thorsson) writes in *Sigurðr: Rebirth and the Rites of Transformation* (originally his master's thesis at the University of Texas): "All of the above concepts and functions [the *hamingja*, the *fylgja*/fetch, and several other parts of the soul] are closely interwoven and probably should be best understood as various aspects of the same basic 'material.'"[3] All of them spring from consciousness, will, and the progressive use of the magical power associated with the breath.

The ego, or sense of self-identification, is central to this whole process. In normal consciousness, we are aware of only a small part of who and what we are. We know, of course, that we are in a body and we will have some awareness of mind, memory, and breath. We seldom or never experience ecstasy. Almost none of us have any conscious contact with our personal power, much less with the fetch. As we experience these different parts of ourselves, integrating them into our being and

2. Smithville, Texas: Rûna-Raven, 2003, pp. 153–56.

3. Stephen E. Flowers, *Sigurðr: Rebirth and the Rites of Transformation* (Smithville, Texas: Rûna-Raven, 2011), p. 58.

bringing them under our control, our sense of who we are grows. This is our goal—to extend our sense of self, becoming fully conscious of what we truly are, or at least what we can potentially be.

Our ancestral Lore provides a map for personal development, a virtual "science of the soul" by which those who choose to do so can walk the very Path of the Gods.

Understanding the parts of the soul complex is also essential to comprehending what happens to us after death—the subject of our next chapter.

Chapter 16

What Happens After We Die?

The sagas and the Eddic poems offer us several ideas on what happens after death. Unfortunately, these ideas are, at least on a superficial level, contradictory.

The best-known version of the Nordic afterlife is not based on the traditional literature but owes its popularity to novels and Hollywood movies. It is the romantic idea that a Viking has to die with his sword in hand so he can go to Valhalla, Odin's hall. This is not quite what our ancestral faith taught—gripping a sword is not a prerequisite for Valhalla—but a brave death would certainly improve one's chances of being chosen for this honor. Our lore makes it clear that Valhalla is for the elite. Besides Odin's hall, the other Gods and Goddesses have realms of their own to which their devotees could journey after death. We also read of men who entered into the hills to be with their ancestors after dying. Others led a life in the grave mound that was in some ways much like their earthly life had been. There are even hints of reincarnation in the lore.

What are we to make of all these stories? Which, if any, are true? Can we find some underlying pattern that explains what our ancestors believed about the afterlife, and can we make it relevant to our modern age?

The answer to the question of what happens after we die obviously depends on the nature of the soul. Since we are made up of a number of different soul-parts, the answer is not as simple as going to Heaven or Hell, reincarnation, or whatever. We shall have to fall back on the previous two chapters, where we studied the many parts of the soul as envisioned in the Germanic world.

Let us begin with the simplest and most ephemeral. Presumably, ond simply fades away with the ebbing of life. Likewise, the inspired state or wode, simply ceases to exist.

The fetch (fylgja) and the luck (hamingja), on the other hand, survive death. They go to the realm of Hel (which, despite its name, is not to be confused with the place of torment in Christian doctrine) and are reborn into the deceased person's clan. According to this interpretation of the Lore, each of us is a combination of our own unique consciousness that we receive at birth, plus a fetch and luck inherited from an ancestor.

But when we speak about an afterlife, what we really want to know is what happens to the individual consciousness—to the "us" we know, our self-awareness, our essential ego or ek.

This sense of personal identification is carried in the hugr-minni complex: the mind, made up of its cognition and memory. This "I-ness" goes to one of the other worlds. Some select few will go to Odin's hall, to assume greater responsibilities and continue the path of unending evolution. Others will go to the halls of other Gods or Goddesses, perhaps to Folkvang to be with Freya, or Thrudheim, to sit with Thor. All of these require a certain amount of spiritual development, acquired through accumulated right action—typically, heroic deeds or mastery of the magical arts, or at the very least a life of devotion and adherence to a code of behavior such as the Nine Noble Virtues, covered elsewhere in this volume.

What does it mean to go to the abodes of the Gods or Goddesses? Our lore paints a vivid picture of Odin's chosen warriors in Valhalla. Their postmortem experience consists exclusively of fighting all day and feasting all night, as they prepare to stand alongside Odin at Ragnarok. We can consider this to be a symbolic description, indicating that the Odinic paradise is one with purpose, struggle in service to Life, and continuing evolution. The halls of the other deities remain almost a total mystery to us, but we can make reasonable guesses based on what we know about the different Gods and Goddesses. A mythic afterlife as Thor's guest might entail feasting, good fellowship, feats of strength, and an occasional adventure. Freya's guests can expect beauty, pleasure, and sensual delights. Ullr's friends may go hunting, after which they share the meat of the kill.

All this should be taken metaphorically. Odin's heroes don't really spend century after century drinking mead and swinging swords. All the other activities listed above are likewise symbolic. The important thing is that those humans who make it to the garths of the Gods will find things to do that are in keeping with their interests, inclinations and talents. I believe, also, that the things done in the afterlife will be useful on a cosmic scale (preparing for the struggle at Ragnarok, for example) or helpful to those of us in the world of humankind.

For those whose level of consciousness has been low, who have not bothered to grow, or who have not developed a strong and distinct soul identity, Hel is a likely destination. It is not a place of suffering, but simply a state of low vibration, a vegetative state with no real consciousness or will to speak of. Souls sent to this realm may become undifferentiated, losing their identity in the mass of male or female ancestors, the alfar and disir respectively.

What about reincarnation? The lore tells us that impersonal qualities such as the fetch and luck are reborn, but what about more substantial things like personality and consciousness? Edred Thorsson, perhaps the best-qualified expert on the issue, states that this does not occur. However, there are passages in the Lore that could be taken differently. One of the most important, found in the Eddic poem "Brynhild's Hel-Ride," is Hagen's curse spoken over the body of Brynhild:

Hinder her not   Helward to fare,
whence back never   she be born again![1]

This sounds like a curse uttered against Brynhild as an individual with an ego, not a de-personalized power concept. And Edred himself notes that "The true man or woman desires rebirth in Midgard [the world of

---

1. Verse 45 of "The Short Lay of Sigurth," translated by Lee M. Hollander, *The Poetic Edda* (Austin: University of Texas Press, 1962).

humans in Germanic cosmology] above all things."[2]

E. O. Turville-Petre points out that when rebirth is suggested in the Lore, it is found in conjunction with heroes like the mythical Helgi, supernatural beings such as Svava the valkyrie, or kings. All three of these categories are made up of men or women having great magical/ spiritual power, or hamingja. I believe this indicates that the mightier a person is, the more choices they have. Stay in Valhalla with Odin? Commune with the ancestors? Be reborn as your great-grandchild? Or, like Odin, reach a point where you transcend mortality altogether and become a sort of Germanic bodhisattva? It's all up to you . . . and to the amount of power you can manifest.

Immortality among the Indo-Europeans

Given the confusing nature of Germanic ideas about life after death, it makes sense to examine the beliefs of related Indo-European cultures. By looking for similarities and differences, we can see if our interpretations of Germanic concepts are true to the prevailing trend, or if we have strayed from the general pattern of Indo-European thought.

So just what did the Indo-Europeans, these ur-ancestors of ours, think about the state of the dead?

From the oldest times, our peoples had no delusions about what awaited the average man or woman after death. Most commoners went to Hades or Hel or its equivalent in their culture—not because they were "bad" or "sinful" but because the ordinary person does not cultivate the powers of soul and the permanence of personality needed for a higher condition. There was no suffering in their state, but there was limitation, and relatively little awareness. Not much remained of the human self-consciousness or personality. The best they could expect was a modest level of consciousness and will. At worst, the personality dissolved or became dormant as it merged with the ancestors. Even in this state they interacted with the living and sent us their blessings from the world beyond, but it was very different from the willful,

2. *A Book of Troth* (St. Paul, Minn: Llewellyn, 1992), page 98.

conscious state we know and enjoy in this world.

The dead who are remembered fare better than those who are forgotten. This was why, in many Indo-European societies, the living made sacrifices and offered prayers to their ancestors. The dead need to be remembered and honored, not just by anyone and not just in general terms, but by their own descendants calling them by name, making offerings to them, and telling the tales of their deeds.

Fame—being honored after death by large numbers of people even beyond one's immediate family—meant that one would be remembered by one's extended family, tribe, and nation for a very long time, and thus was a powerful aid to immortality. As Jean Haudry puts it, "Immortality in a form worth having is not conferred but must be conquered. The hero conquers it by his deeds and their fame."[3] Throughout the Indo-European world, not just among the Germans but also in the writings of the Greeks and in ancient India, we find traditional poetic formulas referring to a hero's "imperishable fame" or "undying fame."[4] This idea is still with us: a plaque in Richmond, Virginia, honoring the great Confederate General "Stonewall" Jackson, reads: "Only the forgotten are dead."

Scholars usually assume these formulas mean nothing more than living on in the memory of one's family, friends and enemies, but I believe there is more to them than this. It is as if we, by honoring the dead, share with them some of our own consciousness and will. Blessings flow both ways through the thin curtain separating life and death. We honor the ancestors, thus ensuring their continued existence and status, and they reciprocate by giving us spiritual nourishment and might. This interaction between the dead and the living implies that it is important to continue the family line, so that the ancestors—among whom you and I will someday be numbered!—will have descendants to remember them and pour offerings at their gravesides.

3. Jean Haudry, *The Indo-Europeans* (Washington, D.C.: Scott-Townsend Publishers, 1998), p. 25.

4. Haudry, *The Indo-Europeans*, p. 17.

Indo-European thought reveals two roads in the hereafter.[5] One is the "Way of the Fathers," or in Sanskrit, *pitriyana*. This was the way of the common man or woman, who went to a place like Hades or Hel and became one with the ancestors. In the Lore of the Nordic lands, this could be represented by the idea of passing into a mountain to join one's dead kin, or the concept of continued existence inside the burial mound. Rebirth of certain powers and faculties like the fetch and the hamingja was possible from this state, but the ego or individuality probably remained in the vegetative state, if it continued to exist at all.

The "Way of the Gods" (Sanskrit *devayana*), on the other hand, was the way of the hero and the magician. Through the fame of great deeds, or through the mage's powers to transform and weld together the components of the soul, they strive for immortality, for the status of demigods. Rather than being deprived of consciousness, will, and individuality like the denizens of Hades or Hel, they seek to make these qualities strong and eternal.

The Way of the Gods is epitomized in the cult of Odin. For those who would become permanent and powerful spiritual beings, it is not enough just to worship the God—one must imitate him in transcending the mortal state. Saxo Grammaticus has the hero Biarki tell us that Odin "is seizing for doom no lowly, obscure race, no cheap rabble souls, but enmeshes the rulers and fills his river below with men of fame."[6] Valhalla is indeed for the few!

The differences between these two paths are reflected in funeral practices. Georges Dumézil explained:

> In the case of cremation it is the dead person himself who is thought of above all; he is to have a fitting ascension and a rich existence in the hereafter. With the barrow, it is the country which is central; the dead person is a pledge of plenty, kept in the earth to make it produce rich harvests. In other

5. See *Lords of the Left-Hand Path* by Stephen E. Flowers (Smithville, Texas: Runa-Raven Press, 1997), p. 16, for an elaboration on these two paths.

6. Saxo Grammaticus, translated by Peter Fisher, *The History of the Danes* (New York: Brewer, 2002), p. 62.

words, there is a privileged class of dead which goes straight to Heaven . . . the others stay bound to the soil, imparting to the earth in which they lie hidden the fertilizing virtue which characterized them during their lifetime and which will be transformed by the earth into food for the living.[7]

Of these two ways of dealing with the dead, cremation belongs to the Way of the Gods, and burial in the earth to the Way of the Fathers.

How to Get the Best Possible Afterlife

In this chapter, I have mentioned several ways of acquiring the spiritual/magical power needed to have meaningful options in the afterlife. To restate these: great deeds—the doing of difficult things—builds personal power. So much the better if those feats result in "undying fame." One especially difficult thing is the warrior ideal of dying bravely or, more to the point, dying with the mental discipline and the magical skill to use death to attain a high state of evolution. This, of course, is the truth behind the old "dying with a sword in your hand" stereotype.

However, there are many things besides dying heroically that carry merit. These other "right actions" include religious acts (observing Asatru's seasonal festivals, offering blot to the Gods and Goddesses, and so forth) and honorable behavior in accordance with the traditional values of Asatru. One of the best ways is the practice of spiritual and magical disciplines to nourish and develop the various soul components described in the two previous chapters, bringing them under control of the will, and welding them together in such a way that they survive the death process. This is a highly specialized study and would require a book in itself.

Our Germanic tradition holds no comfort for those who think that a life of laziness and stupidity qualifies them for an afterlife of bliss and glory. The Norns do not award blue ribbons just for participating. Ultimately, the best afterlife is one we earn, either by noble deeds or

7. Georges Dumézil, *From Myth to Fiction* (Chicago: University of Chicago Press, 1973), pp. 144–45.

by the pursuit of wisdom and magical power. The more developed and integrated the soul-components, the better the quality of the afterlife—and this happens only by earnest effort. As always in Asatru, "you get the fate you make."

Chapter 17

Ⴎhe Purpose of Life

Why are we here?

There are a few ultimate questions that face men and women of every era. Where do we come from? What happens when we die? What is truth? Is there a God or Gods, and if so how does that affect us? But arguably the biggest question of all is . . . What is the purpose of life?

You and I may think of these in religious terms, but even atheists want a purpose! Some atheists treat their philosophy as if it was a religion, and they preach it with the fervor of streetcorner evangelists. For communists, the purpose of life is to advance the class struggle and bring about the dictatorship of the proletariat. Saddest of all is the impoverished soul with the bumper sticker that reads: "He who dies with the most toys, wins."

Perhaps we can start by examining what the purpose of life is not.

When I was a Catholic, the Baltimore Catechism told me that God created me "to know Him, to love Him, and to serve Him in this world, and to be happy with Him forever in Heaven." The devout Muslim learns that the goal of life is submission to the will of Allah and attainment of Paradise. The Buddhists say that the purpose of life is to escape life as we know it—to reach Nirvana and thus be released from the cycle of reincarnation.

None of these visions are attractive to Asatruar.

Loving Life in This World

We don't want to submit to God like Christians or Muslims. Nor do we want to escape this world like the Buddhists; we like it here!

Atheism and materialism, on the other hand, strike us as cold, sad, and ultimately just not true.

Many religions (or at least, many religious people) seem to think that the purpose of life lies in getting to some other realm. For them, Earth is only a place where we prepare to receive our eternal reward somewhere else. This world is full of tears and torment, they believe, and we're just passing through. Nothing here matters unless it contributes to our salvation: the beauty of a sunset . . . snow falling silently in the forest . . . the sacrifices of heroes . . . even love itself . . . all these are insignificant things and we must turn our backs on them as we journey toward an afterlife we have never seen.

Asatru emphatically rejects this line of thinking. To us, the purpose of life lies in maximizing wisdom, might, and joy, and in the affirmation of existence. The philosopher Friedrich Nietzsche said it well: "Pagans are those who say yes to life!"

Historians of religion would classify ours as a "world-accepting" rather than a "world-rejecting" faith. We believe life is a blessing, not a curse. We understand that life's challenges and pain are opportunities for us to grow stronger and wiser. Life is good, our lives are good, and the world is good.

Because of this world-accepting approach, our priorities are different. We do not need to be "saved," nor do we want to dissolve into the Absolute, or become "a drop of water in an endless sea." Our concerns have always been down-to-earth-ones. Before Christianity, European religions dealt with practical needs: a bountiful harvest, healthy babies, victory in battle, justice before the law, stability of the social order, increased wisdom. These concerns are as relevant to us today as they were a thousand years ago. But "salvation?" It's just not something we need.

Yes, we care about an afterlife. Elsewhere in this book we discuss this subject in detail. For now, though, it is enough to say that living fully in this world is the best preparation for what happens after death. Being "world-accepting" in no way detracts from our spiritual goals; quite the opposite. Our ancestral religion features heights of mystical experience as grand as those of any faith conceived by man. However, this life in this world is where spiritual evolution actually takes place.

The Sixfold Goals

Earlier, I wrote that life's purpose lies in "maximizing wisdom, might, and joy" and in the "affirmation of human existence." The Sixfold Goals, enumerated by Edred Thorsson, elaborate on this idea.[1] (I have modified some of his terminology for clarity within the context of this book.)

The Sixfold Goals are:

Right. Human beings want to live in a society where truth, reason, and justice are as constant as the North Star. The law under which we live must be administered fairly and consistently by honorable men and women. The values and lore of our ancestral culture must be respected and honored.

Wisdom. We seek wisdom to understand the universe and everything in it, including ourselves. Our curiosity about the world around us is boundless—from the spinning galaxies on the edge of space and time, to the mysteries of our own souls. Matter and energy, men and Gods, are all fit subjects for our ceaseless inquiry and exploration.

Might. In a brutal world, Right and Wisdom need the protection that Might can give! Strength of arm and heart, of brain and will, gives us the ability to defend that which is ours, and to crush those who threaten us. Might represents the warrior instinct within us—the primeval, unapologetic thrill in power and victory.

Prosperity. Wealth is good. Money is the form of energy that makes our modern world function. But prosperity is more than just financial success; it is the increase of all things good and desirable. This includes essentials like food, clothing, and shelter, as well as the luxuries that give us delight. Most important of all is having the right attitude about

1. Edred Thorsson, *A Book of Troth* (St. Paul, Minn: Llewellyn, 1992), pp. 114–17.

wealth—the ability to cherish and enjoy it, without greed and grasping.

Harmonious striving. Our ancestors had a word, frith, which is usually translated as "peace." However, it means much more than that. We want a stable environment within the framework of kin and clan in which we can pursue a full life, but we don't want boredom or stagnation. Struggle is necessary for growth. We need dynamic, harmonious striving.

Love. We treasure love in its purest and most idealized forms, as well as the earthier manifestations of sexual pleasure, passion, and a general lust for life. All too often, frolic and play are forgotten in the frenzied rush of the daily routine. We seek to set right that loss!

Applying the Sixfold Goals

Each of us will pursue the Goals differently. One person will be more interested in Prosperity, another in the experience of Love. Still others will seek Wisdom as the highest good and undertake the task of spiritual transformation. This variety is natural, and people will tailor the Goals to their own needs.

However, there are some basic rules. While we will naturally have our favorites, we must not neglect any of the Goals—they're all important. The idea is to allow individuals to have balanced, energetic fulfillment in a way that is harmonious and productive.

Another rule is this: Right and Wisdom lead the way. All the others must serve them. Without Right and Wisdom, Might is mere bullying, Love slides into decadence, Prosperity descends to greed, and so forth.

Living Fully

The Sixfold Goals reveal a plan for a full life.

Each of us can push these Goals to very high levels, depending on what we want out of life. You can try to become as wise as the greatest sages ... or acquire a vast fortune ... or live a life of lusty adventure and pleasure to rival that of any character in fiction. You are limited only by your ability and determination.

Most of us will settle for a life that is satisfying and successful without necessarily being spectacular. Whether your objectives are modest or grandiose, however, the choice is yours—there is no predestined fate setting your limits, and no "God's will" to which your own sovereignty must be subordinated.

The Sixfold Goals are a life-affirming declaration of limitless possibilities for each of us. But their application does not stop there, for we do not live in a vacuum. There is always the dynamic balance between the individual and the group. That balance lies in knowing what things we owe to ourselves, and what we owe to others.

Things We Owe Ourselves

We owe ourselves the ever-increasing wisdom that comes from living life to the fullest. It can be cosmic wisdom or folksy wisdom, and it can be humble or sublime, but in any form it is the treasure that takes life to its summit.

We owe ourselves strength of body, mind, and spirit that allows us to protect ourselves and those who are dear to us. The weak will always be targets. Only when we are secure in our strength, only when we have the power to choose, can we afford to extend a hand in friendship to others.

We owe ourselves joy, prosperity, love, and pleasure. Life is good, and we should experience that goodness every day, in one form or another. The idea that we should feel guilty for wealth or for enjoying life is entirely alien to Asatru.

Our potential for wisdom, strength, and joy is vaster than we can imagine. We have the delightful duty of exploring these endless possibilities!

Things We Owe the Community

In Asatru, we aim to live productive, honorable, and happy lives. These three things are of course related; when we are productive and self-fulfilled, carrying out our responsibilities to others and to ourselves, we are most likely to find that elusive quality called "happiness."

The best life is neither one of narrow self-absorption on the one hand, nor a life that ignores our own needs, on the other. There must be balance between our interests and those of the communities of which we are a part.

What are these communities, and what do we owe them?

To our ancestors, we owe remembrance, respect, and loyalty. From them we received a cultural heritage, a lineage, and a family name. It is our duty to never bring shame to any of these. Instead, we should try to add to their glory by our own deeds.

To our living family, we owe loyalty. We should strive to get along with family, even when it is difficult. Sometimes we cannot honestly claim to love all our kin, but the least we can do is honor the blood that flows through their veins by performing our duties in regard to them.

To our descendants, we owe the chance to exist. Not everyone can have children for all sorts of reasons, but passing on the torch of life to the next generation is the ideal. In some historical Indo-European societies, the firstborn child was considered to be the debt owed to the ancestors in return for the gift of life. Our descendants are the future, and we must do everything possible to ensure that they thrive and fulfill the highest destiny of which they are capable.

To all men and women descended from the indigenous tribes of Europe, we owe brotherhood. They are our Greater Family. Unfortunately, this family has dwindled to about eight percent of the Earth's population, and continues to shrink not only as a percentage of the whole, but also in absolute numbers. There are fewer of us today than there were yesterday. For our own sake, we need to understand our common roots and stand beside each other.

To all men and women on Earth we owe honorable behavior, the right to work out their own destiny, and the understanding that their ancestral way is as holy to them as ours is to us. Their Gods live in them, as our Gods live in us. Let us respect each other, and the holiness within us.

To the Earth itself we owe love and care. Our Lore considers her a Goddess—sometimes identified with Frigga, other times with Nerthus or with Jord. She is our mother, and our neglect of the Earth and all her living systems has brought us to the brink of disaster. None of us working alone can reverse the damage that has been done, but every one of us can do his or her part. It is our moral duty to refuse to willingly participate in the destruction of life on this planet.

To the Gods and Goddesses themselves we owe respect and awe, but not slavish submission. We are like them in essence, but the difference in magnitude between the Holy Powers and ourselves should keep us from treating them trivially, or with too much familiarity. Furthermore, Asatruar have a sacred duty to ceremonially observe the turning of the seasons and other holy days, for this makes us participants in the cosmic drama and brings the world of humankind and the divine world into harmony.

The Purpose of Life: A Summary

The purpose of life is to experience ever-greater Right, Wisdom, Might, Prosperity, Harmonious Striving, and Love—now and always!

Happiness comes to us when we do our duty to others, while at the same time looking after our own needs and promoting our own growth. Life is an open-ended adventure, a quest that challenges us and forces us to the highest level of greatness we are capable of attaining!

The purpose of life, in short, is to LIVE in the fullest, most vigorous, and most expansive meaning of the word!

Above: Preparing the feast at the first Althing. **Facing page, top left:** The late David James, who was active in Asatru since the early 1970s. **Top right:** Steve performing the first Odin blot in North America. **Facing page, bottom:** Steve with Valgard Murray, founder of the Asatru Alliance.

Performing blot, late 1990s.

Left: Steve and Sheila McNallen outside the Burke Museum at the University of Washington, where the remains of Kennewick Man were deposited in 1998.

A gift calls for a gift! Promotional photo, 1990s.

Above and below: Bosnia at the start of the war, 1992. Above: Steve with friends near a Slivovitz (plum brandy) still.

Above and below: Travels in Burma (now Myanmar) with Karen freedom fighters in the early 1990s. The Karen are an ethnic minority on the Thailand-Burma border in Southeast Asia.

Above: Steve and Tibetan political activist Jamyang Norbu in 2002.
Below: Tibetan freedom rally, San Francisco, California, 2007.

Above: Communing with the ancestors, McNallen family burial ground, County Tyrone, Northern Ireland. **Below:** Pouring a libation for *Conan the Barbarian* creator Robert E. Howard, Brownwood, Texas.

Above: Blessing a meal with Asatruar in Denmark, 2013. **Below:** Steve in ritual garb in the Pocono Mountains, Pennsylvania, 2012.

Above: Steve's work with endangered species, and especially elephants caught in the ivory trade, remains a priority. **Below:** Asatru Folk Assembly booths at the "Nevada County Food & Toy Run" in Grass Valley, California.

Above: Gravestone of Clark Wullenweber, Vietnam veteran and Asatruar. The Hammer of Thor was added to the list of symbols approved for engraving on Veteran's Administration headstones in 2013.

Above: Relaxing with a drink among the trees. "I like to describe Asatru in terms of connections: with the ancestors who gave us life . . . with our descendants yet to come . . . with our living kin . . . with the divine powers, or Gods . . . and with the natural world around us."

Part Two:
PRACTICING ASATRU

Chapter 18

Why Ritual?

It is not my purpose in this book to give "how-to" instructions on the performance of Asatru rituals. My main goal is to introduce the philosophy of Asatru, and to demonstrate the meaning and the relevance of our faith for men and women in the modern era.

Nevertheless, it is important to include a few chapters on our ceremonial practices. Ritual plays a key role in our spiritual path, and I cannot give a well-rounded description of Asatru without at least touching on this important element.

So why do we need ritual, anyway? Isn't it enough to study the beliefs of our ancestors and try to live our lives accordingly?

There are many benefits to be gained from the symbolic religious acts that come under the broad heading of ritual. I have listed some of these benefits below. Not all will apply to every rite, but many of them will be found in even the simplest blessing of food, or the greeting given the morning sun and the pale moon overhead.

Here are some reasons Asatruar express our faith ceremonially:

The inborn human need for ritual. Humans are ritual-building beings. Anthropologists have defined us as "tool-using animals" and as "time-binding animals," and even as "symbol-using animals." I will pass over the question of whether or not we are animals,[1] but surely the building of rituals encompasses all three of these—a sense of time and symbols, as well as the ability to construct tools (spiritual ones, in this case). Evidence for deliberate ritual can be found in Neanderthal burial customs, so it's clear we've been doing this sort of thing for a long time. For some reason, ritual innately appeals to us and it makes sense,

---

1. Biologically, of course, there is no doubt that we are animals. However, the question of to what extent the "lower animals" have the same soul components as humans is certainly open to discussion.

then, that we ought to be doing it.

Contact with the Holy. Many rituals provide an awareness of, and contact with, "the Holy"—a quality which can be terrifying, awe-inspiring, and attractive all at the same time. Intense ritual can immerse us in this might and glory, taking us beyond the concerns and experiences of ordinary life, and opening up the universe in a way we normally do not perceive. This contact with the Holy is perhaps the underlying motivation for humanity's pursuit of ritual, explaining everything from flowers in Neanderthal graves to the intricacies of the Eastern Orthodox Mass.

Communion with the Gods. This can happen on a number of levels. It can be virtually indistinguishable from the "contact with the Holy" described above. However, the Holy Powers are our friends and, even more importantly, our kin. They have distinguishing personalities. We can commune with them on this more personalized level, experiencing them in (usually) wordless delight. The benefits include a more personal, more specific version of expanded awareness and awe.

Becoming more Godlike. Being in the presence of the Gods is, to be sure, a good thing. More significant, however, is the change it produces in each individual. Regular ritual elevates our consciousness, giving us new perceptions and perspectives. It sharpens our appreciation for life and enhances our mental and spiritual faculties. In short, it promotes our personal evolution. We are different from the Gods in magnitude—they are "bigger" than we are—but not in essence, and we become more like them through the long-term internalization of ritual.

Practical, tangible aid. Our ancestors gave offerings to the Gods and Goddesses for down-to-earth reasons. In native religions, people typically pray or sacrifice to get good crops, victory in warfare or in love, a healthy herd of cattle, or healing from sickness. Today, thanks to science, we have more control over these things—so we have the luxury of interacting with the Gods about more spiritual matters, such as our own evolution. Nevertheless, diseases still afflict us, crops become blighted or destroyed by drought, and our enemies torment or threaten us . . . so the basic problems of human existence remain very much a part of our lives. We can seek to mitigate them by appeals to the unseen powers that shape the world.

To those raised in a rationalistic culture, this may seem so much superstition. How can prayer, sacrifice, or magic influence events? The truth is, we do not really know how the universe works. We have a few tentative rules we call science, but the postulates underlying our knowledge change at least a couple of times per century, and the rate of change is accelerating. We do not understand consciousness or its interaction with matter. Dozens of books have been written on the strange zone where religion and science seem to merge in ways that Newton or Einstein would find incomprehensible. Our ancestors were not fools or dupes. They lived their lives with utter pragmatism—otherwise, they would have never survived long enough to have babies, and none of us would be here. We would be unwise to exclude their conviction that the universe, in accordance with laws about which we can only speculate, responds to human will as expressed through ritual.

Helping the world. Insofar as ritual supports our efforts to live better lives and raises our consciousness, it is a factor for creating a better world. Furthermore, Asatru takes stands on specific issues that serve the interest of everyone on the planet, not just those who follow our religion. Foremost among these are an abiding belief in the possibility of human nobility, dedication to the welfare of our kin, and an intense desire to protect the ecology of the beautiful planet on which we live. When we add power to our convictions through ritual, we advance these noble causes.

Some group rites in Asatru include a specific blessing in which the altar (called a horg or harrow) is sprinkled with the sacred mead used in the ceremony. Because the altar symbolizes all of Midgard (the entire world), this commits a portion of the holy might used in the blessing to the weal and welfare of the Earth as a whole, and all the living beings on it.

Healing and awakening our European-descended kin everywhere. Asatru represents the innermost soul of the Northern European peoples. Immersed in the sacred, relating to the Divine through ritual in the manner of our distant ancestors, we are nourished and strengthened. We are connected with all the far-flung sons and daughters of the Germanic lands in ways that are profound yet unseen. Anything that affirms that connection strengthens us all.

It is a strength that many of us have not yet experienced. Our European-descended brothers and sisters are asleep. Rootless, stripped of their heritage and their sense of self-worth, they wander through the world bemused by idle entertainment and material delights. How can they be true to themselves? How can they find the path that leads to our spiritual home? Some of them explore the religions of other peoples—American Indian religion, Voudon or other expressions of African belief, the intricacies of Tibetan Buddhism—without understanding that the way of their own ancestors is the best way for them.

We are a wounded people. Torn from our ancient tribes, riven by sword and burned by fire until we died or accepted foreign beliefs, stripped of our natural pride, filled with guilt—guilt about sex, guilt about power, guilt about the very color of our skin—we are brimming over with poison. The results are clear for all to see: more of us are dying than are being born, our children look to other peoples and cultures for their models, our heritage and history are steadily displaced. This is the road to marginalization and extinction.[2]

There is an answer to this condition, and it is a spiritual one. Without a spiritual rebirth, a revolution in consciousness, nothing else can happen. To be healed, we need to find again the faith that is naturally ours. And it is not enough to find that faith in our heads, we must find it in our souls and, yes, even in our bodies. That is where ritual enters the picture. Moving our limbs, raising our voices, turning our eyes to the bowl of the sky, uniting outer actions with inner states, we find wholeness and holiness. This is the way home.

2. Estimates by the Census Bureau indicate that people of European heritage will make up between fifteen and thirty percent of the U.S. population by the year 2100.

Chapter 19

The Blot or Blessing: "A Gift Calls for a Gift"

The blessing, or blot, is one of the two main rites of Asatru (the other being the sumbel, about which more in the next chapter). The blessing is governed by the principle of exchange: "a gift calls for a gift."

Giving gifts was a vital part of Germanic society. Friends were made by sharing even modest things:

> No great thing needs a man to give,
> Oft little will purchase praise;
> With half a loaf and a half-filled cup
> A friend full fast I made.
> —*Havamal*, verse 52

Once friendship was forged, it was continually renewed with gifts:

> Friends shall gladden each other with arms and garments,
> As each for himself can see;
> Gift-givers' friendships are longest found,
> If fair their fates may be.
> —*Havamal*, verse 41[1]

The giving of gifts, then, creates a bond between the giver and the receiver. The Holy Powers, as we discussed in Chapter 5, are our friends

---

1. Both verses translated by Henry Adams Bellows, *The Poetic Edda* (New York: American-Scandinavian Foundation, 1923).

and our kin—so it is only right that we give them gifts to maintain the relationship and keep it fresh, just as we would with our human friends.

Earlier, we listed the benefits we receive from ritual: inspiration, insight, a feeling of union with the Gods and Goddesses, the power to gradually transform our lives and to evolve upward, are a few of them. There are more tangible gifts from the Gods, as well—the luck that gets us through tight situations, victory in our everyday battles, the answers to help life go more smoothly. But what about the Holy Powers? What do they need from us?

The Gods and Goddesses are subject to the weavings of cause and effect, by the deeds laid in Urd's Well, just as we are. They face great challenges in the ordering of the world and its defense against the forces of chaos, and we have the ability to help them in these cosmic tasks. Our gift to the Gods is summed up in the words of one blot as "our might, our main, our troth"—in other words our honorable deeds, our spiritual power or hamingja, and our loyalty or "trueness" all contribute to the well-being of the Gods and give them strength. We of Asatru share a mutual interdependence with the Holy Powers; we need them and they need us. (Notice how very different this is from the Biblical religions, where humans have no input in the larger scheme of the universe.)

The gifts we give to the Gods and Goddesses, and the corresponding gifts that they give to us, bind us to each other in the rite of blessing.

An Outline of a Blessing

Several essential parts make up the framework of a blessing. Other things can be added to these core elements depending on the circumstances and the creativity of the participants. What I will give here is the framework that I personally use.

Preparation of the Area—First, the place where the blessing will be done is ritually set apart from the rest of the universe and dedicated to the holy purpose at hand. Historically, this can be done by carrying flame around the perimeter, or marking it off with physical objects such as stones, wooden rods, posts, or special ropes. Protective gestures, often employing the symbolism of Thor's hammer, have been used in modern times to accomplish this end.

If the place has been used for blessings over a period of time by the group and especially if it is set off by some physical boundary such as a ring of stones, preparation of the area may consist of a gesture and a few words to renew this "apartness" in the minds of those attending.

Calling of the Holy Powers—Next, the God or Goddess with whom we wish to communicate is asked to be with the participants. This is done by calling them by name, as well as their nicknames as found in the Eddas.

Ideally, this calling should be in verse form, but rousing prose is perfectly acceptable. It should emotionally evoke an image of the God or Goddess in question and remind us of his or her key characteristics.

Intent—Rituals should have clear and concise objectives. Just what is it we hope to accomplish? Whether the purpose of the blessing is to receive the general gifts of the Gods, or whether the community has come together for a specific reason, that should be stated in simple language.

Giving Gifts to the Gods—Since we cannot hand the Holy Powers "our might, our main, our troth" in the same way you pass a plate of food to a friend, we give a symbolic gift that represents the intangible ones we give the Gods on a continual basis, and which we pledge to keep giving in the future. In Asatru, that physical representation of our invisible gift is very often a horn of mead. Holding it aloft, the godi or gydja (priest or priestess, respectively) offers it to the deity to whom the blot is dedicated. Then, the mead in the horn is poured into a blessing bowl which will later be emptied on the ground. If the blessing is done outdoors, the mead can be poured directly onto the earth.

So why do we use mead? Although other things can be used to represent our gifts, mead is particularly appropriate. Long ago, when our ancestors lived in a society based on agriculture and animal husbandry, a beast would be killed for the communal feast. The animal was dedicated to the Gods, and its blood was sprinkled on the altar stones and on the assembled people using an evergreen sprig. The idea was that the blood carried the divine power, which could be transmitted to the worshipers by the act of sprinkling (as well as by consuming the flesh of the animal during the ritual meal).

Today most of us buy our meat wrapped in styrofoam and plastic at the local supermarket. We don't slaughter animals for the sacred feast, so a substitute is needed. Mead, or honey wine, is the ideal choice. Both blood and mead are in some sense "alive"—the one from being the symbolic life of an animal, and the other from fermentation. Additionally, mead figures prominently in our Lore. Odin went on a quest for the magical mead that gave ecstasy and expanded consciousness, and mead is the drink of the heroes in Valhalla. Finally, the sharing of alcoholic drink is universally seen as an act of friendship and hospitality. In short, mead is the perfect substitute for the blood used in the old sacrifice.

Receiving the Gifts of the Holy Powers—A gift demands another one in return, so now the Gods give us their gifts. Again, mead is the medium. A second horn is filled with the liquid and held aloft. The participants ask the Holy Powers to pour their blessing into it, that it may be shared among the people and thus give them the benefits they seek.

The most obvious way of sharing the empowered mead with the participants is for the godi or gydja to carry it around the circle, offering a drink to each individual. If there is any question of contagion, the mead may be poured from the large drinking horn into a smaller horn or a cup (not paper or plastic) held by the person receiving it. Those who do not drink alcohol have the option of the godi or gydja dipping a finger into the mead and placing a drop on their foreheads. When all have taken the mead, any remaining in the horn is poured onto the ground as an offering to the land wights.

Sometimes, particularly if many people are involved, passing the horn may prove cumbersome. One problem is the difficulty of maintaining an intense ritual state for the time that the horn is being carried around. In this case, the mead may be poured from a drinking horn into a bowl, the evergreen sprig dipped in the mead, and the mead sprinkled on the participants. One attraction of this method is that it imitates the ancient practice of sprinkling the blood of the sacrifice.

Afterward, the leftover mead is poured onto the ground as an offering to the land wights. Some is also poured at the base of the tree from which the evergreen was cut, and the branch used in the blessing is placed there, as well.

Closing—The Holy Powers are invited to linger with their human kin, and to enjoy the feasting and companionship of all present. They are asked, when they "wend their way to heavenly hearths," to take with them the love of their worshipers here in this world.

This, then, is the framework of a blessing. To this outline may be added readings from the Lore, songs, dramatic skits or other features to help set the mood, establish communion with the Holy Powers, or in any other way accomplish the intent of the blessing.

When are blessings done? The answer is, anytime they are needed or wanted. As a minimum, blessings are given when we celebrate the turning of the seasons. Some individuals and groups like to offer blessings at the full moon; others like them even more often.

Blessings usually involve a number of people—a local kindred or "congregation" of Asatruar, a family, or a group of friends. However, they can be given by lone individuals, as well.

The blessing, however, is not the only major ritual in Asatru. There is another rite of great importance, in which we draw might from the past, from the Well of Urd itself, and immerse ourselves in it so that we can use that might to work our will in the present. We will now turn our attention to the sumbel.

Chapter 20

The Sumbel: Power from the Past

The sumbel is the second of the two great rituals of modern Asatru. It is simple yet elegant, consisting of ceremonially passing a horn filled with mead, beer, or ale around a circle and making toasts. Do not be deceived by its lack of complexity; the sumbel is laden with might and spiritual impact.

Where the Sumbel Gets its Power

In the sumbel, we access three sources of power.

The first of these is the innate spiritual power contained in alcoholic drink. We mentioned in the previous chapter that alcoholic beverages are—like blood—somehow "alive." They are bearers of the divine energy, giving ecstatic communication with the realm of the holy. Odin won the Mead of Inspiration, and with it, the ability to weld the intensity of rational intellect to the winged flight of creativity. We can taste this awesome power to a lesser degree in the sumbel. Moreover, we can shape it with our will, and with the words we speak over the drinking horn as we make our toasts.

The second source of power comes from imitating the Gods and Goddesses. The Lore tells us that the Aesir and Vanir themselves sit at sumbel, and two of the ancient stories in the *Poetic Edda* show the Gods and Goddesses communing in just this way. The sumbel is not just a casual feast or a drinking session, but a ritually significant act—and when we imitate the significant acts of the Holy Powers, we gain a measure of their nature.

But the greatest power in the sumbel comes from its ability to reach into the past, summon up the might of the great deeds that lie there, and bring them into the present so that we can benefit from them in the here-and-now.

How does this work? In chapter 12 we spoke of the Well of Urd. In the mythic Lore of the Germanic peoples, this well is the repository for "that which has become"—in other words, the past. It contains the essence of all deeds which, although in the past, still exert their influence on the present, or "that which is becoming." The past sets the stage for this ever-changing slice of time called "the present" where we are attempting to work our will in the world.[1]

Consider, for a moment, the great feats of our heroes long ago. Wouldn't it be wonderful if we could call upon the power that made those glorious accomplishments possible? Couldn't we benefit immensely by summoning up the courage, persistence, honor, skill, and other traits of the ancestors who placed these great attainments into Urd's Well? Armed with this spiritual essence, we could apply it to our own lives and overcome all the obstacles that confront us. We could live more successfully, more prosperously—more fully!

But how can we figuratively dip into Urd's Well and partake of the magical fluid? How can we use the power from the past to help us in the here and now?

An Outline of the Sumbel

The word "sumbel" is an Anglicized version of the terms used in the elder tongues of our peoples. It is called *sumbl* in Old Norse, *sumbal* in Old High German, and *symbel* in Old English.

Whatever the language, its original meaning can be traced to *sum*, or coming together, and *ol*, or ale. A sumbel is an event at which we come together to share an alcoholic beverage and, more importantly, to share the magical energy transmitted through that beverage.

The following format shows how the sumbel is typically conducted in the Asatru Folk Assembly. Different groups will have their own versions, some simple like those of the Asatru Alliance and some, like

---

1. The ultimate resource for the sumbel, and for the worldview on which it depends, is *The Well and the Tree* by Paul C. Bauschatz (Amherst: University of Massachusetts Press, 1982). Many of the same concepts are summarized in Bauschatz's article "Urth's Well," found in the *Journal of Indo-European Studies* 3 (1975), pp. 53–86.

those of the Theodish branch of Germanic religion, very complex.

Preparation—Historically, sumbels took place inside a chieftain's hall. This enclosed space was, of course, protected from the weather and from enemies, but it was also protection against the unknown. The hospitable fires of the hearth, the familiar setting of tables and benches, shields on the wall, weapons at hand, the comfort of food and drink and the pleasure of laughter among men and women one knows and loves—these things are powerful and good. They constitute the innangarth, the comfortable realm of human society and order.

Outside the hall, in the dark and cold, was the unknown. Wild beasts and monsters lurked in the forest and the fens, prowling about and seeking advantage to strike at the world of men and women. This was the utangarth, the lawless area outside the walls, fences, and sentries.

The sense of order within the innangarth, of "rightness," is emphasized in the preparation for the sumbel. The room should be neat, tidy, uncluttered. The participants should be seated in a meaningful sequence. The host and hostess, along with guests of honor, sit at a head table. Other especially significant individuals might be grouped nearby—in ancient times, this might have been proven heroes or honored members of the war band. The others present fill the remaining benches. By imposing order on chaos we imitate the Gods themselves in their role as the regulators who set into place the fundamental constants of the universe.

Another key task is the preparation of the drink—typically mead, but possibly ale or beer. Words are spoken over it by the hostess, perhaps with the assistance of one or more chosen women. Men are not present during this traditional women's magic. The sacred drink is poured, blessed, and given to the assembled people by women not because women are servants but because they are in some ways closer to the Divine than their male counterparts.

Opening—When all are seated, the hostess carries a horn of mead to the host and ceremonially hands it to him, while speaking formulaic words urging him to protect those assembled (in the old days, the clan or war band or tribe), to further their prosperity, and to speak wise words over the horn. The formula intoned by the hostess might be something to the effect of "Take this horn, leader of the host, and speak good words over it. Be steel-friend and gold-friend to the folk. Bring us weal and wisdom. Let the Gods and the ancestors be with us this night."

He takes the horn and vows to do so, echoing her language: "I will speak good words over the horn, and will be steel-friend and gold-friend to the folk. I will bring us weal and wisdom. The Gods and the ancestors will be with us this night."

Rounds—The host raises the horn and makes the first toast. Traditionally, it is to Odin, master of the mead and of inspiration, father of the Gods and of the Northern folk. This toast may be in prose or poetic form. Then, handing the horn to the hostess, he gives her the charge—"Give them the gift of the Holy Powers!"

She hands the horn to each person in turn, moving clockwise around the group. The recipient raises the horn to one of our Gods and Goddesses. Their toasts may be as simple as "Hail Thor!" or as fancy as a poem prepared for the event, honoring Freya or another deity.

The second round is to an ancestor, and the charge given the horn-bearer is to "Give them the might of the ancestors!" Early in the Asatru revival, these tended to be generalized ancestors that could be claimed by anyone of Northern heritage—heroes from the sagas like Leif Erikson, or Hermann of the Cherusci, who led the German tribes against the invading Roman armies. As people grew more comfortable with sumbels, however, they became more likely to raise the horn to personal ancestors. Now the most common toasts are to parents, grandparents, the ancestor who came over from England in 1804, and so forth. The person holding the horn tells those present a little about the person being honored, specifically highlighting his or her virtues and accomplishments.

For the third round, the horn-bearer is urged by the host to "Give them the power of the past!" This time, individuals may toast either a

God or Goddess or one of the ancestors. They may tell a (short!) story, sing a song, or recite a poem—always with the idea of conjuring the courage, integrity, loyalty, perseverance, sense of humor, or other traits from the realm of the past.

The third round is also the time to make a boast of some deed accomplished—a test passed, a book written, an athletic feat realized—a victory in life's battles. These, too, become deeds laid in the Well of Urd, adding to the resources on which the group can draw in time of need. All of us can and should hail the person who does great things, and rather than envying them, we ought to go forth and accomplish worthy deeds ourselves.

Another possibility for the third round is to make an oath. Successfully fulfilled, an oath adds to our spiritual power. A failed oath, however, takes away from our store of accumulated might. It also detracts from the might—the "luck," or the hamingja—of the group. It is wise to make oaths sparingly and to take them very seriously once they are made. Words spoken over the horn echo among all the worlds, and reach the ears of the Gods themselves. Beware the urge to make rash oaths!

Finally, gifts may be given during the sumbel. Gifts work in two ways: they bind friends together, and—when given by a leader to his or her followers—they serve as recognition for excellence.

Closing—After the last round, the horn is given to the host. He will make appropriate comments to formally conclude the sumbel and any mead remaining in the horn will be poured out for the Gods, with a share usually being given to the spirits of the land.

Cautions: Guarding the Luck of the Folk

Just as an unfulfilled oath harms the luck of the group, so can other ill-advised actions.

Curses are forbidden. They tend to reflect back on the one who makes them, and sometimes bring "collateral damage" to those sitting with them at sumbel.

Along the same vein, in the Asatru Folk Assembly we do not

toast Loki, whose negativity ranges from mere mischief to much more serious offenses against the world order. At Ragnarok he stands against the Gods and their chosen heroes and helps to bring the ruin of the world. In our experience, toasts made to him are followed by ill-luck.

Drunkenness is strongly discouraged at the sumbel (or at any other Asatru rite!). It leads to offensiveness that disturbs the fellowship of those assembled and opens the temptation to make oaths that will not be kept. Nor is it a good example for children who may be present. All these are harmful to the group as a whole.

The sumbel is a powerful experience that promotes personal spiritual evolution and, more immediately, nourishes the clan, tribe, or kindred that practices it. Its simplicity makes it all the more attractive for those of us who follow our ancestral faith.

Long live the might of the mead!

Chapter 21

The Wheel of the Year

Blot and sumbel may be performed any time the blessings of the Holy Powers or the ancestors are needed. But, like all cultures, the Germanic peoples held certain times of the year to be especially important: the marking of the sun's passage in the sky, the changing seasons, and the agricultural cycle.

There have been many reconstructions of a workable, modern Germanic religious calendar. The names of the holy days vary from one version to another, dates may be a little different, and there are seeming discrepancies. But it was this way in ancient times, too—different tribes gave highest place to different Gods and Goddesses, and the timing of some festivals depended on the local climate. The specifics of the Germanic ritual calendar varied over time and geography. But then as now, the major ideas remained the same—the great midwinter festival, for example, or the harvest, or the coming of spring.

We celebrate for many reasons. There is a resonance between our inner nature as human beings and the changes in the world around us. In spring and summer, we are more active. Our spirits respond to the awakening of life in the field and forest, and to the warmth of the sun. Similarly, in winter we turn inward, become more introverted, and seek the shelter of the fireside against the ravages of cold weather. There is a general principle here that may be summarized: "As without, so within."[1] We are not separate from nature; we are an integral part of it.

The sun and moon were seen as visible manifestations of Gods and Goddesses. To the simple folk, these celestial bodies were

---

1. This corresponds well with the Hermetic axiom: "As above, so below."

185

thought to be the literal Gods and Goddesses themselves, or at least so the Christian chroniclers would have us believe. To those with greater understanding, however, the sun and moon are only physical phenomena, behind which lies an unseen and intangible spiritual essence conceived as a spirit or deity—the *numen*, as the renowned psychologist Carl Jung called it.

Given this way of looking at the world, in which the sacred permeates all of nature, we can understand why our ancestors were interested in events involving the sun and moon. As the days get shorter and the weather turns colder, the sun seems to lose its power, its ability to warm us and to give life. This weakening progresses until the winter solstice, the very lowest point of the sun's might. Then, gradually, the days grow longer again and the sun's power grows in the heavens. Life returns to the world around us. Eventually, six months after the winter solstice, the sun's influence peaks at the summer solstice (Midsummer) and the cycle repeats itself.

Similarly, the phases of the moon exhibit a shorter cycle, moving from fullness to waning and then to the "new moon," when it disappears entirely. The moon then reappears as a tiny sliver of itself and waxes again toward fullness.

These astronomical movements, which we take for granted, are nevertheless of huge symbolic, or archetypal, significance. They demonstrate the fundamental cycle of birth, life, death, and rebirth which is found throughout nature in many forms. Combine this with the idea of the sun and moon as being Gods and Goddesses, and we can see why our ancestors marked their passage with ritual. In regard to the sun, this religious observation centered around the winter and summer solstices, and the midway points we call the fall and spring equinoxes. Similar rites could be expected at the full and new moons— and indeed such ceremonies are common for many Asatruar today.

Although the markers of the year are important from a religious standpoint, there are very practical matters associated with the coming and going of the seasons. The cycle of the sun drives another important series of events, those of agriculture. Preparation of the field for planting, sowing the seed, maintaining the crops as they grow to ripeness—all culminated in the harvest and its attendant festivals. The bounty of the crops determined whether there would be enough food to get through the winter. Producing a plentiful supply of food was a matter of life and death—and where we find matters of life and death, we find humans appealing to the Holy Powers.

Taken together, the astronomical and agricultural cycles constitute the "Wheel of the Year."[2] Graphically, this is represented by a circle with the winter solstice (Yule) at the top, the summer solstice (Midsummer) at the bottom, and the spring and fall equinoxes (Ostara and Harvest) on the right and left midpoints, respectively. The other holy days are sprinkled around the perimeter of the circle. Significant festivals fall approximately midway between the equinoxes and the solstices, so that the whole arrangement forms an eight-spoked wheel. The year begins at Yule or winter solstice, and proceeds clockwise through the various holy days until it arrives again at its ending/starting point.

In addition to the holidays based on astronomy and agriculture, there are special days in memory of Asatru martyrs and heroes. Although not of ancient origin, these "Days of Remembrance" are widely celebrated by modern Asatruar.

Now let's start at the top of the circle, and work our way around the Wheel of the Year.

A Trip Around the Wheel of the Year
Yule—Approximately December 20 through December 31

To moderns, Yule is just another word for Christmas. However, before the coming of Christianity, Yule was the great midwinter celebration of the Germanic peoples. Many of the things we associate with Christmas have pagan roots. The evergreen is a symbol for enduring life, the candle and the Yule fire represent the reborn sun, and the giving of gifts and the emphasis on kin were Germanic themes long before they were Christian ones.

Because of these common features, the Asatru celebration of Yule

---

2. The term "Wheel of the Year" apparently originates with the Wiccan and neo-pagan movements, rather than being a strictly Asatru metaphor. In any case, it is a vivid way of thinking of the turning (which is what wheels do, after all) of the seasons.

The Wheel of the Year

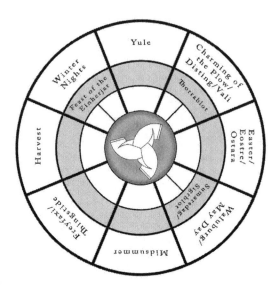

looks a lot like what our Christian friends do at this time of year. We erect Yule trees, which for us symbolize the World Tree. We decorate them with pre-Christian sun-symbols and runes. If we have a star on top, it stands for the North Star; or perhaps instead of an angel we have a valkyrie. Our homes are decked in wreaths and evergreens. Asatruar get together with kin and friends and exchange gifts, just like everyone else.

Yule is not just a single day, but rather a whole miniature season of its own. The common expression "Yuletide" suggests this—"tide" meaning a span of time consisting of a number of days. In modern Asatru, at least in the United States, Yule typically starts on December 20, which is on or just before the winter solstice. We call this first day of Yuletide "Mother Night" because it gives birth to the sun and to the new year. Celebrations continue for the next twelve days. On Twelfth Night, December 31, the season ends by swearing oaths for the year to come.[3] Interestingly, the modern custom of "New Year's resolutions"

---

3. Notice that this is different from the Christian tradition, in which the Twelve Days of Christmas begin on December 25 and run through January 5.

goes back to a pre-Christian tradition: in the Norse sagas, we read how the Yule boar was led around the hall, so the folk could place their hands upon it while making oaths.

Several major religious ideas come together at Yule. One is the rebirth of the sun. At the winter solstice, the year's longest night, the spell of winter is broken and the days will gradually become longer. This turning point was extremely important to our ancestors, who by this time were wondering if they would have enough food to survive until milder weather.

Another crucial idea at Yule is the continuity of the clan. Yule is a time of family—not just the nuclear family, or even the extended family, but the family line itself as a time-transcending unity encompassing the ancestors, the living, and the descendants yet to come. At Yule, the veil between the worlds is thin and the ancestors are with us in a special way. Because of this, we may prepare an "ancestors' plate" before sitting down to the Yule feast, thus inviting those men and women who gave life to join in our festivities.

Thorrablot—on or near the Friday between 19 and 25 January

Thorrablot is a cure for the "cabin fever" induced by the long Nordic winters. It is not as well known as some of the other festivals; maybe four-wheel drive and the Internet keep us from being as isolated during the winter as in olden times.

The origins of Thorrablot are speculative. It may, however, be related to the first glimmers of the Germanic awakening, which was becoming evident in Scandinavia only a few centuries after the Christian conversion. By the 1700s, Icelanders were greeting the fourth month of their calendar—Thorri—with *Thorrablottar* or "sacrifices to Thorri." Folklorists speculate that this is a half-forgotten memory of a winter spirit with the same name.

Alternatively, Thorri may have been none other than Thor himself. Perhaps his name became garbled over time, or maybe it was deliberately camouflaged to ward off Christian zealots. In any case, what better God to shake off the wintertime blues? Thor is gregarious, cheery, and possessed of a great appetite for food and drink. No one could stay depressed for long in his presence!

Asatruar who celebrate Thorri realize that religion should warm the heart and lift the spirit—and Thor is always up for a good time. It's a perfect occasion to get together with friends and lift a glass with the traditional Icelandic toast: "Let us greet Thorri with great courtesy, for he is a brave fellow. He is extraordinarily brave and powerful!"

Disting/Feast of Vali/Charming of the Plow— around February 14

This festival may have different names and themes from one Asatru group to another, but there are underlying connections. The name "Disting" means "Thing of the Goddesses"—*thing* in this case being the word for the old Germanic tribal or regional assembly. Thus, Disting was a gathering or assembly dedicated to the female deities, especially Freya and Frigga. The ideas of fertility and rebirth dominate this event. In the old days, this might have meant saying prayers over the plow and ritually placing grain cakes into the furrow, hence the alternative name of "Charming of the Plow." Asatruar sometimes bless their gardening tools at Disting and remind themselves that we are just as dependent on the soil for our sustenance today as we were thousands of years ago.

The connection with Vali is more problematical. Some connect it with Valentine's Day. In the mythic lore, Vali is the God who avenged Balder's death by slaying Hod. Only by this act of revenge could Balder be reborn after Ragnarok.

Ostara/Eōstre/Easter—around March 20, the spring equinox

This festival takes its name from a Germanic Goddess of the springtime, rebirth, and dawn. Variations of her name are found in Old High German as *Ostara* and in Old English as *Eōstre*. Our modern word Easter is a direct descendant. I am always astounded that the most important celebration of the Christian faith bears the name of a pre-Christian deity!

At Ostara we take pleasure and comfort from renewed life. The fields are green again after winter's abuse, and newborn animals totter around on wobbly legs. We think on the quickening of life and what it means for ourselves, as parts of the natural order.

Many Christian Easter customs are directly lifted from pagan lore. Eggs and hares have long stood for birth and rebirth. Even the common Christian "sunrise services" make more sense for a dawn Goddess than for celebrating a resurrected Christ!

I am not trying to poke fun at Christianity by pointing out these pagan origins. On the contrary, I am trying to show how much we have in common: eggs and hares to be sure, but more importantly the return of life and the promise it holds for each of us.

Sumarsdag/Sigrblot—on or near the Thursday between April 9 and 15

In old Iceland, Sumarsdag or "Summer's Day" was the first day of summer. For most of us, that's not particularly relevant. Few of us live in Iceland, and we have another festival—Midsummer—that marks the warmer half of the year. Sumarsdag becomes a piece of exotica, if viewed from this limited perspective.

However, early April was also when sacrifice was given to Odin for victory in the raiding-and-trading season that began with warmer weather. This rite was known as the Sigrblot, or "victory sacrifice." Many Asatruar combine these two themes into a holy day welcoming the more clement weather, and at the same time invoking Odin for victory. No, not victory in sacking monasteries or raiding coastal cities—times have changed. But what has not changed is our need for victories in the daily battles of our lives, as individuals and as a community. Victory is good! Winning is better than losing! To Asatruar, victory or sigr is a spiritual quality—and Sigrblot is an ideal time to strengthen this quality in ourselves.

Waluburg/May Day—April 30 and May 1

A second-century seeress named Waluburg won renown for traveling with Germanic troops serving the Roman Empire in Egypt.

Today, many Asatruar honor Waluburg, as well as deities like Holda, Frigga, or Freya, on April 30 and May Day. Freya is especially suitable because she is patroness of the magical arts of seidr, a form of seership. Waluburg becomes a time for the mysteries of the Earth, for the working of magic, and for inquiring into the future. The tone is one of nighttime revelry and the practice of the occult arts in hidden places—which is, of course, just how things must have been with the threat of Christian persecution hanging over the heads of all dissenters.

If Waluburg is characterized by the concealing shadows, May Day is bright and sunlit. The startling polarity of darkness and light, of the underworld mysteries and the miracle of renewed life, jolts us into a heightened awareness of both. May Day sings of birth, renewal, and deeds brought to fruition. It is a day to celebrate the world around us, and especially the return of life to the world and to our own hearts.

Midsummer—on or around the summer solstice, about June 21

At Midsummer, the hours of daylight are at their longest. From this point onward, the nights gradually lengthen as we begin the long slide into winter.

Midsummer is still celebrated in modern Europe, and is a time of dancing, festivity, and continual reminders of our pre-Christian past. Some of these remnants include flaming sunwheels rolling down hillsides, and, of course, the all-night bonfires around which people congregate for merrymaking.

Why the bonfires? Why the flaming sunwheel? Perhaps we wish to actively play a part in the cosmic scheme, to encourage the sun and give it strength along its decline and the descent toward eventual rebirth at Yule.

At Midsummer, Asatruar remember that we are a part of the drama of existence, and we seek out our connections with those we love as we gather against the growing darkness.

Freyfaxi/Thing's Tide—around August 23

In parts of Viking Age Scandinavia, a horse festival was common in August. Horse fights were a part of these events, with the power of the animals taken as an omen of the harvest's bounty. No specific name for this festival is recorded in the literature.

When I was assembling a religious calendar for Asatru back in the late 1970s and early 1980s, I called this festival "Freyfaxi," or "Frey's Mane," after the horse belonging to the fertility God Frey. Any gathering connecting horses and harvest would certainly have been a suitable time to honor Frey, keeper of the holy might of virility, fertility, and plenty.

August was also a common time for hosting the thing—the rough equivalent of a legislative session combined with a law court, as well as more casual visiting, bargaining, romancing, and gossiping, with a little feuding thrown in for good measure. Hence another name for the August festival, "Thing's Tide." The thing opens and closes with a blot to Tyr, God of justice and law.

Harvest/Winter Finding—on or about the Fall Equinox, around September 21

For our ancestors, the harvest was a matter of life or death. The coming of winter could be chilling in more ways than one if the storage rooms were not well stocked with food. Would the tribe thrive, or starve? How many precious animals would have to be slaughtered to allow the folk to survive? The season of cold and ice was a severe test in ancient Europe. While this was a curse for individuals, it was a blessing for us as a group. The reputation of the Germanic peoples for planning, foresight, and delayed gratification stems from many generations of harsh Darwinian selection in which snow and starvation were nature's culling knife.

We are just as dependent on the Earth's bounty as were the Teutons of old. Supermarkets are not, after all, the ultimate source of the food we eat. Fewer of us are farmers than at any other time since the introduction of agriculture in the Neolithic Age—but the soil provides for us all, regardless of how we earn our bread and meat.

In a widespread economic or societal collapse, our vulnerability would become gruesomely obvious within days.

During the harvest season, we give thanks for what we have produced with the help of the Earth and Sky. We ask for continued plenty in the future, and prepare both spiritually and materially for the challenges of the coming months.

Winter Nights—the Saturday between October 11 and 17

At Winter Nights we recognize the female spirits of fertility, plenty, and well-being known as the disir. These beings are often equated with the women of the ancestral line, looking on from the Otherworld to bless their descendants with luck, love, and inspiration. The disir are there to give us a helping hand when things get a little too much for us to handle.

The disir remind us that death is not a brick wall, but rather a thin veil through which the ancestors send gifts to their descendants. In return they ask (1) to be remembered and honored, and (2) for the family to continue into the future. After all, if their line dies out, who will pour them libations? Who will tell their stories?

We recall our female ancestors at Winter Nights, often invoking them ritually by name to join their living kin for an evening of feasting, laughter, and storytelling.

Feast of the Einherjar—November 11

The einherjar are the heroes chosen to go to Odin's hall, Valhalla, after death in battle.

Once in Valhalla, the lore tells us that the slain warriors feast on endless pork and quaff horns of mead carried to them by beautiful valkyries. Every day they fare out and fight each other, inflicting the most horrible wounds. When evening comes, however, they are miraculously healed so they can feast that night, then go out the next day and do it all again. This seemingly pointless activity is actually practice for Ragnarok, the great battle at the end of this cycle of time, when Odin and the other Gods will need all the heroes they can muster. To be listed among the einherjar is the highest honor the

Teutonic warrior can attain.

The myths surrounding the einherjar are a symbolic expression of several spiritual truths. First, the afterlife is not a place of rest, but of continued struggle, growth, and purpose. These things are, after all, the very essence of life, on either side of the transition we call death. Second, human actions make a difference. We can aid the cause of the Gods, fighting alongside them either literally or metaphorically. Third, there is a path of transcendence, a way of becoming a demigod, by paradoxically utilizing the power of death to overcome death. The lesson here seems to be that immortality is attainable only by those not afraid to die.

November 11 is, of course, Veterans Day in the United States. It is also the birthday of the famous and controversial General George Patton—a true warrior mystic. Patton believed that he had been reincarnated as a warrior many times throughout history. He even experienced what today we'd call a "near-death experience." Thrown from his horse and unconscious, he "dreamed" that he was being carried off a battlefield on a shield borne by two Viking warriors. They set him down when they realized it was not yet time for him to die.

This chapter has introduced Asatru's seasonal holy days. Now let's look at a different kind of observance.

Chapter 22

The Days of Remembrance

The Days of Remembrance are modern inventions. I composed them when I was relatively new to our faith—a mere fifteen years or so into my spiritual journey. The Viking influence, in contrast to my later pan-Germanic approach, is strongly apparent in them. They are not "traditional" in the sense of being twelve hundred years old, but they are "traditional" insofar as they date back to the earliest days of the Germanic religious revival in the Unites States, and that in itself is a worthy thing.

It is good to remember those who fought and died to keep our religion alive during the long centuries of Christian persecution. The constant effort to imitate the bravery and sacrifice of these men and women builds our character and makes us better people.

Asatruar, if they are true to their faith, constantly seek self-improvement. This is especially so when it comes to the heroic virtues conjured as we read the Days of Remembrance—courage, honor, loyalty to one's faith and one's ancestors, prowess in battle, sharpness of wit, dedication to kin. Each of the heroes, martyrs, and accomplished men and women in this list can show us the way to be more and to do more.

How do we celebrate these Days of Remembrance? Simply reading about them reminds us of the men and women being honored, but this in itself is hardly enough. We should spend at least a few moments in reflection—to consider how these heroic individuals relate to our own lives and how we can use these special days to make ourselves a little more like them.

January 9—Day of Remembrance for Raud the Strong

When King Olaf Tryggvason was making Norway Christian by
fire and sword, there lived a man named Raud the Strong. He was
a follower of our Gods and had little time for the newly mandated
faith. Raud was not only strong, he was rich and influential—which
made him an especially tempting target for royal wrath. Tryggvason
had him captured and demanded his conversion. Raud refused, so Olaf
forced him to swallow a snake, resulting in his death. This got rid of
an influential Asatruar and cleared the way for the king to confiscate
Raud's land for himself.

February 9—Day of Remembrance for Eyvind Kinnrifi

Eyvind was led into a trap and captured by Olaf Tryggvason's men,
who tossed him at the king's feet. At first, Tryggvason and his bishop
tried to persuade Eyvind of the new faith's rightness. When that didn't
work, they bribed him with gifts and a share in the royal revenues.
Eyvind refused, so they set a bowl of red-hot coals on his abdomen
and cooked his organs while he was still alive. According to the saga,
Eyvind's stomach burst under this torture and he died.

March 9—Day of Remembrance for Olvir

Olvir, like most of the men and women in the district around
Trondheim Fjord, remained true to the Aesir and Vanir long after
King Tryggvason declared Christianity the one true faith of the land.
To get around the royal decree, a group of men secretly organized
the traditional festivals. Olvir was a leader of this resistance. When
Tryggvason found out about this, he brought his army and killed Olvir
as well as many of his companions. Those who were less involved were
driven out of the country or fined.

March 28—Ragnar Lodbrok Day

On this day in the year 845 CE, a viking named Ragnar attacked Paris
and caused major destruction, not the least of which was the burning
of three churches. It is probably not a coincidence that this happened
on Easter Sunday. The perpetrator is reputed to have been none other

than Ragnar Lodbrok, one of the greatest Norsemen, and hero of the saga which bears his name.[1]

If raiding Paris on Easter Sunday and burning churches sounds like a religiously motivated attack—well, it may have been. Historians used to think that the Viking Age arose solely from a desire for loot and land. More recently, historians have made the case that many Norsemen were defending our native religion and culture in the face of the deliberate, aggressive, and intolerant expansion of Christian missionary activity into the Northlands. No doubt three medieval churches in Paris would be worthy targets because that's where gold and other fine things were kept ... but why on Easter Sunday? Ragnar was striking a blow for his Gods and his people.

April 9—Day of Remembrance for Jarl Haakon

Haakon Sigurdsson joined forces with the king of Denmark to conquer Norway and defeat its king, Harald Fairhair, a Christian. In return, Haakon was made jarl (or "earl") over the western part of the country.

Jarl Haakon was a devout follower of the Gods and a defender of the traditional freedoms that went with Asatru. He brought back the ancient rights of chieftains and farmers, rebuilt the temples that had been destroyed, and allowed the folk to once more follow their ancestral way. Peace ruled the country, and the people prospered. Even the crops in the fields seemed to respond to the restoration of freedom and holiness. This period lasted many years, then a dispute broke out with some of the residents of the Trondelag area. Haakon lost support as the inhabitants sided with newcomer Olaf Tryggvason, who was later to become king and renew the persecution of Asatru. Jarl Haakon was eventually murdered.

May 9—Day of Remembrance for Gudrod

King Olaf the Stout of Norway, later known as Saint Olaf, continued the tradition of persecuting anyone who held true to the Gods. Along with this religious oppression came the consolidation of political

---

1. Available in *The Sagas of Ragnar Lodbrok*, translated by Ben Waggoner (New Haven: Troth Publications, 2009).

power in royal hands, and the revocation of the rights of the freemen.

This caused much muttering among the people. A meeting of the regional Uppland kings was called to debate these issues. Indecision prevailed until Gudrod, king of Gudbrand's Dale, rose to speak. According to the saga, his words were these:

> We are here five kings, and none of less high birth than Olaf. We gave him the strength to fight with Earl Svein, and with our forces he has brought the country under his power. But if he grudges each of us the little kingdom he had before, and threatens us with tortures, or gives us ill words, then, say I for myself, that I will withdraw myself from the king's slavery; and I do not call him a man among you who is afraid to cut him off, if he come into your hands here up in Hedemark. And this I can tell you, that we shall never bear our heads in safety while Olaf is in life.[2]

These bold words carried the day, and the Upplanders rose in opposition. A traitor carried word of the plot to Olaf, who moved against them and captured them all. The king had Gudrod's tongue cut out.

June 8—Lindisfarne Day

The Viking Age officially began on June 8 in the year 793, when three ships loaded with Norwegian raiders descended on the monastery of Lindisfarne, off the coast of England. Since the Holy Isle—as the Christians called it—was a center for missionary activity, and because the attack had come with no warning, Christian kingdoms everywhere stirred with panic.

Lindisfarne Day was one of the first "days of remembrance" we established early in the Asatru revival. It, along with Ragnar Lodbrok Day, shows how attached we were to the romantic figure of the Vikings during the 1970s.

Both these holy days celebrate Norse military victories over

2. *The Heimskringla*, translated by Samuel Laing (London: Longman, Brown, Green, and Longmans), vol. II, p. 81.

Christianity. Our Christian friends may not understand this, since they've been taught that the conversion of the North was accomplished peacefully. The truth, however, is that the Viking world was under cultural, political, and religious attack by the Church. The Norsemen struck back against centers of the Church's power, and Lindisfarne was thus a prime target.

June 9—Day of Remembrance for Sigurd the Volsung

No Teutonic hero overshadows Sigurd. Of all the great warriors and striding conquerors, of all the brilliant poets and stubborn martyrs, none can match his fame. His saga was passed on to us by both the Continental and the Scandinavian branches of the Germanic peoples. Richard Wagner adapted this epic tale of love, valor, and betrayal for his great Ring Cycle. Sigurd, the slayer of dragons and winner of the cursed treasure, will be known and praised for as long as our Folk lives to hear of his deeds.

July 9—Day of Remembrance for Unn the Deep-Minded

Unn was a powerful woman from *Laxdaela Saga* who emigrated to Scotland to avoid the hostility of the Christian monarch, Harald Fairhair. She established dynasties in the Orkney and Faroe Islands by carefully choosing mates for her granddaughters. When Unn settled in Iceland she continued to show all those traits which were her hallmarks—a strong will, determination to control events, dignity, and a noble character. In the last days of her life, she solidified her line by selecting one of her grandsons as heir. Unn died during the grandson's wedding celebration, having accomplished her goals and worked out her fate here in Midgard. She received a typical Norse ship burial, surrounded by her treasure . . . and by the shining glory of her reputation.

August 9—Day of Remembrance for King Radbod of Frisia

Christian missionaries in Frisia had done well, and King Radbod had agreed to accept the new faith. As the day of his baptism drew near, the king voiced one nagging doubt. What about all his ancestors who had died without recourse to Christ? Where were they spending eternity? The monkish reply was swift and certain: all the heathens were writhing in hellish agony.

The king, showing that the noble blood still flowed through his veins, proudly responded: "Then I would rather be suffering there with them than go to heaven with a parcel of beggars." The baptism was canceled, the priests were sent scurrying, and Frisia remained free of the Christian yoke for many years to come.

September 9—Day of Remembrance for Hermann of the Cherusci

Few heroes have served our Folk as greatly as Hermann, leader of the German tribe called the Cherusci. When the Romans crossed the Rhine to push deeper into German territory, Hermann organized a confederation of tribes to oppose them. The invasion ended abruptly when Hermann's forces annihilated three of Varus's legions in the Teutoburg Forest, in the autumn of 9 CE.

Thanks to Hermann's rallying of the Cherusci and affiliated tribes, Roman ambitions were largely frustrated. Without his efforts, Roman settlements would have sprung up in the Germanic heartland, ultimately changing the very character of the people. Hermann gave us the time and territory we needed—and made possible the Germany we have come to know.

October 8—Day of Remembrance for Erik the Red

Erik the Red is commonly remembered as the father of his more famous son, Leif Erikson. Each October, as the country gets ready to celebrate Columbus Day, jaded newspaper reporters and the Sons of Norway remind us that, after all, the sailor from Genoa was about five hundred years too late. Leif gets the spotlight, but standing not far back in the shadows is that old rogue, Erik.

Back in the early 1980s or so, I decided that Erik deserved more prominence. When I learned that October 9 had been formally declared Leif Erikson Day, I decided to give Leif's stalwart sire a day of his own. Since October 9 was already Leif's day, we opted to celebrate it the day before—hence the departure from our usual pattern of celebrating Days of Remembrance on the 9th of every month.

Erik was a dedicated follower of Thor. He stayed loyal to his blustery God even when his wife converted to Christianity and wouldn't sleep with him anymore. I don't imagine Erik went without a bedmate—and his wife got a little chapel, built right over the hill where her heathen husband wouldn't have to see it when he looked out of the house.

November 9—Day of Remembrance for Queen Sigrid of Sweden

Sigrid, widow of King Erik the Victorious, was an attractive woman whose hand was sought by one royal suitor after another. She rebuffed them, some of them violently, and it wasn't without reason that history gives her the nickname "Sigrid the Haughty."

However, one proposal finally won her over—that of Olaf Tryggvason, king of Norway. Olaf, you may remember, was a zealous Christian who slaughtered Asatruar from one end of his domain to the other.

There was one catch: Olaf insisted that Sigrid must give up the Gods and become a Christian. She refused, saying "I do not mean to abandon the faith I have had, and my kinsmen before me. Nor shall I object to your belief in the God you prefer." The king swore at her and slapped her across the face with a glove he held in his hand. Sigrid rose, stared at him coldly, and warned him that this deed might well be his doom.

Clearly, the wedding was off. Years went by. Sigrid married King Svein of Denmark and produced a son, Olaf, who became king of Sweden. He, along with King Svein and Earl Erik of Norway, went to war against Tryggvason—largely at Sigrid's instigation. Tryggvason was defeated, and killed himself by leaping off his ship and drowning. Sigrid had, indeed, gotten her revenge.

Asatruar today remember Sigrid for standing by the Gods rather than marrying Olaf, despite the king's fame and reputation. Her steadfastness deprived Olaf of her considerable political power and possibly slowed the Christianization of Scandinavia.

December 9—Day of Remembrance for Egil Skallagrimsson

Viking Egil Skallagrimsson was a rare synthesis of action and introspection, of daring and thoughtful complexity.

How do we explain such a man? Extremely violent when angered, broad-shouldered, taller than most, with craggy and harsh features, Egil was a ferocious fighter who embodied the Viking image. Odin was his God, and the blood of berserks and shapeshifters ran in his veins. His lust for gold and fame drove him from land to land, from one adventure to the next, in a powerful saga that some consider the best in Icelandic literature.

But Egil was also passionately devoted to his friends. He was generous to those who found his favor. Egil's hard warrior heart was torn when tragedy took his sons, and in his grief he gave us the unforgettable poem *Sonatorrek*—"The Irreparable Loss of Sons." The same brain that directed axe-blows and planned raids also seethed with poetry and expressed it with a skill that calmed the anger of hostile kings; Odin's inspiration showed itself in skaldic metaphor and meter as truly as in berserk fury and splintered shields.

Egil Skallagrimsson lived a life of the sword and of poetry. To say that he was a remarkable man, deserving of our remembrance, is an understatement.

With the mighty Egil we bring this chapter to a conclusion. It has been a long journey, from the purpose of religious festivals, to the Wheel of the Year, and finally to the Days of Remembrance. These are some of the ways in which modern Asatruar observe their faith.

It is important to remember that no single set of holy days will recreate the ritual life of our ancestors: this was always a product of the local culture, the social leadership, and even the climate. What we have presented here is a general template offering a reasonable reconstruction for men and women living in the twenty-first century. It is as true as we can make it to the underlying spiritual concerns of our forefathers and foremothers.

And what were those concerns? The same as ours

today—connection with the Holy Powers, with the natural world, with our ancestors, with our living kin, and with our descendants yet to come . . . in short, the very gifts that Asatru bestows on its practitioners, whether in the tenth century or the day after tomorrow.

Chapter 23

Runes: Mysteries of the Universe

Runes you will find, and readable staves,
Very strong staves,
Very stout staves,
Staves that Bolthor stained
Made by mighty powers,
Graven by the prophetic God.

—*Havamal*, verse 142[1]

The twiglike figures writhe across ancient stones, eroded by time but still whispering from the past. Some of them march single file on bits of bone and sticks of yew. Others stand somberly on the hilts of steel swords and rust-speckled spearheads. Today, more than two thousand years after their birth, these mysterious shapes are cut into bits of wood, or carved into a drinking horn, or scratched into metal or bone amulets.

The figures are called runes. They look like some bizarre alphabet from a magician's diary . . . and so they are, in a sense, though they were never designed to be letters, and they are not organized in alphabets, but in rows called futharks.

Runes are the very heart of Germanic magic and mysticism, an integral part of our religious heritage. More than any other facet of our faith, runes have acquired a certain amount of fame in the modern world. Much has been written about them—some of it wisdom, and

1. *The Elder Edda: A Selection*, translated by Paul B. Taylor and W. H. Auden (New York: Random House, 1969).

more of it nonsense.

Runes look like letters, but they were not designed for the writing of ordinary words. Their original functions were purely religious and magical. It was only in later and more degenerate times that they were put to work writing the medieval equivalents of grocery lists and love notes. Writing with runes was possible because, as we shall see, runes had sounds associated with them, just like our modern letters. In the earliest of times, however, those sounds were used to create magical incantations and charms—they were for communicating with the Gods, not humans.

If runes are not letters, what are they? Technically speaking, the written figure we see carved on stones and pieces of wood is not really a rune. The real rune is the sacred concept or mystery for which the figure stands. We sometimes call the written symbol a "rune stave" to differentiate it from the invisible, spiritual mystery it conceals, but for convenience we usually end up calling both the stave and the hidden concept "runes." In this book, I will use "rune" to mean either the stave or the concept that lies behind it.

In the traditional lore, each stave is given a name. These names are suggestive of the hidden concept the rune represents. The stave also has a certain phonetic value—that is, it corresponds to a particular sound, just like our letters—and it has a specific order in the runic "alphabet," or futhark.

The charts in this chapter show how this works. For example, look at the table for the rune row we call the Elder Futhark. Now find the first rune listed: it looks a lot like our capital "F." Its name is *fehu*, which can mean either "cattle" or "wealth" in the early Germanic language. Both these words are connected with the deeper concept of the rune, which has to do with a mobile form of property or power, among other things. Since *fehu* is the first rune of the Elder Futhark, it has the value of "one" for numerological purposes.

The Evolution of the Rune-Row

In the Bronze Age, spiritual leaders among the Germanic tribes used many symbols with precise religious and magical meanings. We can

Pre-Runic Symbols

still see them carved into rocks all over the Nordic lands today. Some of these glyphs remind us of the runes we know, but others are quite different—sunwheels, circles, and simple geometric forms of many kinds.

A century or more before the Christian era, however, this simple collection of images was replaced by something much more sophisticated: new symbols—the runes—were created. Each was given a specific meaning, just like the earlier symbols, but the runes were also assigned phonetic values, and placed in a designated order. Additionally, the runes were interrelated in complex patterns of meaning. The runes were immensely more powerful as a metaphysical system than the older set of unordered and unrelated Bronze Age signs. The oldest rune row, made up of twenty-four symbols, was called the Elder Futhark. It dominated the religious landscape of Northern Europe from about the second century BCE to approximately 800 CE. The Elder Futhark seems to have been the work of a specific group of people, an ancient guild of magicians or spiritual technicians that cut across tribal boundaries.

About nine hundred years later, the Elder Futhark gave way to a condensed rune row called, predictably, the Younger Futhark.

ᚠ	f	*fehu*	cattle
ᚢ	u	*ūruz*	aurochs
ᚦ	þ	*þurisaz*	giant
ᚨ	a	*ansuz*	god
ᚱ	r	*raiðō*	ride
ᚲ	k	*kēnaz*	torch
ᚷ	g	*gēbō*	gift
ᚹ	w	*wunjō*	joy
ᚺ	h	*hagalaz*	hail
ᚾ	n	*nauþiz*	need
ᛁ	i	*īsa*	ice
ᛃ	j	*jēra*	year
ᛇ	ei	*eihwaz*	yew
ᛈ	p	*perþrō*	pear
ᛉ	r	*elhaz*	elk
ᛊ	s	*sowilō*	sun
ᛏ	t	*tīwaz*	Tyr
ᛒ	b	*berkanō*	birch goddess
ᛖ	e	*ehwaz*	horse
ᛗ	m	*mannaz*	man
ᛚ	l	*laguz*	water
◇	ng	*ingwaz*	Ing
ᛞ	d	*dagaz*	day
ᛟ	o	*ōþila*	estate

The Elder Futhark

Times were changing. The Elder Futhark had served well for almost a millennium, but with the beginning of the Viking Age the society of runemasters decided that it needed revision. They dropped the number of runes from twenty-four to sixteen, while preserving certain important relationships between them. We know this was done for magical reasons, not linguistic ones, for a simple reason: the variety of sounds in the Germanic languages had increased over the centuries,

ᚠ	*fé*	wealth
ᚢ	*úr*	drizzle
ᚦ	*þurs*	giant
ᚬ	*áss*	God
ᚱ	*reið*	ride
ᚴ	*kaun*	sore
ᚼ	*hagall*	hail
ᚾ	*nauð*	need
ᛁ	*íss*	ice
ᛅ	*ár*	good year
ᛌ	*sól*	sun
ᛏ	*týr*	Tyr
ᛒ	*bjarkan*	birch
ᛘ	*maðr*	man
ᛚ	*lögr*	water
ᛣ	*ýr*	yew bow

The Younger Futhark

yet the runemasters went the other way—they chose to reduce the number of symbols. If their motivation had been to accommodate changes in the language, they would have added runes rather than dropping a third of them! This revised futhark lasted through the Viking Age—from about 800 CE to 1100 CE.

There were other rune-rows which, while perhaps less significant as historical benchmarks, also deserve mention. One was the English Futhorc (futhorc rather than futhark, because the language was Anglo-Saxon and the sound values changed accordingly). This consisted initially of twenty-six runes, and expanded eventually to thirty-three as the language became more complex. It is used in only about sixty surviving inscriptions over a span ranging from before 650 CE up to the eleventh century.

Another runic system of note is from Frisia—a coastal nation extending from what is now the Netherlands across northwestern

Germany, to the border of Denmark. This area was culturally conservative in ancient times, and the sixteen or so inscriptions in Frisian runes are strongly religious and magical in character. Unfortunately, no complete Frisian rune row has been found, so our knowledge remains somewhat sketchy. The Frisian runes appear closely linked to the English ones.

With the destruction of organized Asatru after the end of the Viking era, the runic system degenerated. Within a few centuries of our religion's eclipse, Scandinavian scholars would begin studying the runes anew, and they continued to be used for magic—but the deeper elements of runic wisdom sank into the folksoul, there to await the inevitable revival. Glimmers of light would shine through the darkness as the years went by, but a full-fledged resurgence would have to wait almost eight hundred years.

The late nineteenth and early twentieth centuries witnessed a revival of all things Germanic. This awakening was largely spurred by the creation of a unified German nation in 1871. Many Germans were disappointed with the resulting state; they had expected something more spiritually enriching than the prosaic politics of the day. Idealists, mystics, and romantics of all sorts reacted against this limited vision. One of the leaders of the resulting Germanic folk movement was a man named Guido von List, who, depending on who you ask, was either a crackpot or a gifted visionary.

List rose to fame in the late 1880s with the success of his novel *Carnuntum*, which is set during the conflict between the German tribes and the Roman Empire. In the years that followed, he used psychic methods to explore the Germanic landscape (*German Mythological Landscape Images*). He also wrote a book summarizing his worldview (*The Invincible: An Outline of Germanic Philosophy*).[2] List had been a follower of the God Wotan, or Odin, since his youth and he wrote extensively on Germanic society as it had existed in prehistory—or rather, as his psychic talents told him it had been.

More relevant to our discussion of the runes, however, is the fact that List endured eleven months of virtual blindness following

2. Guido von List, *The Invincible: An Outline of Germanic Philosophy*, translated by Stephen Flowers (Smithville, Texas: Rûna-Raven, 1996).

ᚡ	f	primal fire
ᚢ	u	resurrection
ᚦ	th	thunder
ᚨ	o	mouth
ᚱ	r	primal law
ᚴ	k	world tree
ᚼ	h	hail
ᚾ	n	fate, necessity
ᛁ	i	ice, iron
ᛆ	a	leadership
ᛋ	s	sun power
ᛏ	t	rebirth of sun God
ᛒ	b	birth
ᛚ	l	*örlog*
ᛉ	m	man
ᛣ	y	now (rainbow)
ᛦ	c	duality, marriage
ᛎ	g	gift of life

The Armanen Futhark (or *Futharkh*)

cataract surgery in 1902. During that time, he immersed himself in introspection and meditation. His efforts were rewarded: the secrets of the runes were unveiled to him in a profound spiritual experience. The revelation was of an eighteen-rune futhark based on verses in the Eddic poem *Havamal.* It was very similar to the Younger Futhark, but with two additional runes. There were also fundamental differences in the ways the rune names were used, as well as other features that took it outside the stream of traditional rune lore. This new rune row became known as the Armanen Futhark—named after the Armanen, which List claimed had been the priesthood of ancient Germany. Von List set forth his insights in a book titled *The Secret of the Runes,* published in 1908.[3]

Virtually no scholars give credence to List's work. Nevertheless, it is magically effective and perhaps we should let time render its judgment.

After all, our religious tradition is a living one. The Gods still speak to their Folk, and from time to time some of us hear them! Since there was no equivalent to the ancient network of runemasters when List had his vision, one could speculate that the Gods chose to show him the revised futhark.[4] While we should not uncritically accept everything List wrote, many of his teachings have merit and should not be rejected out of hand.

But what does one do with runes, regardless of the futhark in which they are found? In ancient times, our ancestors used runes in three main ways: to divine the future or seek advice, for spells or charms to magically change the world in some way, and to advance the rune-worker to a higher level of spiritual evolution.

Divination—Advice from the Gods

Divination with runes is effective because the futhark, taken as a whole, is a perfect representation of the universe. All the mysteries of the individual runes, added together, describe the forces at work in the exterior universe and in the human soul. Create wooden lots with the runes carved on them, toss them in accordance with the right methods, and the rune staves conform themselves to the forces in the universe at that moment.[5]

This may sound unbelievable to anyone raised in

---

3. Guido von List, *The Secret of the Runes*, translated by Stephen Flowers (Rochester, Vermont: Destiny, 1988).

4. Or, to use a different metaphor, perhaps the new runic system had been "uploaded" in the collective unconscious by the impersonal Nornic forces, ready for "downloading" by a talented and persistent individual.

5. There are other theories to explain why divination works. Some believe that the Norns, entities involved in determining orlog or "fate," actually manipulate the runic staves. Another view is that the runes are only devices allowing us to access our own innate wisdom and to move the staves psychokinetically. Regardless of the mechanism that may be involved, my experience is that they do, in fact, work!

twenty-first-century materialism, but my own experience tells me it is true.

Many years ago, in the midst of a prolonged spiritual crisis, I blindly drew one rune stave per day out of a set of twenty-four (the Elder Futhark) for five consecutive days. The staves were carved on wooden pieces that could not be distinguished from each other by feel. Each of the five days, my hand drew forth the same stave. The odds against such a coincidence are approximately eight million to one. The stave that kept coming up was not just any old rune, but one named *perthro*—whose meaning is connected to the divinatory process itself. Years later, I read that this particular stave often comes up when one is not supposed to know the answer to a question.

Drawing individual runes out of a bag or cup is good for a quick summary of one's current standing in the universe, and thus can provide hints to the right action one ought to take. Many Asatruar make this simple practice a part of their daily routine. But Tacitus, a Roman chronicler who shed much light on the ways of the Germanic tribes, describes a somewhat more complicated rite practiced in the first century CE:

> For omens and the casting of lots they have the highest regard. Their procedure in casting lots is always the same. They cut off the branch of a nut-bearing tree and slice it into strips; these they mark with different signs and throw them completely at random onto a white cloth. Then the priest of the state, if the consultation is a public one, or the father of the family if it is private, offers a prayer to the gods, and looking up at the sky picks up three strips, one at a time, and reads their meaning from the signs previously scored on them.[6]

Edred Thorsson uses Tacitus's description as the basis for a simple

6. Cornelius Tacitus, *The Agricola and the Germania*, translated by Harold Mattingly (London: Penguin, 1970), p. 109.

but elegant runic divination ritual in his book Futhark.[7] He has the inquirer cast the runes onto a white cloth and then take up three runes. The first describes past events as they relate to the question. The second indicates where things stand at the present moment, and the third represents the probable (but not predetermined) outcome. Endless variations have been devised, some of which are quite complex. The best single source on the theory and practice of runic divination is Thorsson's *Runecaster's Handbook.*[8]

Today, some two thousand years after Tacitus, sets of "runestones" are sold in occult shops across the country so that people can "read their fortune." These "runestones" almost always consist of runic characters painted on small stones or scratched into ceramic tiles. Sometimes the sets contain a very nontraditional "blank rune," which has no rune on it at all. Historically, however, small runic artifacts such as charms and talismans were always inscribed on wood, bone, or metal—never on stones. The only authentic stones with runic inscriptions are hefty ones, often weighing hundreds of pounds, erected to protect graves or to serve as memorials ... not exactly the kind of objects one would toss for divination!

Spells and Charms—Changing the External World

Divination is a comparatively passive art. More active forms of rune magic were used in ancient times for a multitude of purposes—for curing people and animals or cursing them, or for obtaining things like gold, or a maiden's love, or protection in battle. *Egil's Saga* tells a story of a poorly made runic charm that actually made a girl sicker instead of healing her, until Egil corrected the runes and cured the patient. Likewise, we read how Egil scratched a rune on a drinking horn filled with poison, causing the horn to burst asunder in his hand. More than a thousand years later, in twenty-first century California, runes carved into wooden stakes have successfully guarded a home against thieves.

Again, our logical minds remain skeptical—but experience proves

7. Edred Thorsson, *Futhark: A Handbook of Rune Magic* (York Beach, Maine: Weiser, 1984).

8. Edred Thorsson, *Runecaster's Handbook: The Well of Wyrd* (Boston: Weiser, 1999).

that logic is not enough by itself to explain the world. We are just beginning to understand the ways in which consciousness interacts with the physical universe.

Long ago, when I was very inexperienced in the way of runes (Weiser Books had just published *Futhark*), I was forced by circumstances to try a simple act of runic magic.

I was visiting an out-of-town friend when she hysterically informed me that her former sister-in-law had called. This woman was not merely someone with whom she had a disagreement; my friend felt that this person was truly evil in a way that went beyond like and dislike, or even love and hate. More to the point, she was coming over to pay a visit from which no good could come, and she was due to arrive imminently.

Wanting to help, I hastily improvised a simple ritual. It involved mentally tracing the rune stave *thurisaz* on the front door, with the strong intent of warding against all ill, just as Thor's hammer wards against the giants in our Lore. (In retrospect, another rune might have been more suitable and some would say that *thurisaz* is a dangerous rune for the beginner to choose—nevertheless, that is what I did.)

The woman did not come over that night . . . or any other night for about eight years. No explanation was ever given for her failure to appear. Was it the power of the runes, or coincidence? You decide.

As mentioned above, runes were traditionally carved on fragments of wood, bone, or metal for magical purposes. These could be carried on the person or placed in an appropriate location—perhaps the bed of a sick person, under a doorstep, or hidden around the house. Runes were inscribed on boulders to protect graves or to give blessings to the departed. They were not always written on material objects; runic incantations could be—and still are—chanted for magical effect. Runes are flexible and potent magical tools that can be used in a variety of ways to change the world around us. For example, there is a whole subset of runic practice in which one assumes postures resembling the runes while chanting a galder (*galdr*, a sort of runic mantra).

Runes for Personal Evolution

The greatest purpose for rune-working is to allow the dedicated, persevering individual to follow in the footsteps of Odin and evolve into a higher being—a sort of Germanic *bodhisattva*, a spiritual version of the Nietzschean superman. Few will attain this lofty goal, but many lesser souls, striving upward, will nevertheless reach greater heights than otherwise would have been their lot. At the very least, they will lead interesting lives!

Divination and magic play their role in this transformative process. When tossing the runes, one constantly interacts with the force of wyrd, the flow of cause-and-effect that shapes events. The runecaster acquires a deep intuitive understanding of the way things are, and how things work on a fundamental level—which is the essence of wisdom. Given the universal scope of the runes in both the macrocosm and the microcosm, this wisdom is comprehensive. You don't just find out if you'll get that new job, or if you should date the girl from work; you gradually acquire insights of a much deeper order.

A man or woman who throws the runes imitates the Gods in a meaningful action. In *Runecaster's Handbook*, Edred Thorsson writes: "The first 'runecaster' was Ódhinn himself, and in casting the runes the diviner is actually participating in the divine process in an imitative way . . . in the context of the ritual act the runecaster has assumed the status of 'a god.'"[9] Acting in this exalted manner, the aware individual, one who is consciously motivated by the prospect of spiritual evolution, rises to higher levels.

More active forms of rune magic also contribute to this evolutionary process. Even the most humble acts of "low magic" convince those who perform them that the world does not necessarily obey Cartesian logic and Newtonian mechanics (although both are valid in everyday, nonmagical situations). This breakthrough in awareness opens many doors to higher development. Like the runecaster, those who carve runes and sing incantations take on some of the attributes of Odin himself, shaping the very fabric of the universe to work their Will.

---

9. Thorsson, *Runecaster's Handbook*, p. 12.

The Lore teaches us how Odin hung nine days on the World Tree, starving, weakened by thirst, and wounded with a spear, to win this sacred knowledge. Those humans who can muster comparable will and determination to Overcome can rise to the level of the Gods themselves.

Chapter 24

A Holy Reserve

We must approach the Gods and Goddesses in the right spirit. We live in a cynical society where everything is open to ridicule. Irreverence is considered a virtue and it is unfashionable to take anything very seriously.

The Holy Powers must not be exposed to this attitude. Before rituals of any sort we must remind ourselves that some things matter, and that they are not to be approached in a casual or overly familiar way. This is not to say that our rites must be grim-faced affairs; in sumbel, particularly, a wide range of emotions come forth and laughter often echoes among those taking part. Always, though, there is an awareness that what we are doing is holy, ultimately serious, and that the Gods and Goddesses are not to be mocked or trifled with.

The Experience of the Holy

From the beginning of the Asatru resurgence in America, we have been very open in our practice. We have allowed outsiders to attend, to take photographs, and to take part. I believe that this was a mistake, and I have been guilty of it myself. There is a difficult balance here. On the one hand, we need to give people some idea of what we do. Secrecy builds distrust, and people's imaginations will fill in the gaps with all sorts of fantasies, most of them unpleasant. Nevertheless, it is vital to protect the dignity of what we do and to maintain an awareness that this faith is ours, not something that can be expropriated by passersby. Over time, we must evolve protocols that meet both these requirements.

Why does it matter so much? The German theologian Rudolf

Otto, in his book *The Idea of the Holy*, examines the essence of the "numinous experience"—the human encounter with the Divine. This meeting between man and divinity cannot be adequately described in words because it lies beyond the life that we know. We can only approximate a description of the numinous through analogy, and through the feelings of awe and majesty it induces in us. The experience of the numinous is one of overwhelming power, of inspiration and even of ecstasy. It is in this sacred state that we commune with the Gods and with our ancestors.

Our encounter with the Holy Powers is set apart from the mundane world. One early Germanic word for holiness, *wihaz*, implies exactly this sort of awe-filled separation. The *vé-bönd*, or sanctuary rope, that marked off the ritual area in Viking times was a physical sign of this protected, holy enclosure in which every word and gesture took on special significance. It is inappropriate to invite the merely curious, the whimsical, the scoffing, or the outsider into this space.

Maintaining the Dignity of the Holy Powers

Quite apart from the essential nature of the holy in Germanic religion, there are other very good reasons to safeguard our rites from the eyes of the outside world. Though our ceremonies consist of nothing more shocking than pouring libations to the Holy Powers, making certain gestures, or passing a horn around a circle and making toasts, they will look strange to some outsiders. It all comes down to what people are used to seeing. The Catholic Mass—complete with a priest in vestments, bells, and incense—would look very peculiar except for the fact that we are familiar with it.

So it is with Asatru. We know why we do the things we do, and for us they make sense, but to others they may simply look bizarre. It is our duty to protect the Gods and Goddesses from the scorn of nonbelievers.

Keeping Some Things Private

The problem is, then, that we must give outsiders some idea of what we do while not compromising our relationship with the Gods.

This is something that American Indians have done very well, and we can learn from their example. As my friend Stefn pointed out elsewhere in this book, anyone can come to a powwow and watch the drumming and the dancing. Sometimes, selected non-Indians may be invited to take part in other events, but ultimately there are rites to which only Indians are invited. Some Indian groups are very militant in stressing the proprietary nature of their practices—which of course gets them labeled "racists" by petulant moderns who feel they have a right to practice the religion of any group whatsoever.

Historically, native religions have been guarded about their religious practices. When the father of a household in Vedic India performed the daily sacrifice before the hearth, only family members could be present. Even good friends were excluded. Similarly, lower castes and outsiders were not even allowed to hear certain verses of the *Rig Veda* spoken aloud. This was definitely not a "come one, come all" religion!

In more modern times, the Mormons maintain the privacy of their religion against the casual curiosity of others. If you're not a Mormon, you won't be allowed inside the temple. Fraternal lodges like the Masons and their many offshoots keep the same policy of exclusivity.

There is a place for privacy. Modern Asatru is still wrestling with this issue, but eventually a workable balance will be established.

So what are my personal thoughts on what is appropriate or not? We need to be choosy about the people we allow to participate in, or even to observe, our rituals. Strangers or outsiders can have my hospitality and my friendship, but this does not necessarily give them a right to share my connection with the Divine.

I will not allow my rituals to be photographed. Nor will I appear in public in ritual garb or clothing from another historical era. Years ago I did this sort of thing, and I was mistaken.

A dignified, reserved, reticent attitude toward the rites of our religion can win us the respect of the modern world. Most importantly, it will deepen our contact with the Holy Powers.

Chapter 25

The Future of Asatru

Most books on Asatru concentrate on our past, or on our beliefs and practices today. Very seldom does anyone attempt to look at the future of Asatru. We're going to do that in this chapter. We can't predict everything that will happen in Germanic religion in the long term, but we can at least look at the likely features of our faith over the next few generations.

The Awakening and Healing of the European-Descended Peoples

If Asatru rises to prominence, it will do so as part of the spiritual awakening of the European-descended peoples. Unless tied to that awakening, it will remain one more minor choice available to the rootless and alienated. As a factor in our resurgence, on the other hand, it will be loaded with the power of Odin, the very expression of divine will and energy.

What do I mean by an "awakening of the European-descended peoples?"

First, I mean that we as a group must reclaim our native spirituality, and that this spirituality must help shape our view of ourselves and the universe around us. I do not mean to say that every person of European heritage should become Asatru. There will still be Catholics and Protestants, Buddhists and atheists. However, regardless of religion, every thinking person of European heritage would at least be aware that we have a deep culture and religion, and would acknowledge it as a part of their heritage. The power of Asatru to connect us—with our Gods, our ancestors, our kin, and with nature itself—can be a healing paradigm for all of us, regardless of faith or the lack of it.

Second, we must understand that we are indigenous Europeans, even if we live in the United States, Australia, or a scientific outpost at the South Pole. A lack of continuous residence in Europe does not keep us from being indigenous Europeans: the line of ancestors ties us to Europe. Our bodies and souls are forever shaped by those long millennia in the European environment. My immediate ancestors have lived in America for only 250 years or so, but my forefathers and foremothers were in Europe forty thousand years before that. The bones of my ancestors validate my claim to indigenous European status.

Third, we must realize that as indigenous peoples we have certain needs, rights, and interests, and that it is natural for us to defend these. Like every other group, we have our own problems that we must overcome. Our teenage boys have the highest suicide rate of any group in the United States. Our teen girls have the lowest self-esteem in the nation. We are the only group against whom discrimination is often mandated by law. Any form of group self-interest on our part is greeted with ridicule or by suspicion. Our population, worldwide, is in free fall—we are so materialistic, so separated from our ancestors, that many of us have no interest in the continuation of our people. All these things indicate spiritual sickness of a very serious degree, and only a return to the life-affirming ways of our people can cure us.

In the subtitle above, I wrote of the awakening and healing of Eurofolk. Awakening must be accompanied by healing for the sake of balance. We have been ill—a people in pain, cut off from our soul, which has gone wandering in lands of confusion. As we heal ourselves, our awakening will not be an angry lashing-out, but a confident, centered expression that will benefit us and the other peoples of the world.

Fourth, we must learn to love ourselves. In much of popular culture and academia, we European-descended people are the "evil Other," the "white devil" who is the source of all the wrongs in the world. If you doubt this, take a look at some of the indoctrination courses on "diversity" and "whiteness" to which entering college freshmen are subjected. We must reject these influences for the hateful lies they are, while at the same time acknowledging our very real faults and mistakes. If we do not love ourselves, if we do not love our people, how can we say we love our ancestors or the Gods?

Our awakening won't be the first time that a return to native religious roots has been connected with the revival of a people. Perhaps the best example is the reawakening of American Indian pride and self-assertion during the Sixties. Inspired by the progress of African-Americans, Hispanics, and other groups during the Civil Rights era, the American Indian Movement was formed in 1968. AIM began addressing the needs of its people in a radical way. The occupation of Alcatraz Island and the seventy-one-day takeover of Wounded Knee were two of their best-known actions, but there were hundreds of others—speeches, demonstrations, and occupations all across the land.

The AIM founders realized they had two tools they must use to the utmost: their native religion, and their link to the land. A group of AIM leaders sought the advice of Crow Dog, an elder on the Rosebud Sioux reservation. He told them that

> if they were to be a successful Indian organization, they had to have the spiritual involvement of our medicine men and our holy people. And that is actually when the American Indian Movement was first born; because we think that AIM is not only an advocate for Indian people, it is the spiritual rebirth of our nation . . . So now, the American Indian Movement relies very, very heavily on the traditional elders and the holy men of the various tribes—to give them the direction they need so they can best help the Indian people.[1]

The awakening of Eurofolk may or may not involve the same tactics and attitude used by AIM. But whatever form our revival takes, it will have power and validity only to the extent that it recognizes and

1. Jeremy Schneider, "From Wounded Knee to Capitol Hill: The History, Achievements and Legacy of the American Indian Movement," *Indian Nation*, vol. 3, no. 1 (April 1976).

honors our ancestral religion.

Obviously, an awakening of the European-descended peoples is good for Eurofolk, but who else stands to benefit? The answer is: everyone. Which leads me to my next comment on the future of Asatru.

Cooperation with Other Indigenous Peoples

The words I've written above may seem scary to some readers. We are not used to hearing Eurofolk speak honestly about their needs or interests as a people. (Indeed, I've been told that Eurofolk "have no legitimate group needs or rights worth defending.") I want to speak the truth that I feel, not with anger and demands, but with calm assertiveness, and with malice toward none.

Consider the guiding document of the Asatru Folk Assembly, our Declaration of Purpose. Point Five of the DOP speaks of

> the promotion of diversity among the peoples and cultures of the Earth, in opposition to global monoculture: the world should not be one uniform, unvarying mass. All peoples should be allowed to be different, to relish that difference, and to work out their own destinies. Only in our uniqueness can our respective Gods fully manifest.

I have made this principle a part of my life since those words were written some thirty years ago. I have worked hard for the rights of Tibetans, and lived with Karen freedom fighters in the Burmese jungles. I have written of the sacrifice of people like Ken Saro-Wiwa, the great Nigerian democracy activist.

The more I have come to value the unique nature of my own, European-descended people, the more I have come to appreciate other peoples and cultures. While this appreciation comes to some extent from the things we share as part of our common humanity, that is not the whole story. Indeed, it is our differences that I value more than our similarities. Differences are good, and ought to be respected and preserved. Blending human cultures into a mish-mash of "diversity" destroys the flavor, the unique quality of all of them.

I received my multicultural education not in the classroom nor on carefully insulated tourist jaunts. I rode endless miles in the back of trucks through Africa, crowded in with the locals. I shared food with bus passengers in Algeria, and sat around the fire in the Sahara with Arab truck drivers. I shared tea in the homes of Tibetan rebels. I walked through minefields with villagers in rural Burma. By sharing travel, food, and danger in the company of men and women of many cultures and races, I acquired a balanced respect for the peoples of the Earth. Nothing in this experience lessened my love for my own people, or my determination to serve my people as best I can.

The problem is not with men and women of other races and cultures; there is good and bad in all of us, both individually and collectively. The problem is those few who want us to all be the same, to surrender our identity and our self-determination. Their motivation may be ideological, a conviction that humankind MUST, for some reason, become homogeneous. The goal is, perhaps, one of absolute equality, a sort of metaphysical Marxism. My response to that is simple. "Equal people are not free, and free people are not equal."

From a point of view diametrically opposite that of the Marxists, there are those who seek globalization and uniformity not because of ideology, but for love of profit. Modernization brings wealth, and wealth means that more people, from pole to pole, are "free" to drink Pepsi and buy the latest permutation of the cell phone. Indigenous cultures, traditional cultures bound to kin and to the earth, are an obstacle. Material things—especially the "stuff" we have been trained, by advertising and by peer pressure, to need—just are not that important to them. Those cultures have to be erased, by gradual seduction where possible and by forced relocation from their ancestral lands when necessary.[2]

Caught between the Marxists and the marketers, the indigenous peoples are outnumbered and outgunned. They need allies. Some of those allies will be other tribal peoples like themselves, facing exactly

2. The best book I have ever read on this theme is *In the Absence of the Sacred* by Jerry Mander (San Francisco: Sierra Club, 1992).

the same situations. But we, people of European blood and heritage in the First World, also can and should be their allies. We might have more money and trinkets, but we too have been ripped out of our ancestral context, colonized and exploited in ways that differ only in that we are, for the moment at least, richer. For us, colonization started with the coming of Christianity, and continues even as I write these words. Many indigenous peoples are experiencing the same process that we endured a thousand years and more ago.

Ironically, our fight to preserve our people and culture against the globalist onslaught may best be furthered by aiding other peoples around the world who are similarly threatened. The forces seeking to absorb the Tibetans, the Karen, the Sioux, and hundreds of other indigenous groups are the same forces trying to make Eurofolk part of the produce-and-consume global plantation. Points of cooperation might include our respective religious rights, the practice of our ancestral cultures, and the preservation of our lands and environments. We can help each other.

Defending Life On Earth

Asatru serves life. The Aesir and the Vanir are forces of life and consciousness, always in opposition to the stasis, negation, and entropy represented by the giants. This is indeed a "life-or-death struggle" in the most literal sense possible. The unrestrained victory of the nihilistic force we call the giants would be the devastation of all that we know and love, and would leave our planet lifeless.

It follows, then, that one of the great tasks of Asatru in the years to come will be the preservation of Earth as a place hospitable to life—and specifically, to life of a sort we know, including our Folk and all humankind.

Is life on our planet endangered? Any rational study of the issues renders a resounding "Yes!" I cannot possibly say it any better than radical environmentalist Lierre Keith:

> The hour is late. It's too late for the creatures who went extinct today. Somewhere a tiny green frog sang the song

of his species one final time. A small bird found no mate, and her last ovum is withering inside her. Another eighty-one million tons of carbon were added to the fragile blanket of our atmosphere, that long, ancient work of our good, green ancestors who made animal life possible. A cascade of starvation strains the links of the food chain again, from plankton to salmon to grizzly bears; it's anyone's guess how long it will hold.[3]

Two hundred more species become extinct ever day. Not from natural causes, but overwhelmingly from human activity. And not just obscure snails and butterflies, but fish in the ocean, and wondrous beasts deep in the jungle that we've just discovered (because we're in the process of chopping down their home), and animals whose names we learned as children—elephants and rhinoceros and polar bears. It's no wonder biologists are calling this the "sixth great extinction."[4] How many strands in the net can we snip before it fails to hold, and we all slip into the dark abyss of nonexistence?

Nuclear weapons and climate change have finally made it possible for humanity to literally kill everything on Earth. We are faced with soil depletion, peak oil, and a population that will hit 9 billion around 2050. The ocean is acidifying ten times faster than during a mass extinction event 55 million years ago. Climate change is already disrupting food production and making natural disasters worse, and we're heading for temperatures that will produce massive famine and population relocations around the world. All these problems are political and economic ones at one level, but they are fundamentally spiritual. Human actions depend on human values, and on our attitudes toward other people and the world around us. If we change our values and our attitudes—and then put those values and attitudes to work on the social and political structures around us—we can overcome these

---

3. Aric McBay, Lierre Keith, and Derrick Jensen, *Deep Green Resistance: Strategy to Save the Planet* (New York: Seven Stories, 2011), p. 193.

4. See *The Sixth Extinction: Patterns of Life and the Future of Humankind* by Richard E. Leaky and Robert Lewin (New York: Anchor, 1996).

challenges.

But just what beliefs and feelings do we need to change?

First, we must understand that the natural world is not just a "resource" to be dismembered for human use. The Bible, in Genesis, tells us to take dominion over the Earth and subdue it. This is wrong. Unfortunately, the Abrahamic religions pretty much control the planet, and the idea of dominance is at the heart of our problem. We must relearn a forgotten truth—things in nature exist for their own sake, not for ours. They have meaning in themselves. Can we use the things in nature for our own benefit? Of course. That, too, is the way of nature. But our use must be balanced, in proportion, and done with an understanding of the impacts on other people and other systems.

Second, we must realize that while profit is good, it is not more important than our souls. Some radical environmentalists want to see an economic leveling, a drastic redistribution of wealth so that no one has much more or less than anyone else. I do not. I believe in a market system that maximizes both freedom and prosperity. However, individuals and corporations alike should not be allowed to despoil those things we all use—the air, the water, wilderness, and our climate. Nor should the wealthy or their corporations be allowed to buy candidates or to unethically pervert the legislative process.

Third, we must relearn that the Divine is found in nature. Our first step is to personally seek out a natural place (not easy for many of us these days) and simply *be there*—to immerse ourselves in the experience of nature. When we learn to approach nature on its own terms, to let it define itself and to not impose our preconceptions on it, we can with time and patience reconnect with the divine essence, the numen, that lurks behind the phenomenon. This is, to put it mildly, a powerful experience.[5]

Fourth, we must put these spiritual factors to work in our own lives. The old cliché "Become the change you wish to see in the world" is true. It implies lifestyle choices favorable to the environment, and I'll use myself as an example: I recycle, drive moderately, minimize my use

5. The most informative book I have read on how to see the divine in nature is *Summoning the Gods* by Collin Cleary (San Francisco: Counter-Currents, 2011).

of electricity, and gently encourage others to do these things. But we must not stop with our personal lifestyles—we must act to affect the political and economic structures that are speeding us toward global disaster. For me, that means voting (as hopeless as that sometimes seems), signing petitions, and sending donations to organizations that actually produce results.

I will close this part of the chapter with an observation, a musing, and a call to action. Charlemagne, who spent much of his life forcibly converting the Saxons to Christianity, ordered the slaughter not only of pagans, but of bears. Why? Michel Pastoureau, author of *The Bear: History of a Fallen King*, tells us that

> the bear was sometimes venerated as a god . . . particularly among warriors. Bears had to be absolutely eradicated to convert these barbarians to the religion of Christ. It was a difficult, almost impossible task, because these cults were neither recent nor superficial.

But the Christian psychosis goes even beyond this. Pastoureau goes on to say that

> relations that human beings have had with [the bear] have always been passionate. They are still . . . and they will remain so whatever measures are taken to try to save the animal. In killing the bear, his kinsman, his fellow creature, his first god, man long ago killed his own memory and more or less symbolically killed himself. It is too late to turn back the clock. . . . the bear is doomed to disappear.[6]

The polar bear has, until recently, fared much better than his land-bound brothers. But that is changing. A few days before I composed these words, the Arctic ice shrunk to the lowest extent ever recorded.

6. Michel Pastoureau, *The Bear: History of a Fallen King* (Cambridge: Belknap, 2011), p. 239.

The state of the ice determines the fate of these fur-clad lords of the North. An ice-free Arctic summer may be only a few years away, and hope for the existence of the polar bear dims with the setting Arctic sun.

Has Charlemagne and the Church won? Is Pastoureau right? Have we effectively killed the bear—and ourselves—by allowing politicians and corporations to play to our own greed and shortsightedness?

We are a heroic people, filled with will and capable of vast deeds. Our fate is what we make it. As for me, I stand with the bears, and with all life on Earth.

Asatru Communities

The things discussed so far—the healing and awakening of the European-descended peoples, cooperation with other indigenous groups, and the imperative of maintaining our Earth as a suitable home for life—deal with the conditions Asatru faces in the twenty-first century and beyond. These and other factors will determine our "operational environment" for the next few generations.

Asatru communities, on the other hand, are one way of dealing with these challenges.

What is a community? A community is any group of people bound by common interests, origin, or purpose. We speak of the homebrewing community, the African-American community, members of the local Baptist church, or the citizens of a town. Using that definition, there are hundreds of Asatru communities scattered across the country and around the world—local kindreds, informal groups in meetups, and national organizations, just to name a few. These kinds of communities are essential to Asatru and we must never underestimate their importance.

But there is another kind of community—the "intentional community."

In this case, people typically live together on a piece of land owned by the group as a whole. They may have jobs outside the community, but the community and its members are a major focal point of their lives. One very successful example of such an entity exists an hour's drive from where I sit: Ananda Village occupies nine hundred acres, and was founded in 1968. Despite a difficult beginning and a few crises through the years, this community has continued under its original leader and has not wavered from its program.

Some years ago we attempted to start an Asatru community in the Sierra foothills, but it foundered for a number of reasons. Our plan was somewhat different from that of Ananda. Rather than having the members live communally on the land, our concept was that we would all live in the general vicinity on our private homesteads, coming together for worship and for community endeavors several times a week. We wanted to put in an orchard and provide a space where families could have garden plots. There would have been a burial place for our dead, and possibly even facilities for some light industry. This scheme—a sort of tribe dispersed across an area, with special land for the things we do together—provides a good balance between privacy and communal needs. I still think this is a workable plan, and the AFA is actively working toward realizing it or something like it.

We intend to ultimately have many such communities across the country. Ideally, they should be close enough together that you could leave your home, drive a day's distance, and find yourself at another community (no more lousy budget motels!). These communities would not be identical, but they would be unified in belief and purpose, and together they would constitute a mutually supportive network.

How would we use these communities? What would be their purpose? First, they would be places we could come together with people of common belief and heritage. Being with each other on such a frequent basis would help our spiritual lives and our material lives to bloom and prosper. We would rediscover the joys of connection with others, and specifically with people of like mind and soul.

Our communities would be laboratories for experimenting with the traditional social structures of our Folk—extended and multi-generational families, clans, and tribes. We could develop our own internal customs and systems of governance based on Germanic (for example, Anglo-Saxon) law.

We could sink our roots in the soil. To realize our nature as an indigenous people, we must intimately know the land, plants, animals, and weather of the place we inhabit. We will learn to listen to the unspoken wisdom of these places, to let every aspect of the world around us speak to our hearts.

We can and should invite ordinary people from outside the community to come and learn about us. We could host classes in organic gardening, give living history lessons, or have stargazing parties. Communities must not become compounds, walled off from their neighbors. Isolation brings fear and paranoia—within and without the community. A certain degree of openness is essential.

Intentional communities could be test-beds for environmentally friendly technology. Asa-folk can teach energy-efficient home construction, or sponsor testing for advanced solar technology. It might be possible to cooperate with local colleges, universities, and companies to provide space for such innovations.

Finally, if any of the various end-of-the-world scenarios come true—economic collapse, peak oil, civil war, or whatever—communities will allow us to survive and to help those around us.

In short, in this age of crumbling empires when, as Yeats wrote, "the center cannot hold," communities can be the seeds of a new and better world. We must build them, and we will build them.

Conclusion

The future will be what we make it—which is why there is no term for the future as such in the Germanic languages. Old Norse has only the word *skuld*, which means "that which should be, given the present situation." It is yet to be determined, open to the exercise of our will. Let us, then, will a future for Asatru that heals and awakens all Eurofolk, and allows us to live honorably with all peoples of good will in a world of bounty and beauty.

And beyond that—an even more wonderful destiny. When our descendants many generations from now look up at a star-dusted sky, may they be able to point there … and there … and there … and know that our Folk, the Folk of the North, filled with the might of their holy Gods and Goddesses, have homes in that great immensity. This we will give to our distant sons and daughters to come.

And we will be there with them.

Appendix One
THE DECLARATION OF PURPOSE OF THE ASATRU FOLK ASSEMBLY

Below are listed the purposes of the Asatru Folk Assembly. The first one is obvious—to celebrate our religion. Others are less clearly theological, and the casual observer might say they have more to do with social or even political aims than with religious ones. The preservation of the European peoples and the protection of our culture? The promotion of global diversity? The exploration of the universe? What does this have to do with religion?

The answer is . . . everything! All religions have implied social goals. For the Christian it might be world peace or charity toward the poor. Asatruar are perhaps unique in that we place the highest priority on values such as the survival of our people and traditional culture, freedom from tyranny, and a world that has a place for the heroic ethic.

The Asatru Folk Assembly, in short, exists to serve our Gods and Goddesses and our Folk, and to make the world a better place. The following points constitute the purpose of the AFA:

1. The practice, promotion, development, and dissemination of the religion of Asatru:

We are a religious organization dedicated to practicing and spreading Asatru. Since that religion lives and grows, its development is a continuing process.

Asatru today is a modernized version of what our ancestors practiced. We have adapted it to the context of life in the twenty-first century, but the essence remains the same. The code of honor and nobility that spoke to our forebears' souls speaks to ours as well. In the AFA, we don't have to dress up like Vikings to live true to the Gods, nor do we turn our backs on the age in which we live. We practice Asatru in the here and now, and make it available to our kin.

2. The preservation of the Peoples of the North (typified by the Scandinavian/Germanic and Celtic peoples), and the furtherance of their continued evolution:

Ours is an ancestral religion, passed down to us from our forebears from ancient times and thus tailored to our unique makeup. Its spirit is inherent in us as a people. If the People of the North ceased to exist, Asatru would likewise no longer exist. It is our will that we not only survive, but thrive, and continue our upward evolution in the direction of the Infinite.

All native religions spring from the unique collective soul of a particular people. Religions are not arbitrary or accidental; body, mind, and spirit are all shaped by the evolutionary history of the group and are thus interrelated. Asatru is not just what we believe, it is what we are. Therefore, the survival and welfare of the European peoples as a cultural and biological group is a religious imperative for the AFA.

The belief that spirituality and ancestral heritage are related has nothing to do with notions of superiority. Asatru is not an excuse to look down on, much less to hate, members of any other race. On the contrary, we recognize the uniqueness and the value of all the different pieces that make up the human mosaic.

3. The issuance of a call to all our brothers and sisters of the People of the North to return to this, their native religion, and way of life:

We would impose Asatru on no one. But we earnestly invite those whose heritage it is, to return to the belief that is a part of them as surely as blood and bone.

Asafolk have traditionally been restrained when it comes to seeking converts. However, we do feel that our brothers and sisters will be healthier and happier once they have returned to the religion that expresses their heritage. Also, we need them! The restoration of our ancient ways, and the building of a secure future for our religion and our people, is a huge undertaking that calls for all the willing hands we can find. For these reasons, we call our kin to rejoin the great family of men and women who honor the sacred ways of the Northland.

4. The restoration of community, the banishment of alienation, and the establishment of natural and just relations among our people:

Our ancestors had religious and social folkways that gave them a feeling of continuity and community, yet jealously preserved individual rights. We can and will reestablish this natural order among our people. Let us have an "Ingathering of the Folk!"

The religious values of Asatru encourage sound families, and provide an extended family or tribe to support the basic family unit. We help each other materially, socially, and religiously. At the same time, we respect the need for privacy and allow individuals and families the "space" they need to run their own lives. Our general feeling is that society would work better if families and the communities of which they are a part were encouraged to take care of each other, rather than relying on coercive "help" from outside sources such as government—which always has strings attached.

5. The promotion of diversity among the peoples and cultures of the Earth, in opposition to global monoculture:

The world should not be one uniform, unvarying mass. All peoples should be allowed to be different, to relish that difference, and to work out their own destinies. Only in our uniqueness can our respective Gods fully manifest.

Difference is the very spice of our existence. The melting pot, carried to its natural conclusion, results in a sludgy soup of sameness. The AFA supports the efforts of all cultural and biological groups to maintain their identity, and opposes the plans of the world-managers to reduce all of humanity to a lowest common denominator. People of all cultures and races must stand united against the forces that would transform us into perfectly interchangeable economic units dominated by a financial or governmental elite.

6. The fostering in our people of a deep love of freedom and a hatred of all forms of tyranny:

Asatru implies strong, vigorous, free people who do not grovel before other humans, the state, or the Gods themselves. Our Gods are not slavemasters, but rather want us to grow in freedom and responsibility that we may better imitate them.

The Gods do not want us to be submissive, meek, and mild. Rather, they want us to evolve towards ever-greater freedom, exercised in wisdom and awareness. Similarly, we will never bow before human tyrants. Totalitarianism, the ant hill, and the mass-mind are the antitheses of the European ideal.

7. The use of science and technology for the well-being of our people, while protecting and working in harmony with the natural environment in which we live:

Technology and science are part of our intellectual inheritance, and we can use them to make life better for ourselves and our children. However, greater freedom has the price of greater responsibility. We must use our abilities wisely, keeping the balance of the natural world from which we sprang.

We do not live in the Viking Age or in the Germanic tribal era. It makes no sense to repudiate the scientific and technological progress of the last thousand years. However, we have tremendous ability today to change the world around us—for better or worse. Our knowledge must be applied in a way that is not harmful to the environment in which we live, for the Earth is our mother and—while we retain our wonderful human free will and individuality—we are also part of the web of life.

8. The exploration of the universe, in keeping with the adventurous imperatives of our kind:

We are a wide-faring Folk. Odin is a wanderer, and those who follow our Gods have typically been horizon-seekers. The longship has been replaced by the spaceship and the electron microscope, but the spirit of exploration remains the same.

There is a connection between our love of freedom and our craving for frontiers. Stagnation brings regimentation and tameness. Liberty needs a frontier; there is no place for the hero in a world grown regulation-riddled and over-organized.

9. The affirmation of the eternal struggle and strife of life, the welcoming of that strife as a challenge, the living of life wholly and with joy, and the facing of eternity with courage:

Life's struggle is the whetstone that sharpens the sword of spirit. We should not regret the obstacles that confront us, but use them to grow ever stronger and wiser. Nor should we let them drain away our enjoyment of life. Let us live our lives with vigor—and when it is time to die, let us do that with dignity, honor, and grace.

Appendix Two
ODIN BLOT

This is a sample blot to Odin, written in an instructional format.

Before the Blot

It's always a good idea to remind people of the essence of blot—that it is an exchange of love and power between the Gods/Goddesses and ourselves. Likewise, make it clear what the purpose of this specific blot is, so that everyone has the same intent. Tell them a little about the attributes of the deity with whom you will be trading gifts, and if the event is a seasonal festival, explain what it is about. You don't need to give them a full-length lecture, but a three-minute briefing helps get people into the right spiritual space.

This is also the time to give the participants any special instructions regarding what they need to do or say. Don't assume that people will somehow just know what to do. The better prepared they are, the smoother the ritual will go and the more powerful it will be.

Preparation of the Area

Next, the place where the blessing will be done is ritually set apart from the rest of the universe and dedicated to the holy purpose at hand. Historically, this can be done in many ways—by carrying a flame around the perimeter, or marking it off with physical objects such as stones, wooden rods, posts, or special ropes. Protective gestures, often employing the symbolism of Thor's hammer, have been used in modern times to accomplish this end.

If the place has been used for blessings over a period of time by the group, and especially if it is set off by some physical boundary such as a ring of stones, preparation of the area may consist of a gesture and a few words to renew this "apartness" in the minds of those attending.

The Warding

Face the folk and say:

Be all here blessed. May all ill be cast out, and weal and well-being prevail, that we may listen to the wisdom within us and without us. So may it be!

Turning to the horg, make the Hammersign (while holding a ritual hammer or simply using a clenched fist), and say:

In the sign of the Hammer, and in the holy names of Odin, Balder, Frey, and Thor!

Holding fist or hammer high, continue:

I hallow the horg to Odin, and bless the place of blot! May all that is unholy flee before the might of Mjolnir! May our minds, too, be hallowed and whole, given to the good of the Gods and the Folk! As Heimdall guards Bifrost Bridge, may this place be warded against all ill!

Calling the God

Going into *elhaz* statha (arms upwardly extended to the sides at 45° angles), say:

Odin, we hear you in the rustling leaves of the grove, and in the wild fury of the full-blown tempest! You speak to us in the cry of the raven, and in the call of the wolf on a winter's night. You are there in the shout of the warrior, and in the words of the skalds. Unseen by the eyes of mortals, you ride with furious abandon on your eight-legged horse across the soul of your people—and now, Odin, we, your Folk call out to you again as All Father! Hear us as we summon

you by your ancient names:

Helmed God!
High One!
Lore Master!
Stirrer of Strife!
Father of Victory!
God of Cargoes!
Runemaster!
Mead Thief!
Odin!

The Asking

We stand before you and ask these things:

[Here, say the intent of the blot, the thing or things the folk need. It may be as general as might and main, or wisdom, or success in some endeavor. In some cases, if the folk are few, it may be appropriate for participants to state their needs by turns, each in a single sentence. Prior preparation will of course be necessary for this to proceed smoothly.]

Giving the Gift to Odin

. . . but before getting your gifts, we give our gifts to you!

We carry the horn before the folk, that—from heart to hand to horn—they may fill the mead with their might, their main, their *troth*!

Walk around the circle, pausing for about two seconds in front of each worshiper. During that pause, the worshiper places his or her hand on the horn and by an act of will pours his or her might and main into it. It is important to keep the tempo moving; a simple chant can help in this regard. When every person has had a chance to give his or her gifts, face the horg, raise the horn high, and say:

Odin, we give you blot—not of blood, but the gift of our might, our main, our troth! May it aid us, Gods and human-folk alike, in our fight against those who would war against Asgard, or seek to bring gray slavery to Midgard! Odin, take our gifts, not as from slaves, but as a sign of our love and kinship!

Pause and mentally offer the horn to Odin with great intensity, then pour the mead into a bowl or, if outside, onto the ground, while saying:

I pour out the mead, and our gifts rise to Odin!

Taking Odin's Gift

Take a second horn of mead from a horn-bearer and say:

A gift calls for a gift, and I hold high the horn in trust born of kinship. Fill it with your power, making it for us a true mead of might, that we may share it among us!

Hold up the horn for a moment, that Odin may place his might in the mead. Lowering it, take a drink—pause to experience the mead-might—then one of two things happens, depending on how Odin's gift is to be transmitted to the assembled folk:

First option: passing the horn. Although more satisfying in some respects, this is feasible only if there are a relatively small number of participants—say, a dozen or fewer. Otherwise, people's attention wanders and focus is lost. Carry the horn clockwise around the circle, saying to each person in turn: "I give you the blessing of Odin!"

Second option: sprinkling with an evergreen sprig is good if there are many folk in the circle. The method is in some respects very traditional; in the old days, the hlauttein or "blood twig" was used to bless the folk by sprinkling them with the blood of the sacrificed animal. Pour the mead from the horn into the bowl, dip the evergreen in it, and say words like the following (feel free to improvise under the power of

Odin's inspiration!):

I give you the blessing of Odin! May Sleipnir's hooves thunder across your soul. May the Master of the Mead whisper in your dreams, give you luck, send might your way. May his gifts bring you wisdom and victory!

Then, striding purposefully and with measured footfall, walk clockwise around the circle, sprinkling the participants with sweeping gestures. Completing the circle, place the horn or bowl on the horg, turn to face the folk, and say:

The blot is done. May it fill us with might and main! May it fill us with love of the Gods, and the Folk. May we strive all the greater to live lives of worth, trusting our strength, and honoring the bonds of kinship, until we are gathered to the Gods!

Turning now to the horg, arms high, say:

Odin! Feast with your folk! Share in our joy and laughter this day— and as you wend your way to your heavenly hearth, take with you the gifts of your sons and daughters in Midgard!

Face the folk, and signal them to depart the circle. All should quietly exit the ritual area and spend a few moments alone in contemplation before joining with others and resuming mundane activities.

Appendix Three
GLOSSARY

This list of words is by no means exhaustive. However, it covers most of the terms in this book which may puzzle the reader who is not familiar with Asatru or Norse mythology.

Aegir (*Ægir*)—The God of the sea. He has a reputation as a brewer and as a hospitable host.

Aesir (*Æsir*)—The largest family of Gods, the other being the Vanir. The Aesir are typically associated with government and with war.

Agnarr—In *Grimnismal*, Agnarr helps Odin escape the tortures inflicted by his father, King Geirrod.

alfar (*álfar*)—The elves. Sometimes the alfar are classed with the Vanir, and other times they are considered the male ancestors. Not to be confused with the "cute and cuddly" elves of modern folklore.

Asatru (*Ásatrú*)—A modernized reconstruction of the native pre-Christian religion of Northern Europe.

Asgard (*Ásgarðr*)—The dwelling place of the Aesir.

Ask (*Askr*)—In *Voluspa*, one of the first humans created by the trinity of Odin, Hoenir, and Lodur.

Audhumla (*Auðumla*)—The cosmic cow whose milk nurtured Ymir.

Audhumla also frees Buri, the ancestor of the Aesir, from the ice.

Balder (*Baldr*)—The son of Odin and Frigga. Balder's death plays a crucial role in ushering in the final battle at Ragnarok.

Beli—A giant who fights Frey at Ragnarok. Frey comes armed only with an antler, as he has given his sword to Skirnir.

Bestla—The mother of Odin, Vili, and Ve.

Bifrost (*Bifröst*)—The rainbow bridge between Asgard and Midgard, which is guarded by the God Heimdall.

blot (*blót*)—A sacrifice or blessing. Along with the sumbel, one of the two main rites of Asatru.

Bor (*Borr, Burr*)—The husband of Bestla, and the father of Odin, Vili, and Ve in the Norse cosmogony.

Bragi—The God of eloquence and poetry.

Brisingamen (*Brísingamen*)—Freya's marvelous necklace. The myths tell us that she made love with four dwarves in exchange for this piece of jewelry.

Buri (*Búri*)—The ancestor of the Aesir in the *Prose Edda*.

disir (*dísir*)—Female spirits of fertility, plenty, and well-being. These beings are often equated with the women of the ancestral line, looking on from the Otherworld to bless their descendants with luck, love, and inspiration.

Disting—A gathering or assembly dedicated to the female deities, especially Freya and Frigga. In modern Asatru, Disting is celebrated around February 14.

Donar—German name for Thor.

Easter (variations *Eōstre*, *Ostara*)—Saxon Goddess of fertility, the dawn, and the coming of spring. Her festival is on the Spring Equinox.

einherjar—The heroes chosen to go to Odin's hall, Valhalla, after death in battle.

Eir—A Goddess associated with healing.

ek—The Old Norse term for the ego.

Embla—In *Voluspa*, one of the first humans created by the trinity of Odin, Hoenir, and Lodur.

etin (*eoten*)—Old English word for a giant.

Eurofolk—An informal term for the Folk, or people of European descent.

Fenris (*Fenrir*)—The monstrous wolf fathered by Loki, who bursts his bonds at Ragnarok and slays Odin.

fetch—See *fylgja*.

folk—Any group of people identified by a common heritage, ancestry, religion, language, geographical range, and a desire to associate. Examples include the Goths and Iceni of ancient times, or the Sioux, Sámi, and Afrikaners today. Also, the people of Germanic heritage.

Folk, or The Folk—Collectively, the people descended from the European tribes, wherever they may live or whatever their religious belief.

Folk Within—People of European descent who have returned to

Asatru or to another spiritual expression of native European belief.

Folk Without—People who are of European descent, but who have not returned to some expression of native European belief such as Asatru.

folkish—Having to do with the Folk.

folksoul—The spiritual connection and repository of past action which encloses and unifies all people of a given ancestral heritage. Similar concepts are the Jungian collective unconscious, the morphogenetic field of Rupert Sheldrake, and the Well of Urd.

Folkvang (*Fólkvangr*)—Freya's hall. This is also the dwelling place of half of all the warriors who die in battle.

Forseti—Son of Balder and Nanna. According to Snorri, he is associated with law and legal disputes. His name means "presider" or perhaps "lawspeaker," as at the assembly or thing.

Frey (*Freyr*)—God of fertility and prosperity in Norse lore. One of the Vanir, he is twin brother to Freya. Frey is often depicted with an erect penis.

Freyfaxi—A festival in modern Asatru named for Frey's horse, Freyfaxi. Celebrated around August 23.

Freya (*Freyja*)—Goddess of beauty, love, and fertility, but also with a martial and a magical aspect. Freya is one of the family of deities known as the Vanir.

Friagabis—Frisian Goddess, whose name may mean "Giver of Freedom."

Frigga (*Frigg*, Old High German *Frija*)—Mother of the Aesir, wife of Odin, and a Goddess associated with childbirth, the family, and wisdom. The Langobards are said to have especially worshipped her.

frith—Fruitful peace, happiness within the community.

Fulla—A Goddess listed by Snorri as a handmaiden to Frigga. She appears to be linked with gold. Some Asatruar consider her to be identical with Freya or with Frigga.

futhark (*fuþark*)—The rune-row, or sequence of runic figures comprising a sort of mystical "alphabet." Examples are the Elder Futhark, Anglo-Saxon Futhorc, and Younger Futhark.

fylgja—May be thought of as one of the parts of the soul we are not normally aware of but which manifests as a holy being of the opposite sex, or alternatively considered as an independent entity, i.e., a valkyrie. Also called the "fetch."

Gefjon—A Goddess in Old Norse lore. The best-known tale about Gefjon describes how she turned her sons into bulls, put them before a plow, and separated the island of Zealand from Sweden. Also spelled "Gefion" and "Gefjun."

Geirrod (*Geirröðr*)—The father of Agnarr, who hangs Odin between two fires in *Grimnismal*. Geirrod had been a favorite of Odin, so this betrayal was especially egregious. The name Geirrod means "spear-reddener."

Gerd (*Gerðr*)—A giantess whom Snorri describes as the "most beautiful of all women." The best-known story about Frey concerns the wooing of Gerd.

Ginnungagap—In *Voluspa*, the yawning void from which creation proceeds.

Gna (*Gná*)—Goddess described as a handmaiden of Frigga, who delivers Frigga's messages. She is mentioned only by Snorri.

godi (*goði*)—Priest or chieftain.

Grimnismal (*Grímnismál*)—The Eddic poem "The Lay of Grimnir" (Grimnir is one of Odin's many nicknames, or *heiti*). Heavily excerpted by Snorri in the *Prose Edda*.

Gungnir—Odin's spear. The ninth–century poet Bragi (not to be confused with the God of the same name) refers to Odin as "Gungnir's shaker."

Gunnlod (*Gunnlöð*)—Giantess who guards the mead of poetry stolen by Odin.

gydja (*gyðja*)—Priestess.

Gylfaginning—"The Beguiling of Gylfi." The first of four sections of Snorri's *Prose Edda*.

hamingja—1. A soul component consisting of the objectified good luck of the individual, often seen as a sort of protective spirit. 2. The altered appearance taken on by shapeshifters. 3. Personal magical force equivalent to the Polynesian *mana*.

harrow—An altar. See *horg*.

Haustlong (*Haustlöng*)—A poem composed around the turn of the tenth century. Snorri draws on the poem in the sections of the *Prose Edda* dealing with the theft of Idun's apples, as well as Thor's battle with the giant Hrungnir.

Havamal (*Hávamál*)—"The Words of the High One," a poem in the *Poetic Edda* which alleges to be advice given by Odin. The work consists of several parts, the chief of which are prudent and cautionary advice-giving sayings.

Heimdall (*Heimdallr*)—One of the Aesir, and the guardian of the Bifrost Bridge that connects Asgard and Midgard. He is noted for his sharp eyesight and hearing. Traveling as Rig, as described in the poem "The Lay of Rig" (*Rigsthula*), he sets up the three classes of Nordic society.

Hel—The final resting place for those who die a "straw death" of illness or old age, as well as those whose lives are characterized by low levels of consciousness. Also, the personified Goddess who rules over the realm of the dead.

Hermod (*Hermóðr*)—In the *Prose Edda*, the son of Odin who rides to Hel on a failed mission to rescue Balder. He might be one and the same as a figure named in Old English royal genealogies as a descendant of Wodan. He may also be identical with the "Heremod" named in *Beowulf*.

hlauttein—The "blood twig" used to bless the folk by sprinkling them with the blood of a sacrificed animal. In modern Asatru, an evergreen sprig dipped in mead is typically substituted for the hlauttein.

Hlin (*Hlín*)—Goddess listed by Snorri based on lines from the Eddic poem *Voluspa*. Her name, meaning "the protector," defines her role. Many consider her to be Frigga under a different name.

Hod (*Höðr*)—One of the Aesir, a blind God who unwittingly kills Balder with a piece of mistletoe, at Loki's instigation.

Hoenir (*Hænir*)—God listed with Odin and Lodur in one version of the story of human origins.

Holda—Also known as Frau Holle, Holda appears in German

folklore as a fertility figure and a patron of spinning and other female handicrafts.

horg (*hörg*)—An altar, usually consisting of piled stones.

Hreidmar (*Hreiðmarr*)—The shapeshifting father of the dragon Fafnir, Hreidmar is a key figure in the stories concerning the Volsungs.

Hrungnir—A giant whose name means "brawler." Thor fights and kills Hrungnir, but a piece of the whetstone hurled by the giant lodges permanently in Thor's head.

hugr—Thought, or the rational mind, considered as a component of the soul.

Hvergelmir—A spring that lies in Nifelheim. The source of all the waterways in Midgard.

Idun (*Iðunn*)—Goddess who possesses the golden apples which keep the Gods young. One story tells of her abduction by the giant Thjazi and her subsequent rescue by Loki in the shape of an eagle.

innangarth—See *Folk Within*.

Jord (*Jörð*)—A giantess who often functions in skaldic poetry as a personified "Mother Earth." She also gave birth to Thor.

Jormungandr (*Jörmungandr*)—World-circling serpent lying beneath the oceans. He is Thor's greatest enemy, and the two will face each other at Ragnarok.

jotun (*jötunn*)—A giant.

Jotunheim (*Jötunheimr*)—The abode of the jotuns (*jötnar*), or giants.

kenning—Poetic paraphrases typical of Norse and Anglo-Saxon poetry. As an example, the sea might be referred to as the "whale-road." Modern poets like Ezra Pound and Seamus Heaney have also utilized kennings in their literary output.

kynfylgja—The fetch of the entire lineage.

lik (*lík*)—Old Norse word for the corporeal body, conceived of as a part of the soul.

Lodur (*Loðurr*)—A God accompanying Odin and Hoenir when man and woman are fashioned from trees found on the shore. Scholars have tried to identify him with Loki and with Frey; many Asatruar today think of him as an aspect of Odin. There are only two references to him in all the sources available to us.

Lofn—A Goddess, listed by Snorri, whose role is to bring together men and women whose marriage was previously forbidden.

Loki—A resident of Asgard often interpreted as a trickster, who continually causes problems and then generally aids in their resolution. In the tale of Ragnarok he takes on a more sinister and demonic role, but it would not be accurate to dismiss him as a satanic or evil figure in the Christian sense.

Mani (*Máni*)—The moon, personified as a God.

mannsfylgja—The individual fetch.

mead—Wine made from honey, water, and various spices or fruits. It plays a large role in the tales of the Gods, where it is seen as the carrier of the divine inspiration. In modern Asatru, mead is the outward expression of the gifts exchanged between humans and the Holy Powers.

metagenetics—The principle that there are spiritual or metaphysical implications to physical relatedness among humans which correlate with, but transcend, the known limits of genetics.

Midgard (*Miðgarðr*)—The world of humans, translated as the "dwelling place in the middle."

Mimir (*Mímir*)—Possibly, "the wise one." Odin draws wisdom from Mimir's Well, after plucking out one of his eyes for the privilege.

minni—The component of the soul that constitutes "memory," roughly equated with the right-brain functions.

Mjolnir (*Mjöllnir*)—Thor's hammer, the chief defense of the Gods against their foes. Mjolnir was forged by the dwarves Sindri and Brokk. Amulets in the shape of Thor's hammer were popular during the Viking Age, and are worn by many Asafolk today to show their allegiance to the Gods. Also spelled "Mjollnir" and "Miolnir."

Muspelheim (*Muspellzheimr*)—A realm of fiery energy, one of the two primordial worlds that gave birth to the cosmos. It is the abode of the fire giants, the most important of which is Surt, who will destroy the world at Ragnarok.

Naglfar—The "ship of the dead" which will set sail at Ragnarok. Naglfar is constructed entirely from the fingernails of dead men.

Nanna—The wife of Balder in Norse lore. Her name may mean "mother" or "the daring one." In the story of Balder's death, she dies of grief and is burned with him on his funeral pyre.

Nerthus—A Goddess honored by the northern Germanic tribes on an island in the Baltic. As reported by Tacitus, her cult included the procession of a sacred wagon about the countryside.

Nifelheim (*Niflheimr*)— According to the *Prose Edda*, the World of Mist that existed for "many ages" before the formation of the Earth

Njord (*Njörðr*)—A God of the Vanir, and father of Frey and Freya. He is a God of the sea and of seafarers, and is linked to the wealth that comes from the oceans from fishing and trade. There is speculation that Njord is connected to Nerthus, but this is by no means universally accepted.

Noatun (*Nóatún*)—Njord's home. It means "place of ships."

Odin (*Óðinn*)—Chief God in the Norse lore as presented by Snorri. He is leader of the Aesir, and is a God of wisdom and magic. Odin is an aristocratic deity who was often followed by the ambitious and willful chieftains of the Germanic peoples. His name means "master of the divine inspiration."

Odroerir (*Óðrærir*)—1. The mead of inspiration brewed from Kvasir's blood and won by Odin from the giantess Gunnlod. It is the symbol of the divine inspiration itself, the *wode*. 2. The container which, in Norse lore, holds the mead of the same name.

ond (*önd*)—The vital energy associated with the breath, comparable to the Indian prana.

orlog (*ørlög*)—The effect that past deeds and events have on the present; fate. Literally, "primal layers" in Old Norse. The implication is that this is the "fate we make for ourselves" rather than something which is predetermined.

Ragnarok (*Ragnarök, Ragnarøkkr*)—The catastrophic battle in which the Gods and Odin's chosen warriors battle their foes, including the Midgard Serpent and the Fenris wolf. Though the Gods seem to lose the battle, their heroic efforts inaugurate the beginning of a new cycle of existence.

Ran (*Rán*)—Goddess of the sea, and wife of Aegir. The drowned go to her. In her we see the harsh and sinister side of the sea, well known for millennia to folk who dwell on the ocean's shore.

Rig (*Ríg*)—Name taken by Heimdall (some say Odin) as he went through Midgard and founded the social classes of thrall, karl, and jarl among humans by sleeping three nights in turn between men and women representing each class. In doing so, Rig established the ancestral link between humans and the Gods, and thus affirms our kinship with the Divine.

Rigsthula (*Rígspula*)—"The Lay of Rig" which appears in Snorri's *Edda*. Some scholars have speculated that the story may contain Irish influence, since the name "Rig" is related to the Old Irish word for king, *rí*.

rune—1. A mystery or secret; hidden sacred knowledge. 2. A written symbol representing a concealed, holy concept.

rune stave—1. A written symbol or "letter" representing a rune; a single runic character. 2. A piece of wood on which one or more runes are carved for magical purposes.

Saga (*Sága*)—A Goddess, described by Snorri as drinking with Odin. Some see her as Frigga under a different name, but she may be one of a number of separate Goddesses linked with Frigga.

Saxnot (*Saxnôt*)—A God who appears in Anglo-Saxon royal genealogies as the divine ancestor of the Saxons. He is also denounced in a ninth-century baptismal pledge. Some scholars have attempted to identify Saxnot with Frey, while others have suggested that he might be related to Tyr.

seidr (*seiðr*)—A kind of Germanic magical practice which is essentially shamanic in nature. In the lore, it was an art which Freya taught to

Odin.

Sif—The wife of Thor. She is connected with the growth of crops. Her famous golden hair is thought by some scholars to represent the grain which is periodically harvested.

Sigurd (*Sigurðr*)—The hero of the Volsung stories, and perhaps the most important heroic figure in all of Germanic culture.

Sigyn—Loki's wife.

Sjofn (*Sjöfn*)—A Goddess who inspires love and who oversees affairs of love and marriage.

Skadi (*Skaði*)—Daughter of the giant Thjazi. She is a huntress who rides on skis and claims her prey with a bow.

skald (*skáld*)—A composer of heroic court poetry in the Scandinavian Middle Ages. Skaldic poetry is especially notable for its use of kennings.

Skidbladnir (*Skíðblaðnir*)—Frey's magic ship, crafted by the dwarves.

Skirnir (*Skírnir*)—A servant of Frey, who figures prominently in the wooing of Gerd incident portrayed in the "lay of Skirnir."

Skuld—One of the Norns who influences fate or orlog. Her name is associated with the future.

Sleipnir—Odin's eight-legged horse, on which he rides between the worlds.

Snotra—A little-known Goddess portrayed as wise, self-controlled, and of gentle manners. She may be an aspect of Frigga.

Sol (*Sól*)—The sun, personified as a God.

stadagaldr (*staðagaldr*)—"Posture magic"—the Nordic equivalent to the *asanas* or yoga positions. Related to the "runic gymnastics" championed by the German rune magician Friedrich Bernhard Marby in the 1930s.

Sumarsdag/Sigrblot (*Sigrblót*)—For modern Asatruar, a holy day welcoming the more clement weather, and at the same time invoking Odin for victory. Celebrated on or near the Thursday between April 9 and 15.

sumbel—A ritual of toasts to Gods, Goddesses, and ancestors for the purpose of bringing the power of the past into the present. Also spelled *symbel*.

Sunna—The sun, personified as a Goddess in Old High German.

Surt (*Surtr*)—The fire giant who, in the lore, destroys the world at Ragnarok. Frey is his opponent in this battle, and they slay each other. His name means "the black one."

Svava (*Sváva*)—A valkyrie named in heroic poetry. Her name may mean "sleep-maker."

Syn—A Goddess listed by Snorri as being the guardian of the gates.

thing (*þing*)—The assembly of freemen in Germanic society. The thing has legislative, judicial, social, and religious aspects. Each region or tribe might have its own thing, with larger ones for an entire district or, as in Iceland, a special thing—the Althing (*Alþingi*)—for the whole country. Tyr is considered the patron God of the thing.

Thor (*Þórr*)—Son of Odin, strongest of the Gods, and their (and our) special defender against the giants and other threats. Thor is the "friend of men" and one of the most popular Gods in ancient times, as today. He is known for his red beard, his blazing temper, and the great hammer with which he fights his foes.

Thorrablot (*Þorrablót*)—A winter holiday celebrated by modern Asatruar at the end of January.

Thrudheim (*Þrúðheimr*)—The home of Thor.

Thunor (*Þunær*)—Anglo-Saxon name for Thor.

troth—Honor, truthfulness, loyalty, honesty; pledge or compact, the keeping of these qualities.

Tyr (*Týr*)—Norse God of military valor, the sky, and the assembly or thing. Tyr is best known for the story in which he sacrifices his hand so that the threatening wolf, Fenris, may be bound—thus defining the warrior's role of sacrifice and courage.

Ullr—Scandinavian God associated with skiing and with the bow. He is thought to be an archaic God of winter and death. Some scholars have attempted to pair him with Skadi, but there is no actual evidence to support this.

Urd (*Urðr*)—One of the Norns who influences fate or orlog. Her name means "that which has become," or the past.

Urd's Well (*Urðar brunnr*)—One of the wells or springs said in the Eddic lore to lie at the roots of the World Tree, Yggdrasil. It is here that the Norns reside, and the Gods sit in council.

Valhalla (*Valhöll*)—Odin's hall in Asgard, where he collects the einherjar or chosen warriors who will fight beside him at Ragnarok. According to the lore, the heroes feast all night and fight all day, sharpening their skills for the coming conflict. Also called Valhall.

Vali (*Váli*)—Son of Odin and Rind, who avenges Balder by slaying Hoder.

valkyrie—One of the entities who chooses the slain warriors for Valhalla. The word means "chooser of the slain." Described as Odin's daughters, they have been depicted both as beautiful armored maidens astride flying steeds—or as enraged battle demons delighting in blood and severed body parts. The latter conception is probably the older. Some Asafolk feel there is no conflict between these views.

Vanaheim (*Vanaheimr*)—The abode of the Vanir.

Vanir—The family of Gods and Goddesses most associated with fertility, sexuality, and wealth. Chief among them are the twins Frey and Freya, and their father Njord.

Var (*Vár*)—Goddess of love and marriage listed by Snorri. Her name means "beloved."

Ve (*Vé*)—A brother of Odin named in the *Prose Edda*.

ve (*vé*)—A sacred enclosure or shrine.

Verdandi—One of the Norns who influences fate or orlog. Her name means "that which is happening," or the present.

Vidar (*Víðarr*)—Son of Odin who avenges his father's death at Ragnarok. In the story, he places his foot on Fenris's lower jaw and tears the monster apart. It is significant that one cannot be reborn unless they are avenged, so Vídar's action has an importance that is belied by the simple narrative. Also, in folklore, whenever a devouring monster is ripped open, it permits the person who has been eaten to escape—again underlining Odin's escape, thanks to Vídar.

Vili—A brother of Odin named in the *Prose Edda*.

Voluspa (*Völuspá*)—The "Prophecy of the Seeress," one of the most important poems in the *Poetic Edda*. It gives an account of the world from creation to Ragnarok in extremely effective and vivid imagery.

Vor (*Vör*)—A little-known Goddess portrayed as being so wise that nothing can be concealed from her. She may be an aspect of Frigga.

Waluberg—A second-century Germanic seeress. Many modern Asatruar honor Waluberg, as well as deities like Holda, Frigga, or Freya, on April 30 and May Day.

wihaz—A Proto-Germanic word for "holiness."

wode (*óðr*)—The mystically inspired state of frenzy, typically experienced by poets, magicians, and berserkers. Wode is a gift of Odin, symbolized by the mead of inspiration.

Woden (*Wōden*)—Anglo-Saxon name for Odin.

wyrd—A concept in Anglo-Saxon culture roughly equivalent to the idea of orlog. The flow of cause and effect that shapes events.

Ymir—The primordial giant in the Norse creation story. A man and a woman were born from the sweat under his left arm, and one leg begot a son on the other. From Ymir and his offspring come the race of frost giants.

Yngvi-Freyr—An alternate name for Frey, in his guise as divine ancestor of the Yngling dynasty of ancient Sweden.

Yggdrasil—The World Tree, which holds all the nine worlds of Norse cosmology. Though described in some sources as an ash, it is actually a yew tree. The name means "horse of Ygg (Odin)," referring to the God's hanging from it to win the runes.

Yule—The Germanic festival of midwinter. In modern Asatru, Yule is a twelve-day span running from the Winter Solstice to New Year's.

Traditionally, it is a time for celebrating the time-transcending unity of the clan, and for linking the living with their ancestors. Many of our present-day Christmas customs either originate in, or are consistent with, the ancient roots of this festival.

Printed in Great Britain
by Amazon